Programme for International Student Assessment

Are Students Ready for a Technology-Rich World?

What PISA Studies Tell Us

OECD
ORGANISATION FOR ECONOMIC CO-OPERATION AND DEVELOPMENT

ORGANISATION FOR ECONOMIC CO-OPERATION AND DEVELOPMENT

The OECD is a unique forum where the governments of 30 democracies work together to address the economic, social and environmental challenges of globalisation. The OECD is also at the forefront of efforts to understand and to help governments respond to new developments and concerns, such as corporate governance, the information economy and the challenges of an ageing population. The Organisation provides a setting where governments can compare policy experiences, seek answers to common problems, identify good practice and work to co-ordinate domestic and international policies.

The OECD member countries are: Australia, Austria, Belgium, Canada, the Czech Republic, Denmark, Finland, France, Germany, Greece, Hungary, Iceland, Ireland, Italy, Japan, Korea, Luxembourg, Mexico, the Netherlands, New Zealand, Norway, Poland, Portugal, the Slovak Republic, Spain, Sweden, Switzerland, Turkey, the United Kingdom and the United States. The Commission of the European Communities takes part in the work of the OECD.

OECD Publishing disseminates widely the results of the Organisation's statistics gathering and research on economic, social and environmental issues, as well as the conventions, guidelines and standards agreed by its members.

This work is published on the responsibility of the Secretary-General of the OECD. The opinions expressed and arguments employed herein do not necessarily reflect the official views of the Organisation or of the governments of its member countries.

Foreword

Information and communication technology (ICT) is associated with unprecedented global flows of information, products, people, capital and ideas, connecting vast networks of individuals across geographic boundaries at negligible marginal cost. ICT is an important part of the policy agendas of OECD countries, with profound implications for education, both because ICT can facilitate new forms of learning and because it has become important for young people to master ICT in preparation for adult life. But how extensive is access to ICT in schools and informal settings and how is it used by students?

As part of the 2003 survey of the Organisation for Economic Co-operation and Development's (OECD) Programme for International Student Assessment (PISA), students were asked about their familiarity with ICT, principally about their computer use. The results show that almost all 15-year-old students in OECD countries have experience using computers, but the length of time for which students have been using computers differs greatly across countries. Since the PISA 2000 survey access to computers at home and at school has increased and the majority of students now have access to computers in both places. Access to computers at school is most universal, but students report using home computers more frequently.

This report sheds light on how students are using computers and shows that they use them for a wide range of functions and not just to play games. Only a minority of students reported frequent use of specific educational software, but one-half of the students surveyed reported frequent use of the Internet as a research tool and frequent use of word processing software, both of which have educational potential. The vast majority of students are confident in performing basic ICT tasks such as opening, deleting and saving files and students are generally confident about their Internet abilities. While fewer 15-year-olds are confident performing high-level tasks – such as creating a multi-media presentation or writing a computer program – unaided most think they could do so with some help.

This report complements both *Learning for Tomorrow's World – First Results from PISA 2003,* which focuses on knowledge and skills in mathematics, science and reading, and *Problem Solving for Tomorrow's World – First Measures of Cross-curricular Competencies from PISA 2003*, which profiles students' problem-solving skills.

The report is the product of a collaborative effort between the countries participating in PISA, the experts and institutions working within the framework of the PISA Consortium, and the OECD. The report was drafted by the OECD Directorate for Education, principally by Claire Shewbridge and Miyako Ikeda, under the direction of Andreas Schleicher, with advice from the PISA Editorial Group and support from Donald Hirsch, Kate Lancaster, Sophie Vayssettes and John Cresswell. The PISA assessment instruments were prepared by the PISA Consortium, under the direction of Raymond Adams at the Australian Council for Educational Research. Data analytic support was provided by Alla Berezner and technical advice by Christian Monseur, Keith Rust and Wolfram Schulz.

The development of the report was steered by the PISA Governing Board, chaired by Ryo Watanabe (Japan). Annex C of the report lists the members of the various PISA bodies as well as the individual experts and consultants who have contributed to this report and to PISA in general.

The report is published on the responsibility of the Secretary-General of the OECD.

Table of Contents

1

ICT in PISA and Educational Policy

INTRODUCTION

Information and communication technology (ICT) is playing a central role in the development of modern economies and societies. This has profound implications for education, both because ICT can facilitate new forms of learning and because it has become important for young people to master ICT in preparation for adult life. But is ICT living up to its potential in schools and in the lives of young people? To start to answer this question, the extent to which young people are exposed to and making use of such technology and whether those who do so are achieving desirable learning outcomes must be determined. In 2003, the OECD's Programme for International Student Assessment (PISA) collected data to explore these questions. This report explores what the data reveal.

DRIVERS FOR THE INTEGRATION OF TECHNOLOGY INTO SCHOOLS

Every young person will need to use ICT in many different ways in their adult lives, in order to participate fully in a modern society. It is also now possible to estimate the overall value to economies of ICT. Investment in this technology can give competitive advantage in global markets. Figure 1.1 shows the growth of GDP in percentage points directly attributable to investment in ICT. In all eighteen OECD countries for which data are available it is clear that there have been increased gains in GDP directly attributable to investment in ICT between 1990 and 1995 and between 1995 and 2002. This suggests that countries will continue to invest in ICT and that ICT will become

Figure 1.1 ■ **Contribution of ICT investment to GDP growth, 1990-1995 and 1995-2002, in percentage points**

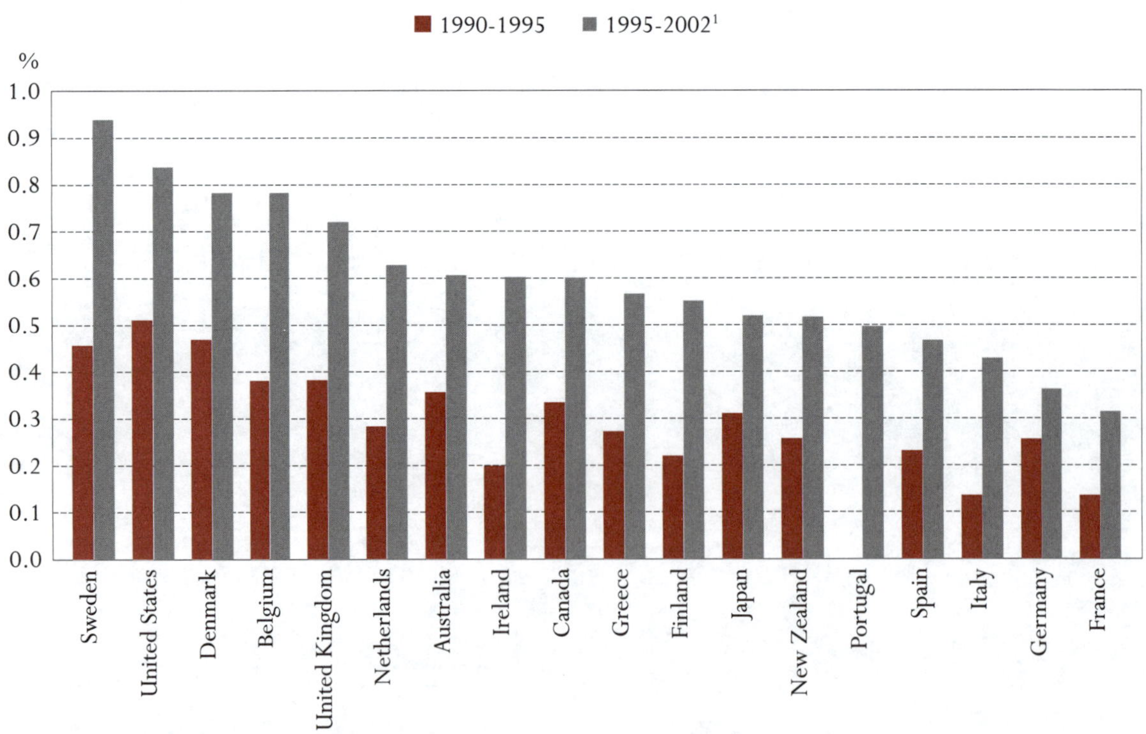

1. Data refer to 1995-2002 for Australia, Canada, France, Germany, Japan, New Zealand and the United States, and 1995-2001 for other countries.
Source: OECD Productivity Database, September 2004 (*www.oecd.org/statistics/productivity*).

commonplace in the workplace. Given this evidence and the extent of organisational and process changes seen throughout professional and personal environments, it is clear that there will be an increasing demand for young people to acquire familiarity with ICT at school, coming from policy makers, parents and even young people themselves.

Moreover, ICT not only makes new demands on schools in terms of desirable outcomes, but also offers an important new tool in the education process. Policy makers and educators have begun integrating technology into schools with the primary aim of improving teaching and learning in different subjects and also with an aim of increasing motivation for both students and teachers. An effective use of ICT in schools can have an immediate positive impact on the schools' learning environments, for example by: creating more dynamic interaction between students and teachers, increasing collaboration and team work in problem-solving activities, stimulating creativity in both students and teachers, and helping students to control and monitor their own learning. Further, a successful use of ICT in schools can help students to develop skills, both specific to ICT and more generally, that will be useful for them in their future academic and professional lives. Whether pursuing further academic or vocational studies or choosing to commence working life directly at the end of compulsory education, students who have effectively used ICT during their compulsory studies should be able to continue to effectively use ICT to control and plan their own projects and to collaborate well with others. Such students will have the advantage of being familiar with different media common to the modern workplace, and should be able to use these ICT skills to access, compile, synthesise and exchange information effectively.

PISA 2003 AND HOW INFORMATION ON ICT WAS COLLECTED

In 2003, PISA ran its second three-yearly survey of student knowledge and skills. PISA is the most comprehensive and rigorous international programme that assesses student performance and collects data on characteristics of students and the institutions where they study. Such contextual data can help explain differences in performance.

PISA is policy driven and aims to provide participating governments with information on how well young adults are prepared to meet the challenges of today's knowledge societies. It therefore assesses students at age 15 who are approaching the end of compulsory schooling. PISA measures how well 15-year-olds can use their knowledge and skills to meet real-life challenges, rather than how well they can reproduce what they have learned.

What did PISA 2003 assess?

PISA 2003 assessed student performance in mathematics, reading and science, as well as in cross-curricular problem-solving skills. In 2003, the domain to which most assessment time was devoted was mathematics. In the first survey, conducted in 2000, the major domain was reading, and in 2006 it will be science. In PISA 2003 the total assessment time of 390 minutes was organised in different combinations of test booklets with each individual being tested for 120 minutes. The time devoted to the assessment of mathematics was 210 minutes (54% of the total) and 60 minutes was devoted to each of the assessments of reading, science and problem solving.

Figure 1.2 ■ **A map of PISA 2003 countries and where the ICT questionnaire was administered**

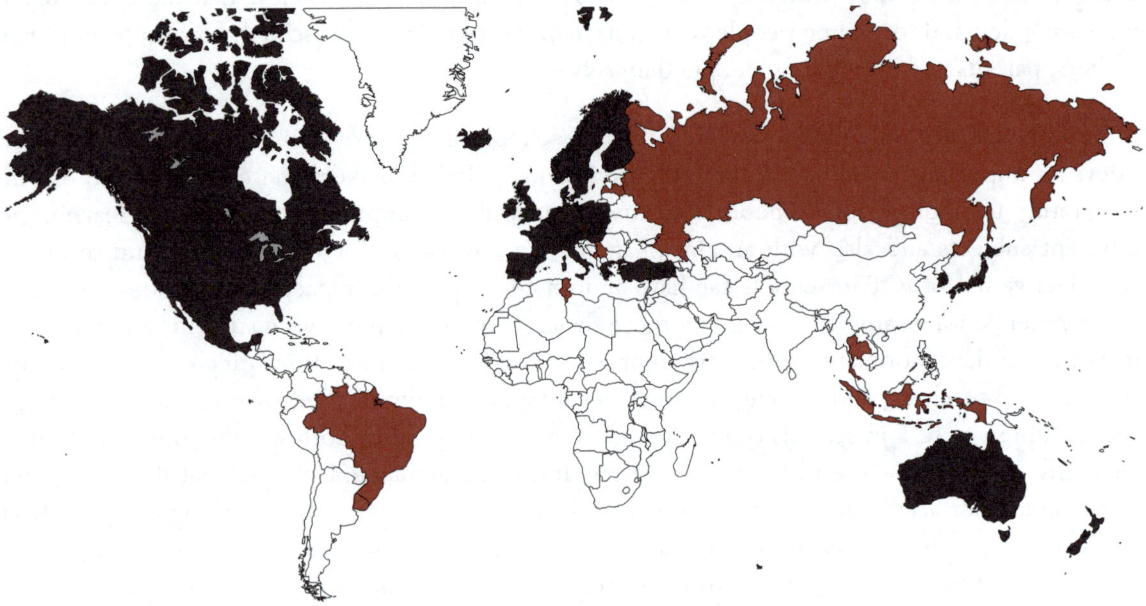

■ OECD countries

Australia
Austria
Belgium
Canada
Czech Republic
Denmark
Finland
France
Germany
Greece
Hungary
Iceland
Ireland
Italy
Japan
Korea
Luxembourg
Mexico
Netherlands
New Zealand
Norway
Poland
Portugal
Slovak Republic
Spain
Sweden
Switzerland
Turkey
United Kingdom[1]
United States

■ Partner countries in PISA 2003

Brazil
Hong Kong-China
Indonesia
Latvia
Liechtenstein
Macao-China
Russian Federation
Serbia and Montenegro[2]
Thailand
Tunisia
Uruguay

Note: Countries that completed the ICT questionnaire are marked in bold.
1. The response rate in the United Kingdom was too low to ensure comparability
2. Data for Montenegro (7.9% of the national population) are not available. Throughout this report "Serbia" is used as a shorthand for the Serbian part of Serbia and Montenegro.

Who participated in PISA 2003?

PISA 2003 was conducted in 41 countries, including all 30 OECD countries (see Figure 1.2). Students participating in PISA 2003 were aged between 15 years 3 months and 16 years 2 months at the time of the assessment. All students of this age were included in the target population regardless of the grade or type of institution they were enrolled in and of whether they were in full-time or part-time education. As a result, the 15-year-olds assessed in PISA 2003 have had different educational experiences, both within and outside school.

How was information collected on students' use of and access to ICT?

All students in both the PISA 2000 and PISA 2003 surveys completed a background questionnaire requesting demographic data on the students and their families, their perceptions of school and how they learned, and details concerning their motivation, engagement and attitudes. In addition, in both surveys countries were given the option of administering a short questionnaire on students' familiarity with ICT. Thirty-two countries took up this option in PISA 2003 (see Figure 1.2). The responses, set alongside other student characteristics and students' performance in the PISA assessment, are presented in this report.

Box 1.1 ■ **How did PISA collect information on ICT?**

Student questionnaire

Students in all participating countries answered a questionnaire that took 35 minutes to complete and that focused on their background, their learning habits and their perceptions of the learning environment, as well as on their engagement and motivation. As part of this questionnaire, students answered questions on whether or not they had a home computer to use for school work, educational software, a link to the Internet and a calculator. The results are presented in Chapter 2 and Annex B1 Tables 2.3a and 2.3b.

School questionnaire

School principals completed a questionnaire about their school that asked them for information on demographic characteristics as well as for an assessment of the quality of the learning environment at school. As part of this questionnaire, principals provided information on the availability of computers at their schools and whether or not their schools ran computer clubs for mathematics, as well as on their perceptions of the extent to which a lack of computers, computer software, calculators and audio-visual resources hindered instruction in their schools. The results are presented in Chapter 2 and Annex B1 Tables 2.4, 2.5 and 2.6.

ICT questionnaire

Students in the countries shown in bold in Figure 1.2 answered a questionnaire that took five minutes to complete about their access to and familiarity with ICT. Students provided information on whether or not ICT was available to them and how they used it, as well as how confident they felt performing certain tasks on a computer and their general attitudes to using computers. Students also provided information on how they learned to use computers and the Internet. The results for the countries that administered this questionnaire are presented in Chapters 2, 3 and 4. For reference, the complete ICT questionnaire is included in Annex A4.

The questions in the ICT questionnaire went into more detail than the basic information about student access to computers elicited by the main questionnaire and focused mainly on how familiar students were with computers rather than ICT in general. Students were asked how often they used computers and where, how they learned to use computers and the Internet, as well as more detailed information on how confident they were in performing certain computer tasks.

The full ICT questionnaire is included in Annex A4. Additional information about ICT in students' schools was provided by the schools' principals, who completed a questionnaire that asked for information about use of ICT in their schools and to what extent a lack of ICT hindered instruction. Box 1.1 presents the sources of information on ICT used in this report.

STRUCTURE OF REPORT

This report presents results from PISA 2003, examining both how equitable access to computers is for students across countries and how familiar students are with ICT as they near completion of compulsory schooling. It looks at how often and where they use computers, how long they have been using them, which tasks they perform on computers and how confident they are using ICT. All of these characteristics are compared to how well students perform in mathematics, the main area of student performance examined in PISA 2003.

Chapter 2 presents a profile of students' access to ICT, examining information provided both by students and their principals.

Chapter 3 shows how students use ICT, including a discussion of gender differences in this usage.

Chapter 4 examines the relationship between students' access to and use of ICT and their performance in PISA 2003.

READERS' GUIDE

Data underlying the figures

The data referred to in Chapters 2, 3 and 4 of this report are presented in Annex B. Three symbols are used to denote missing data:

- *a* The category does not apply in the country concerned. Data are therefore missing.
- *c* There are too few observations to provide reliable estimates (*i.e.* there are fewer than 30 students for this cell).
- *m* Data are not available. These data were collected but subsequently removed from the publication for technical reasons.
- *w* Data have been withdrawn at the request of the country concerned.

Calculation of the OECD average

An OECD average was calculated for most indicators presented in this report. The OECD average takes the OECD countries as a single entity, to which each country contributes with equal weight. The OECD average corresponds to the arithmetic mean of the respective country statistics.

All international averages include data for the United Kingdom.

Rounding of figures

Because of rounding, some figures in tables may not exactly add up to the totals. Totals, differences and averages are always calculated on the basis of exact numbers and are rounded only after calculation. When standard errors in this publication have been rounded to one or two decimal places and the value 0.0 or 0.00 is shown, this does not imply that the standard error is zero, but that it is smaller than 0.05 or 0.005 respectively.

Reporting of student data

The report uses "15-year-olds" as shorthand for the PISA target population. In practice, this refers to students who were aged between 15 years and 3 (complete) months and 16 years and 2 (complete) months at the beginning of the assessment period and who were enrolled in an educational institution, regardless of the grade level or type of institution, and of whether they were attending full-time or part-time.

Abbreviations used in this report

The following abbreviations are used in this report:

ISCED	International Standard Classification of Education
S.E.	Standard error

Further documentation

For further information on the PISA assessment instruments and the methods used in PISA, see the *PISA 2003 Technical Report* (OECD, 2005) and the PISA Web site (*www.pisa.oecd.org*).

2

Students' Access to ICT

KEY POINTS

- Almost all 15-year-old students in OECD countries have experience of using computers, but the length of time for which students have been using computers differs greatly across countries.
- Access to computers at home and at school has increased since PISA 2000 and most students now have access to computers in both places. However, students without computer access at home are likely to come from low socio-economic backgrounds, especially in those countries where overall access to home computers is comparatively low.
- Inequalities across countries in terms of access to resources for home study are wider for computers than for books. Even in countries where the great majority of homes do not have computers, the majority of homes have books.
- The number of computers per student in schools has increased since PISA 2000, but it remains highly unequal across countries, and in some countries a majority of principals believe that shortage of computers is hindering instruction.

Figure 2.1 ■ **How universal is computer access?**

Number of OECD countries by percentage of students who have used and have access to computers

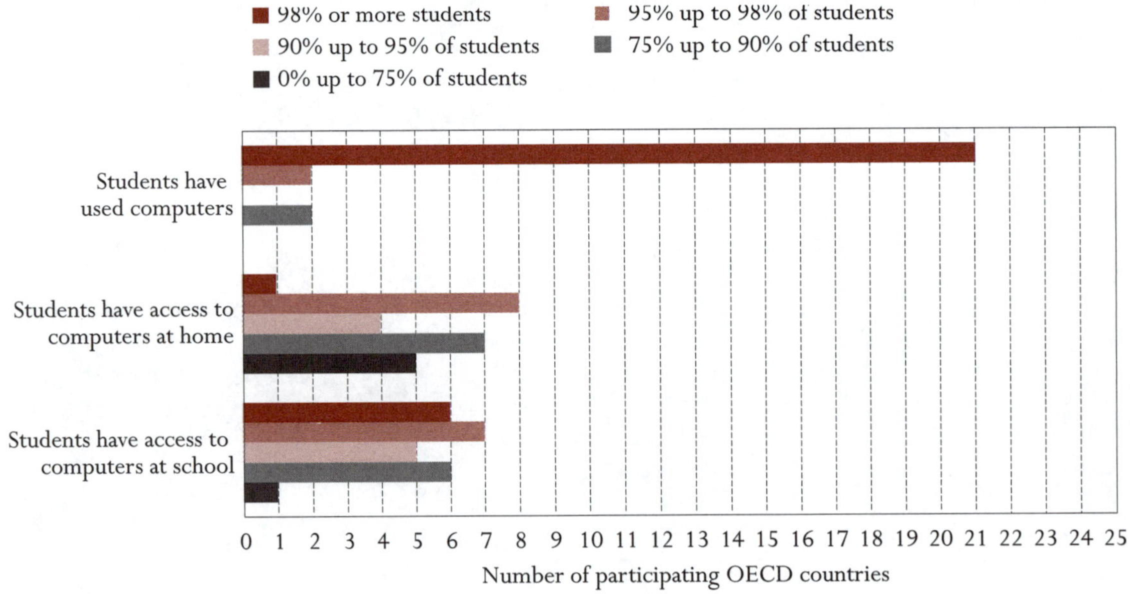

Source: OECD PISA 2003 database, Tables 2.1 and 2.2a.

HOW UNIVERSAL IS ACCESS TO ICT?

In recent years, much attention has been paid to the concept of a digital divide: a gap in the adoption of ICT, both from country to country and between certain communities within countries. To what extent does such a divide still exist among the younger generation? Previous studies have highlighted the fact that households with young families are more likely to have computers and/or access to the Internet (OECD, 2004a). The PISA 2003 data provide an insight into the current level of access to ICT, at home, at school and elsewhere.

When compared to more general survey data on households, the information reported by 15-year-olds in PISA 2003 substantiates the argument that families with young people are more likely to have computers and/or access to the Internet. Figure 2.2 shows that whereas typically between one-half and two-thirds of households in advanced economies have Internet access, in most of these countries between three-quarters and nine-tenths of 15-year-olds report having an Internet connection at home. Although these data come from different surveys, the results are highly correlated.

Yet while it is undoubtedly true that youth access to some kinds of computer resources is now nearly universal in some countries, there remain significant gaps in access in other countries. These gaps can be seen as putting young people at risk of significant disadvantage, in education and in life generally, since the more that computer access becomes usual in a country, the more likely it is that people who lack such access will be unable to participate fully in everyday social, economic and educational activities.

Have students ever used computers? If so, for how long?

A first aspect of access is whether students use computers at all. In most countries, all but a tiny minority have used them by the time they are 15. Only in 12 of the 32 countries surveyed, do more than 1% say that they have never used a computer and only in two OECD countries and three partner countries is this figure above 5% (Table 2.1). The level of such students reached 13 and 14% in Mexico and Turkey, respectively, and 39% in the partner country Tunisia. These data cover only 15-year-olds enrolled in education, however. While more than 90% of 15-year-olds are enrolled in schools in all OECD countries except Mexico and Turkey and in the partner countries Brazil, Indonesia, Liechtenstein, Macao-China, Thailand, and Uruguay, Mexico and Turkey have less than 60% of their 15-year-olds enrolled in education.[1]

There were no gender differences in the percentages of students never having used a computer in most countries. However, in Turkey and the partner country Tunisia, a higher proportion of female students have never used a computer. In Turkey, 21% of female students have never used a computer, more than double the percentage of male students (9%) (Table 2.1).

To what extent do students who have never used a computer come from disadvantaged backgrounds? In most countries, students in the bottom quarter of PISA's index of economic, social and cultural status (ESCS) are not much more likely never to have used a computer than those from the top quarter. However, in all of the five countries where more than 5% of all students have not used a computer, these students primarily have low socio-economic status. For example, in Mexico 29% of students in the bottom quarter by ESCS have never used a computer, compared to only 2% in the top quarter, while in the partner country Tunisia the figure is 70 and 11%, respectively (Table 2.1).

Figure 2.2 ■ **Percentage of 15-year-olds with an Internet connection at home and the percentage of households with Internet access (2003)**

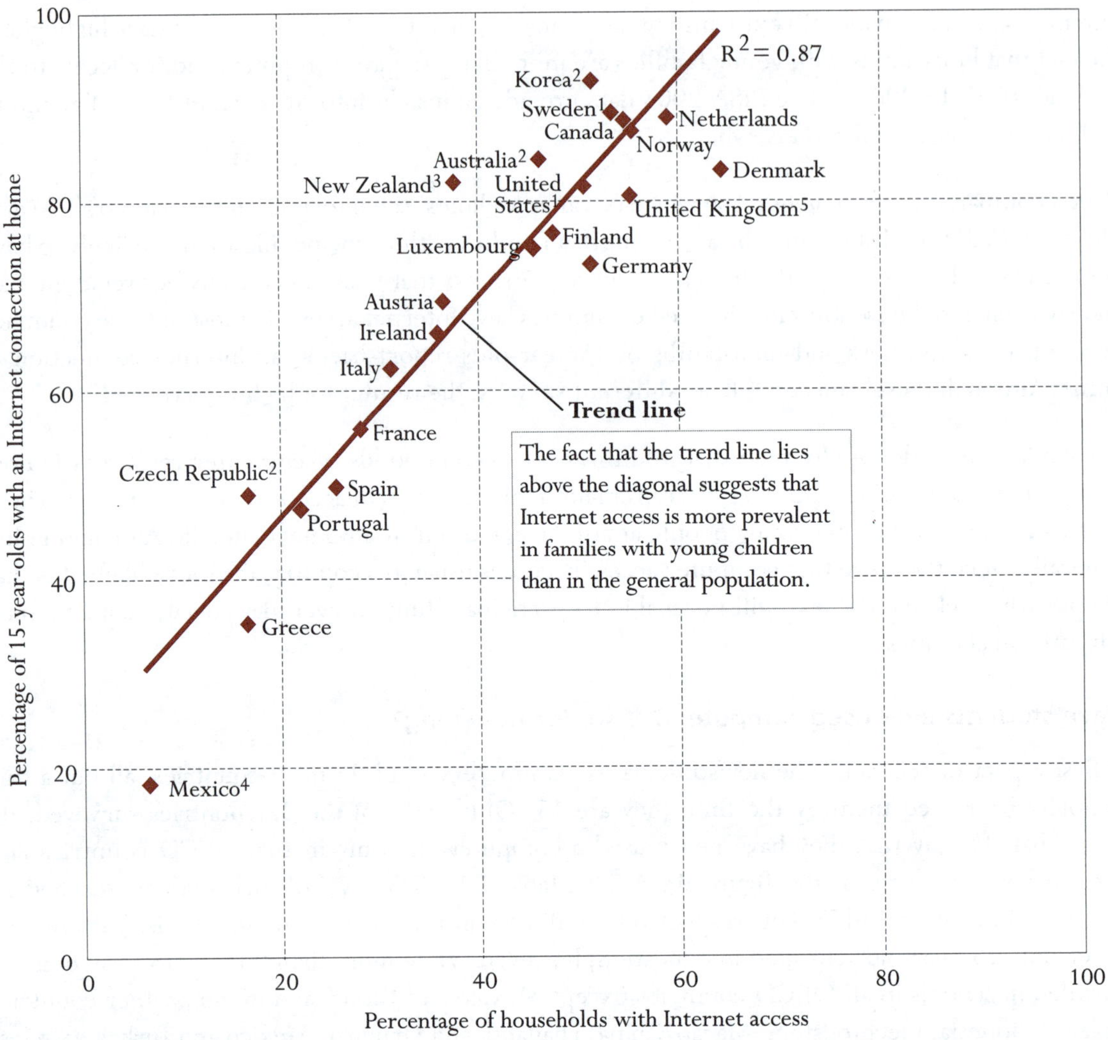

1. Household data for 2001.
2. Household data for 2002.
3. Household data for July 2000 - June 2001.
4. Household data: Internet access via any device (desktop computer, portable computer, television, mobile phone, etc.).
5. Data for 15-year-olds: Response rate too low to ensure comparability.

Source: Data for households taken from OECD ICT database and Eurostat Community Survey on ICT usage in households 2002, June 2003. Included in *OECD Information Technology Outlook 2004*. Data for 15-year-olds taken from the OECD PISA 2003 database.

Among those students who have experience of using a computer, for how long have they been using them? This is relevant partly because computer use has spread relatively rapidly in recent years. Students who first use computers in their mid-teens are less likely to be comfortable in using them than those whose experience dates back to their primary or early secondary school years. Figure 2.3 shows a striking variation across countries in this respect. A majority of 15-year-old students have at least five years' experience of computers in eight OECD countries: Australia, Canada, Denmark, Finland, Iceland, New Zealand, Sweden and the United States. In other countries, newcomers to

ICT are more numerous; in seven OECD countries and five partner countries, at least as many students have started using ICT in the past three years as have used it for longer. Note that in those countries where non-negligible numbers of students have never used a computer, the percentage of all students who are experienced computer users is overstated in Figure 2.3. For example in Tunisia, half of students who use computers have used them for more than one year, but since only 61% of students have ever used a computer, under one-third of all students have used a computer for over a year.

Figure 2.3 ■ **Length of time students have been using a computer**

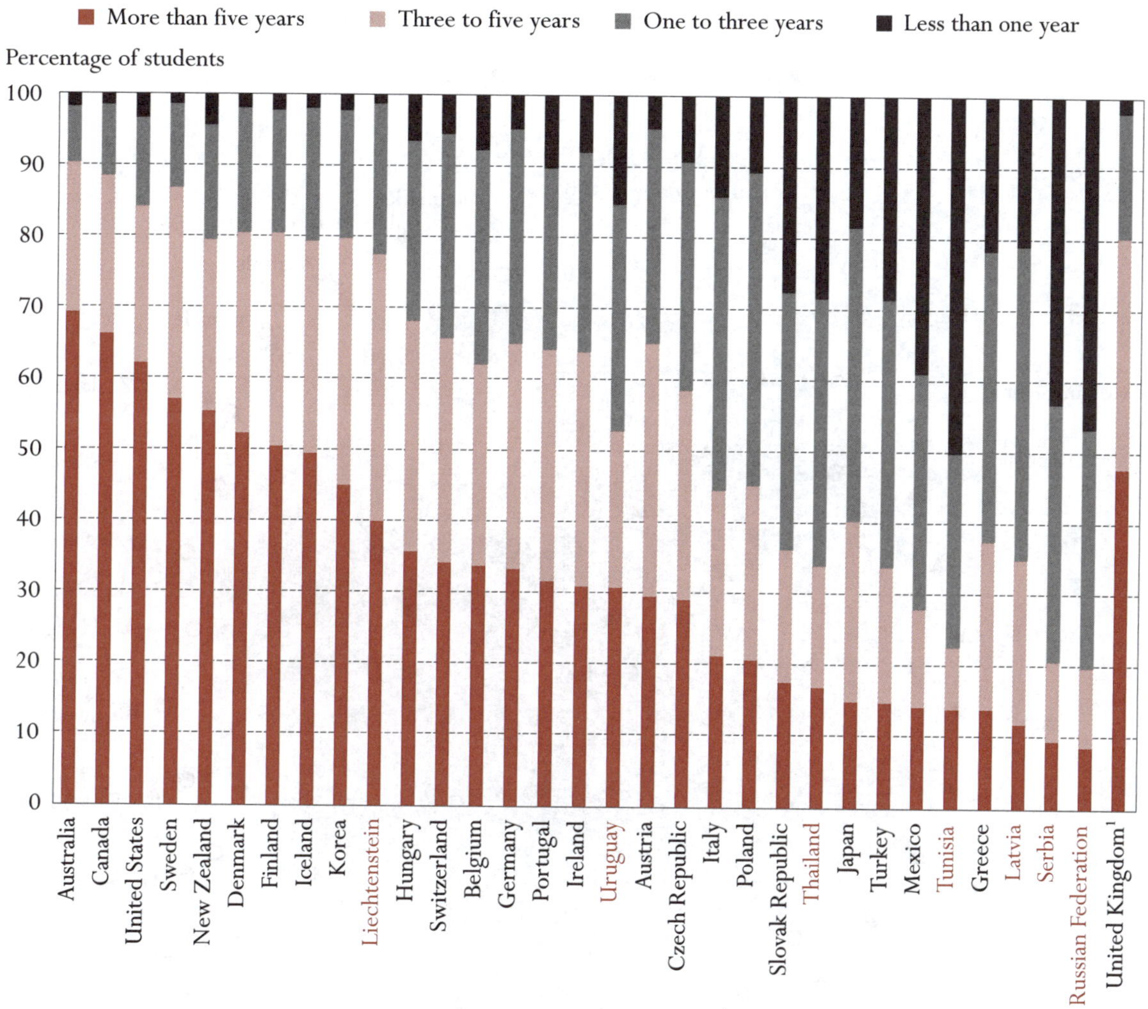

Countries are ranked in descending order of students reporting that they have been using computers for more than five years.
1. Response rate is too low to ensure comparability.
Source: OECD PISA 2003 database, Table 2.1.

Where did students have access to computers?

Students in PISA 2003 were asked about where they had access to a computer. They reported whether or not there was a computer for them to use at home, at school or in other places. This question did not, however, capture the idea of how much time students actually have on computers in each of these places. Students who theoretically have access to computers may not actually spend much time on them or in the case of computers at school may be one of many students sharing a computer. Figure 2.4 reports these results, with countries ordered by the type of access that has become close to universal in most countries: availability at school. In half of OECD countries reporting data and three partner countries, fewer than 5% of students attend schools where they cannot access a computer, and in all but seven OECD countries and four partner countries it is fewer than one in ten. In all participating countries except Turkey and the partner country Tunisia, at least seven in ten students now have school computer access (Table 2.2a).

Figure 2.4 ■ **Percentage of students reporting that there is a computer available for them to use at home, school or other places**

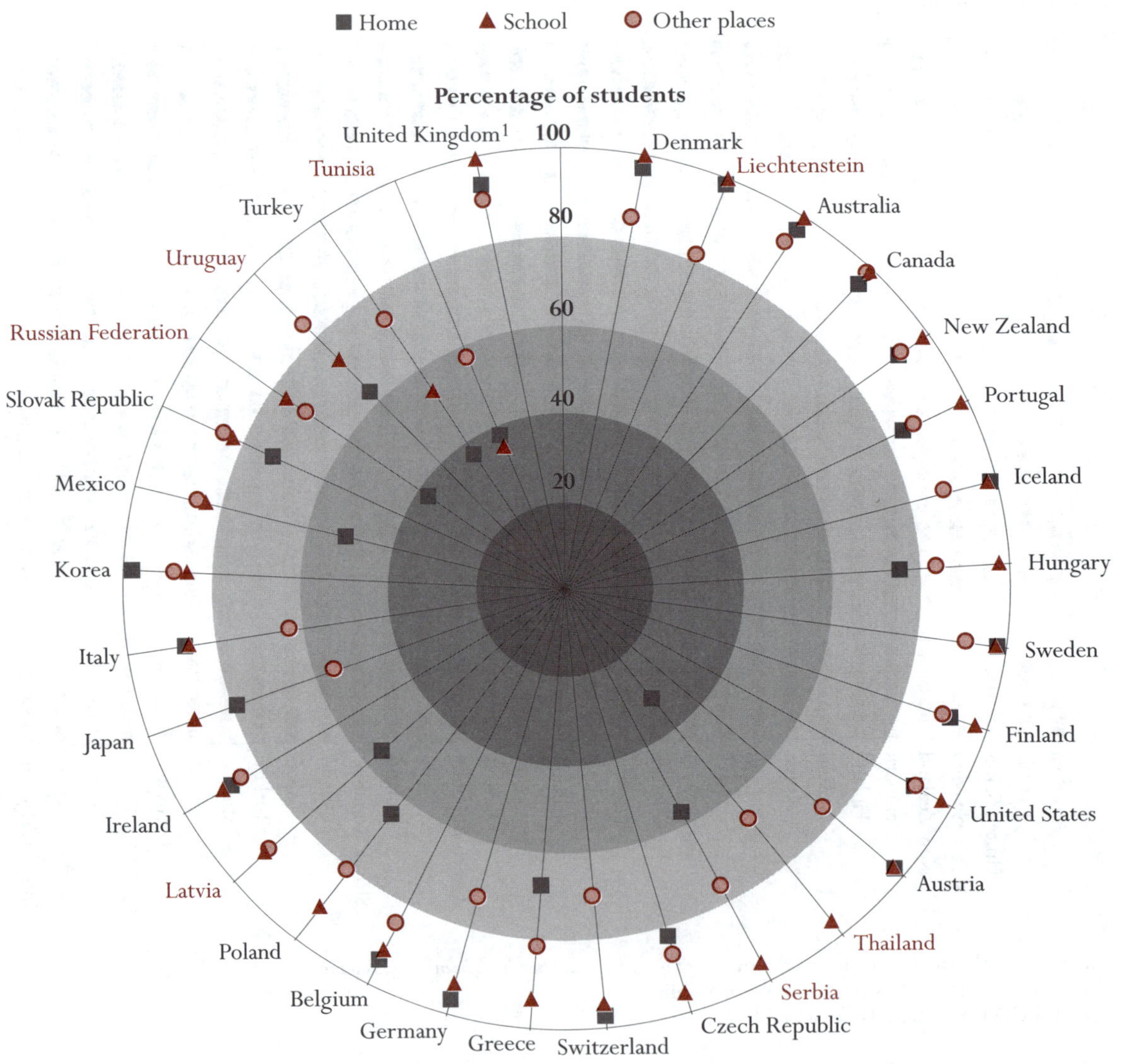

Moving clockwise, countries are ranked in descending order of percentage of students reporting that there is a computer available for them to use at school.

1. Response rate is too low to ensure comparability.

Source: OECD PISA 2003 database, Table 2.2a.

Access to a computer at home remains comparatively less common than access at school in most countries, but nevertheless it is becoming the norm in most places. In the majority of the OECD countries and the partner country Liechtenstein more than 90% of students have access to a computer at home, and the figure is above 70% in all OECD countries except Greece, Mexico, Poland and Turkey. In 18 countries, the proportion of students with access to computers is at least five percentage points higher at school than at home. In other countries, access is similar in these two settings, except in Korea, the only country where substantially more students have home access than school access: 98 and 85%, respectively (Figure 2.4).

This tendency for more students to have computers available at school than at home is especially important in countries with comparatively low levels of access to computers at home, for which the availability of a computer at school may help to compensate. In the partner country Thailand, fewer than one-third of students have access to a computer at home, but almost all (96%) can access one at school. Similarly, in Mexico and the partner countries Latvia and Serbia, only just over one-half or fewer have access at home, but more than 80% have access to a computer either at home or school. However, in a few countries, the inequity of access to a computer at home is only to a limited extent reduced by access to a computer at school. In Turkey and the partner country Tunisia, 40% or more of students do not have access to a computer either at home or at school (Table 2.2a).

Access to computers is not necessarily restricted to the home or school. Students might also, for example, access computers at the homes of relatives or friends or in public places such as libraries or Internet cafes. Students were asked whether they had access to computers somewhere other than at home or school. Many students did not answer this question – in half of the countries, non-response was between 22 and 34%. This in itself could indicate that many 15-year-olds are not aware of the possibilities of accessing computers in places other than home or school, but also means that the responses must be treated with caution. A lower percentage of students reported having access to computers in places other than at home or at school, except in the three countries with the lowest access at school: Turkey and the partner countries Tunisia and Uruguay. For example, in Turkey, only just over one-third of students can access computers at home, about one-half at school and nearly three-quarters in other places. In all countries with available data, except Italy and Japan and the partner countries Thailand and Tunisia, 70% or more of students who responded said that there was a computer available for them to use at places other than home or school (Figure 2.4). However, in few countries is such access close to universal; only in Canada is it over 95%. To some extent this may be a sign that some students with the disadvantage of lacking a computer at home are still unable to access them elsewhere, either because of a lack of supply, a lack of awareness of students that other possible places of access exist, or that the location of computers for public access in places is harder for students to reach independently. However, some students who already have access to computers at home and school may have no need to seek access elsewhere.

Changes in access to computers from PISA 2000 to PISA 2003

In PISA 2000, students in some countries responded to a computer familiarity questionnaire similar to the one administered for PISA 2003.[2] For the countries that administered the ICT familiarity questionnaires both in PISA 2000 and PISA 2003, the changes in access to a computer in the three years between the two surveys are shown in Figure 2.5.[3] Both school and home access rose significantly in almost every country between 2000 and 2003, the sole exception being Finland, where 96% of students already had access to a computer at school in 2000, and this did not rise significantly.

The rise of computer availability at school was particularly rapid in countries where it had previously been relatively low: in Germany it increased from 69 to 93%, in Mexico from 61 to 83% and in the partner country the Russian Federation from 60 to 76%. Home access also rose fastest in countries where it had been relatively low: in the Czech Republic it increased from 58 to 82%, in Hungary from 55 to 75%, in Mexico from 29 to 51% and in the partner country Latvia from 31 to 55%. Thus, in countries where a large proportion of students still lacked computer access at home or at school at the turn of the millennium, this feature of the digital divide tended to diminish in the following three years. This was also true to some extent for access to computers at places other than home or school, although in some countries where overall access is high, this kind of availability seems to have reached a plateau or even fallen slightly.[4]

Figure 2.5 ■ **Access to computers at home or at school in PISA 2000 and PISA 2003**

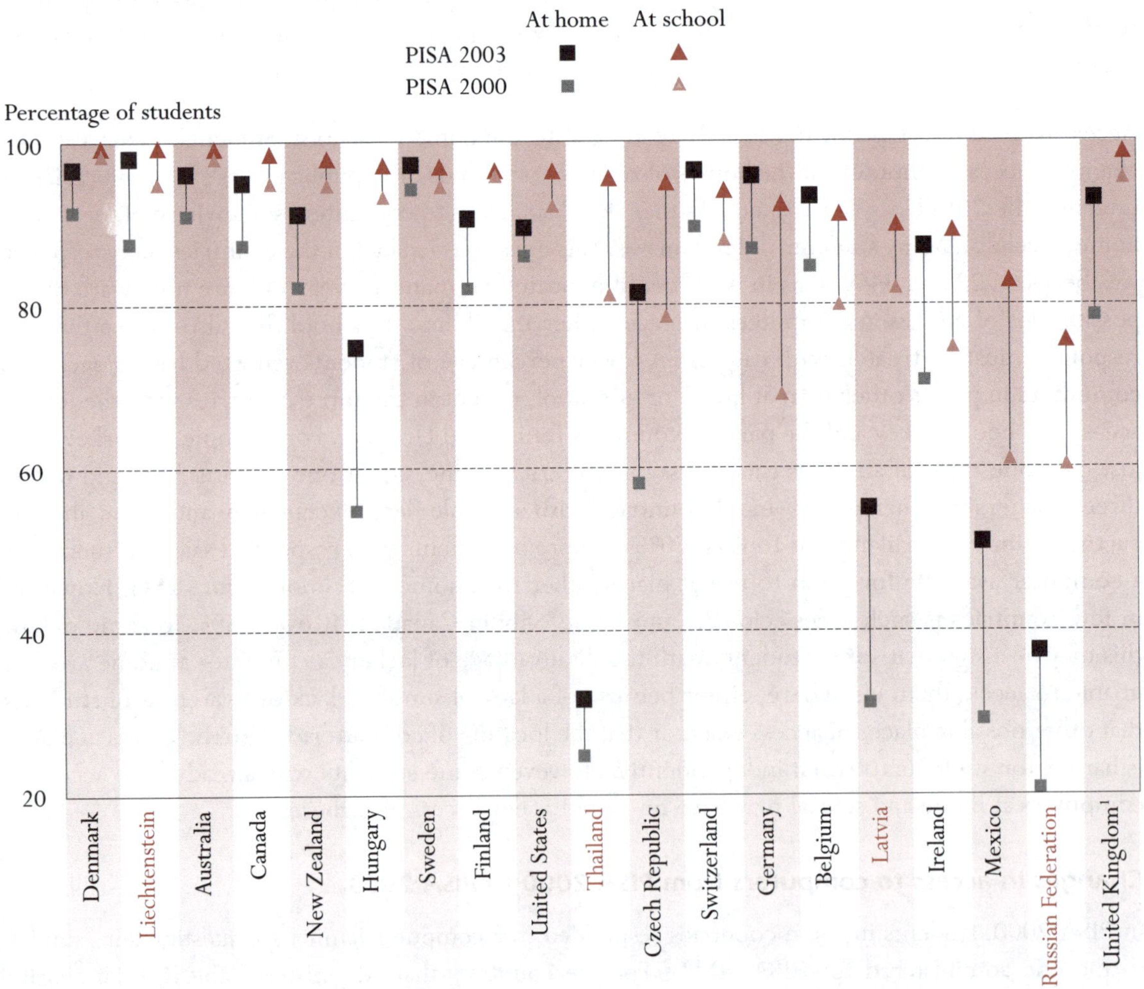

Countries are ranked in descending order of percentage of students having access to a computer at school in PISA 2003.
1. Response rate too low to ensure comparability.
Source: OECD PISA 2003 database, Table 2.2a.

Relationships between access to computers and students' gender and socio-economic background

To what extent do different groups of students – males compared to females, for example, or those students with higher or lower socio-economic status – have different access to computers?

Gender differences in access to computers at home appear in two-thirds of the countries participating in the ICT survey. Male students are more likely to have home computers available than females in 20 countries. In nine of these countries the difference is five percentage points or below, but in Greece, Poland, and the partner countries Latvia and the Russian Federation, it is between 11 and 14 percentage points (Table 2.2b). In contrast, males and females have largely the same degree of access to computers at school, and in the only countries with a gender gap of around five or more percentage points, Belgium, Ireland and Korea, the difference is in fact in favour of females. In 17 countries, males are significantly more likely to have access to computers in places other than home or school, and this difference is as high as 20 percentage points in Turkey, 10 in Italy, and 15 and 11, respectively, in the partner countries the Russian Federation and Serbia (Table 2.2b). In two countries, Ireland and the United States, females are more likely to have access to computers in other places than home or school.

Socio-economic background is a stronger predictor of whether a student had access to a computer at home than is gender, and here again the differences at school and in other places tend to be much smaller than socio-economic differences at home. Figure 2.6 shows these differences by dividing the student population of each country into four equal-sized groups, according to their ranking on PISA's index of economic, social and cultural status (ESCS). In most countries, students from the least privileged quarter of the population by socio-economic background are significantly less likely to have a computer available at home than those in the most privileged quarter. This socio-economic digital divide is starkest in countries where the fewest students overall had home computers access, such as Mexico and Turkey, and the partner countries the Russian Federation and Thailand, where 11% or fewer students in the bottom quarter by socio-economic status can access home computers, compared to at least 70% in the top quarter. However, even in some countries with high overall rates of access, this disguises wide socio-economic differences. For example, 87% of students in Italy have computers available at home, but 33% of those in the bottom quarter by socio-economic background lack this resource, compared to just 2% in the top quarter. On the other hand, some countries have near-universal access in all socio-economic groups: at least 90% of students across the socio-economic spectrum have computers at home in Austria, Denmark, Iceland, Korea, Sweden and Switzerland, and the partner country Liechtenstein.

In many countries, there are no large differences in access to a computer at school among students from different socio-economic backgrounds. However, in Mexico and the Slovak Republic, and the partner countries the Russian Federation, Tunisia and Uruguay, the percentages of students from the bottom quarter having access to a computer at school are more than 10% lower than those from the top quarter. This variable pattern across countries also applies to access to computers in places other than home or school, although here some countries have more substantial differences by background. In the partner country Tunisia, such computers are available to 81% in the top quarter, but only 28% in the bottom quarter. The gap between the top and the bottom quarters is between 20 and 35 percentage points in Mexico, Poland and Turkey, and the partner countries the Russian Federation, Thailand and Uruguay (Figure 2.6).

Figure 2.6 ■ **Students' socio-economic background and access to computers at home, school and other places**

Percentage of students with access to computers at home, school and other places, by national quarters of the index of economic, social and cultural status (ESCS)

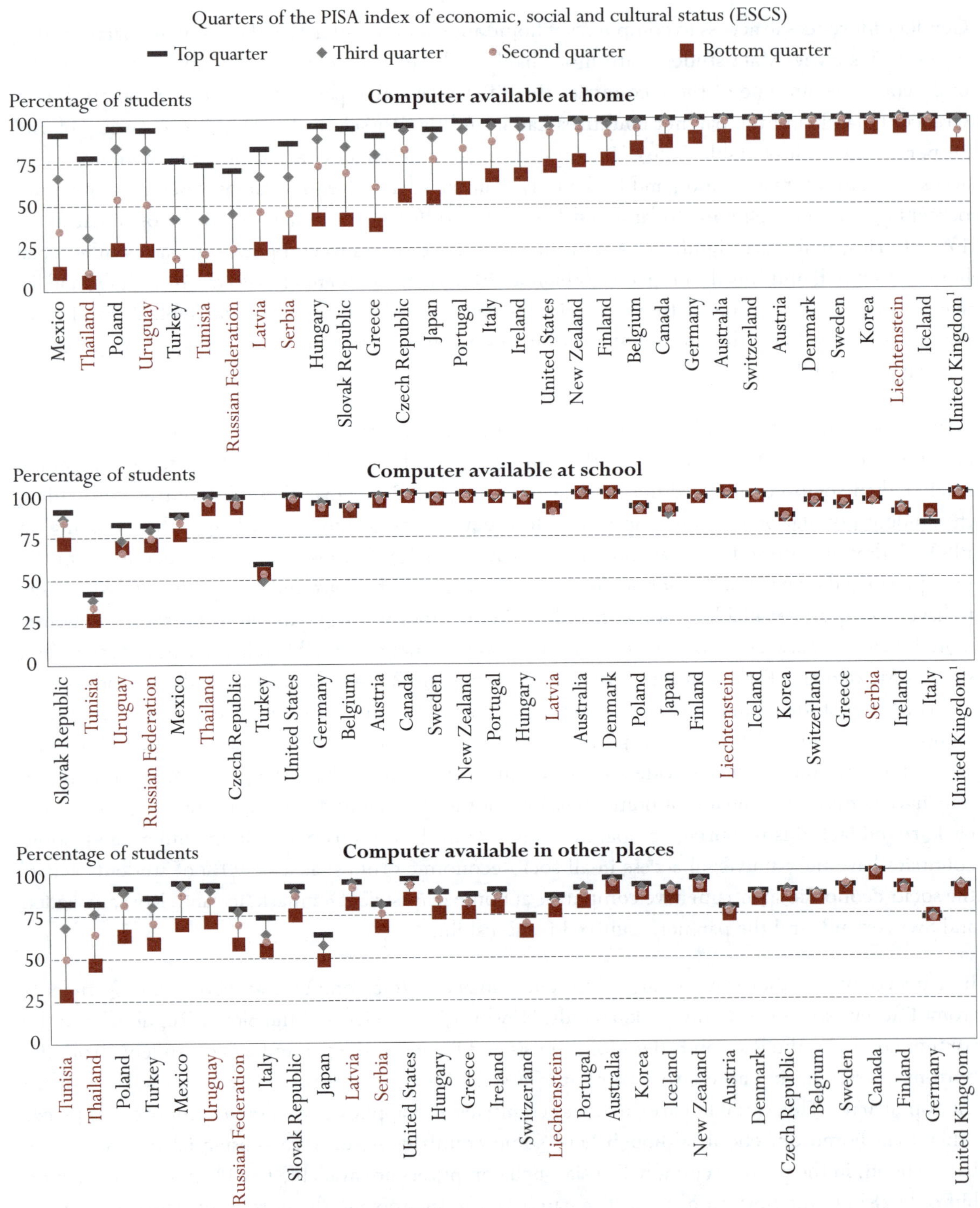

Countries are ranked in descending order of differences between the top and bottom quarters of the index of ESCS for each indicator.
1. Response rate too low to ensure comparability.
Source: OECD PISA 2003 database, Table 2.2c.

ICT AND OTHER EDUCATIONAL RESOURCES AT HOME

To what extent can students' home-based computers and other resources be used for educational purposes? This section presents evidence from students in all 41 countries participating in PISA collected via the student questionnaire (not just the 32 countries that took part in the extra ICT survey). Figure 2.7 shows results of students' reports on whether they had a computer they could use for schoolwork, educational software, a calculator and books to help with their schoolwork at home, with countries ordered by the percentage of students with a home computer to use for schoolwork. This is at least 90% in 14 countries, with Iceland, Korea and the Netherlands having at least 95% of students with this home resource. In each of the 32 countries in the ICT survey, a minority of students who report having access to a computer at home say that they do not have one available for schoolwork (Tables 2.2 and 2.3a). In all but one country, this minority is relatively small – between 2 and 18% of the whole student population. However in Japan, where nearly four-fifths of students have access to a computer at home, less than one-half say it is available for schoolwork.

Not many students report having educational software at home, although over 60% do in Australia, Canada, the Netherlands, the United Kingdom and the United States. Calculators are more common, with at least 90% of students having a calculator of their own at home in 29 countries. However, in Japan and Korea, and the partner countries Indonesia and Tunisia, fewer than 70% of students have a calculator.

In comparison, Figure 2.7 also shows how many students have books to help with their schoolwork at home. In most countries (30 out of 41), at least three-quarters report having this resource, and only in the Netherlands is it below one-half. The percentage of students who report having books at home to help with their schoolwork ranges between 42 and 92% across the OECD countries, which is smaller than the range in the percentage of students who report having computers at home to use for schoolwork (between 23 and 97%). Comparing in Figure 2.7 the number of students with computers with those who have books to help with their schoolwork at home, it is clear that these resources are combined by many students, but that the balance in their availability differs across countries. In about one-half of countries, over 80% have computers for this purpose, and in all these countries fewer have books. In countries where fewer than 80% of students have computers, more have books than computers. In the 11 countries where fewer than one-half of students have a home computer to help with schoolwork, more than 70% have books for this purpose, except in Mexico and the partner country Tunisia.

To what extent does access to ICT and to other educational resources at home depend on the students' socio-economic background? There are large differences in percentages between students in the top and bottom quarters of the PISA index of ESCS, in terms of how likely they are to have computers for use with schoolwork. On average, 94% of students with the most favourable socio-economic background report having this resource, but only 58% of students with the least favourable background (Table 2.3b) do so. Socio-economic background makes less of a difference to the chance of having a calculator, but in the case of educational software, the differences in many countries are quite large: in most, the chance of someone in the top socio-economic quarter having educational software is at least three times that of someone in the bottom quarter. On average in the OECD there is a similar relationship between socio-economic background and the likelihood of having both books and computers at home to help with schoolwork: 60% of students in the bottom quarter have books available at home for this purpose, compared to 95% in the top quarter; this is very similar to the figures of 58 and 94%, respectively, for computers.

Figure 2.7 ■ **ICT and educational resources at home**

Percentage of students with access to ICT and educational resources at home

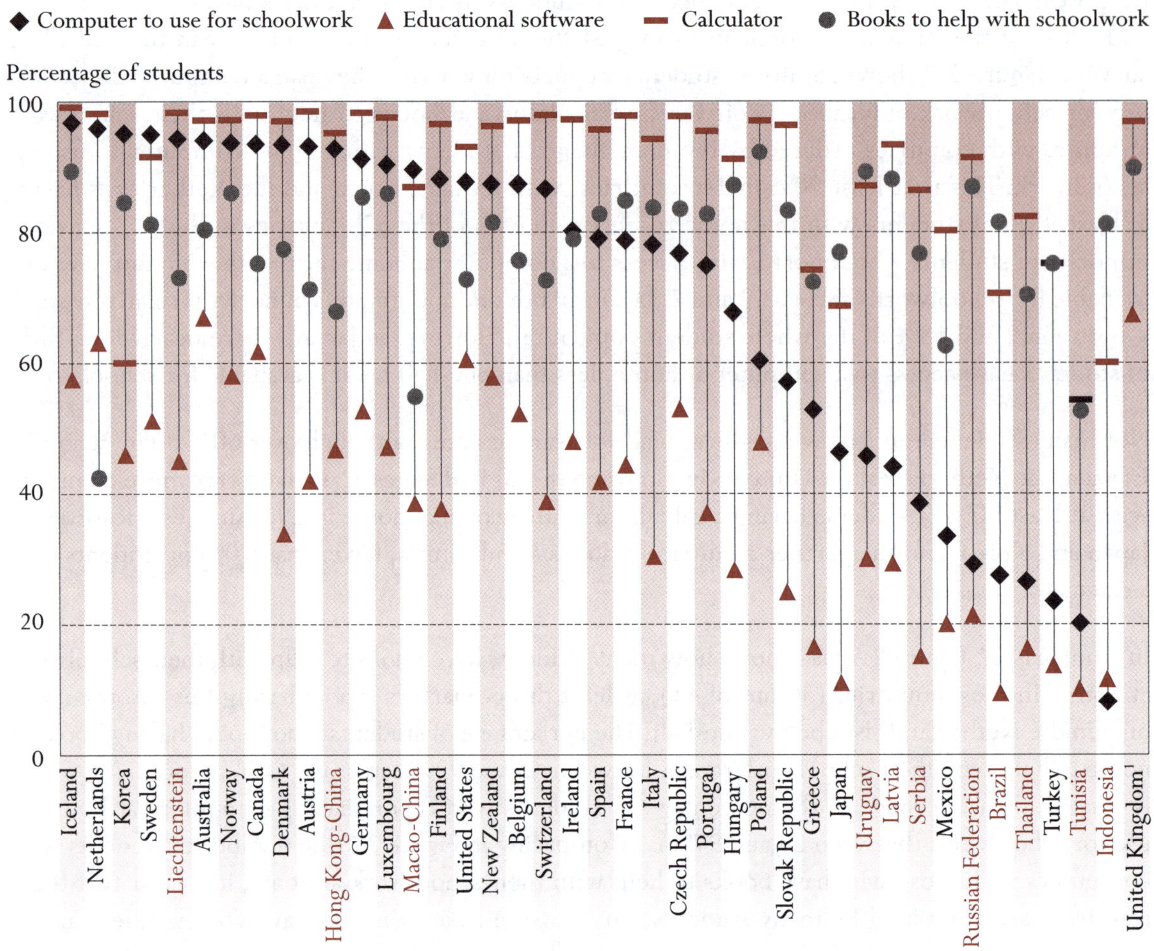

Countries are ranked in descending order of percentage of students with a computer at home to use for schoolwork.
1. Response rate too low to ensure comparability.
Source: OECD PISA 2003 database, Table 2.3a.

ICT RESOURCES AT SCHOOL

The extent of ICT resources available at school

While the great majority of students have some kind of access to computers at school, students' experience of ICT also depends on the number of computers within their schools and on how many of them are available to students, according to principals' responses to the PISA school questionnaire. In all countries except the partner countries Brazil, Indonesia and Tunisia, 99% or more of students are in schools with more than one computer. In Australia, Austria, Canada, Hungary, Korea, New Zealand, the United Kingdom and the United States, and the partner countries Hong Kong-China and Liechtenstein, the number of computers per student is more than 0.2, implying five or fewer students per computer. In Turkey and the partner countries Brazil, Indonesia, the Russian Federation, Serbia, Thailand, Tunisia and Uruguay, the number of computers per student is 0.05 or less, implying 20 or more students per computer (Figure 2.8).

Figure 2.8 ■ **ICT resources at school**

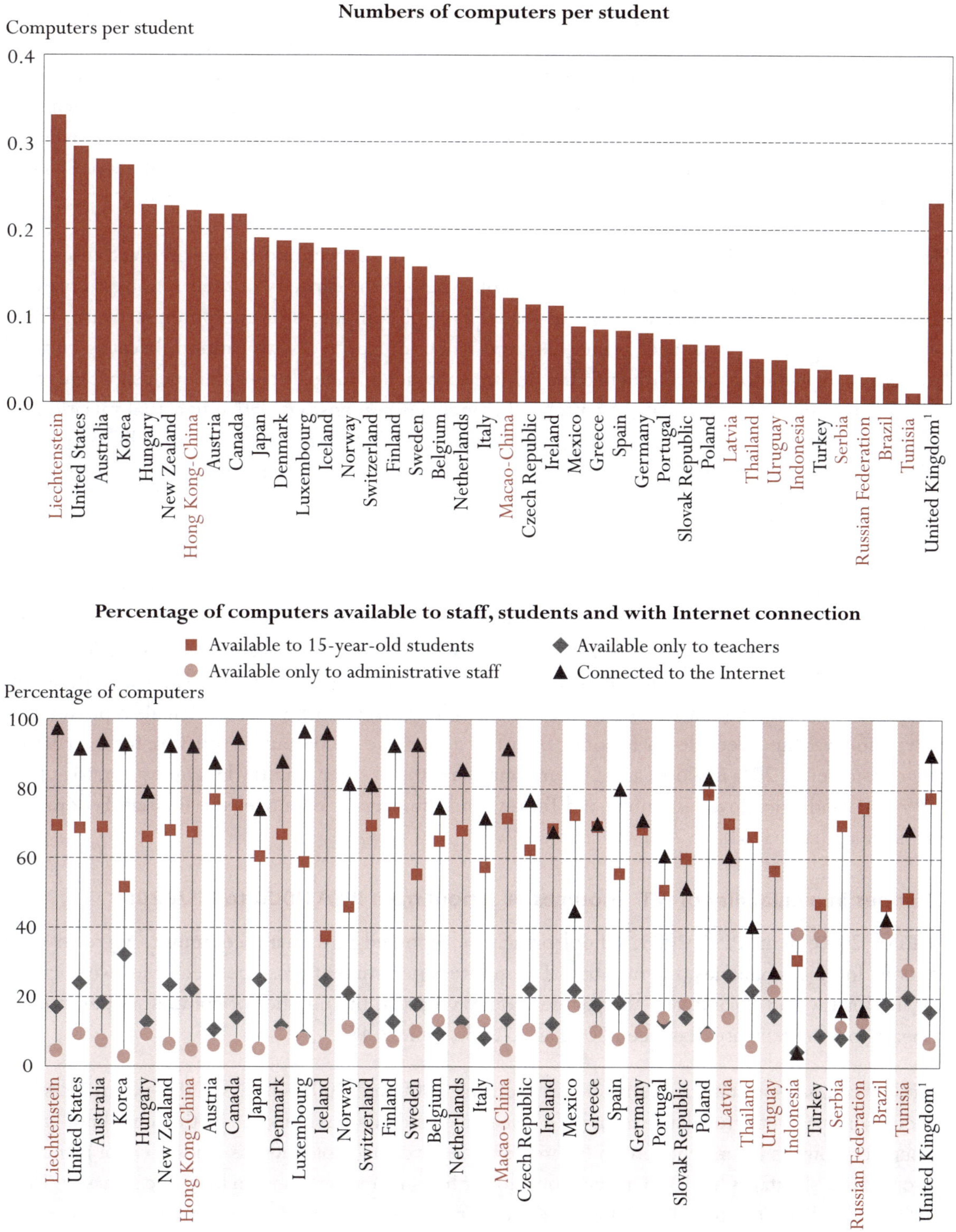

Countries are ranked in descending order of number of computers per student.
1. Response rate too low to ensure comparability.
Source: OECD PISA 2003 database, Table 2.4.

In all countries except Iceland, Norway and Turkey, and the partner countries Brazil, Indonesia and Tunisia, between 50 and 80% of computers in school are available to 15-year-old students. In all countries except Korea and the partner country Latvia, no more than one-quarter of computers in school are for teachers' use only. Also, in all countries except Turkey and the partner countries Brazil, Indonesia, Tunisia and Uruguay, less than one in five computers in school are available only to administrative staff. One-half or more computers in school are connected to the Internet in all countries except Mexico and Turkey, and the partner countries Brazil, Indonesia, the Russian Federation, Serbia, Thailand and Uruguay. In 19 of the participating countries at least 80% of computers in school are connected to the Internet (Figure 2.8).

How does the instructional environment related to ICT resources and ICT-related activities vary between countries? School principals reported on whether the capacity of their schools to provide instruction was hindered by a shortage or inadequacy of computers or computer software. These subjective judgements by school principals need to be interpreted with caution, because cultural factors and expectations may influence the degree to which principals consider such shortage to be a problem. Annex A2 shows that the pattern of principals' responses (relative to actual variations in computer resources within schools) suggests that cultural factors affect the comparability of these judgements across countries, but that within each country the responses can be compared with greater confidence.

The percentage of students in schools where school heads reported that instruction was hindered a lot or to some extent by a shortage of computers for instruction varied from a small minority in some countries to a great majority in others. In Korea and the partner country Liechtenstein, only 10 and 12%, respectively, of students are in such schools, whereas at least 70% of students have principals with these concerns in Norway, Turkey and the partner countries the Russian Federation, Serbia and Uruguay. Similarly, the percentage of students in schools whose principals reported that instruction was hindered a lot or to some extent by a shortage of computers software for instruction range from below 20% in Korea and Luxembourg, and the partner country Liechtenstein, to at least 70% in Poland, the Slovak Republic and Turkey, and the partner countries the Russian Federation, Serbia, and Uruguay (Table 2.5).

Changes in availability of ICT resources at school from PISA 2000 to PISA 2003

In PISA 2000, as in PISA 2003, school principals reported how many computers were in their schools. In most countries, the number of computers per students rose between the two surveys, but in Norway and Poland, and the partner country Latvia, the number of computers per student appears to have decreased between 2000 and 2003 (Table 2.4).

Another comparison that can be made between the 2000 and 2003 surveys is the extent to which school principals reported that learning of 15-year-old students was hindered by the school not having enough computers for instruction. In Figure 2.9, the percentage of students whose school principals reported that shortages hindered instruction a lot or to some extent is shown by vertical bars for PISA 2003 and by diamonds for PISA 2000. In some countries the situation appears to have improved; in others, school principals perceived the lack of computers in 2003 as more of a problem than they did in 2000. This does not necessarily mean that fewer computers were available for learning. It could also mean that school principals in these countries showed greater awareness of the relevance of computers to facilitate learning. The reported effects of shortages has lessened in Germany, Greece, Iceland

Figure 2.9 ■ **Percentage of students in schools whose principals report that instruction is hindered by a shortage of computers for instruction**

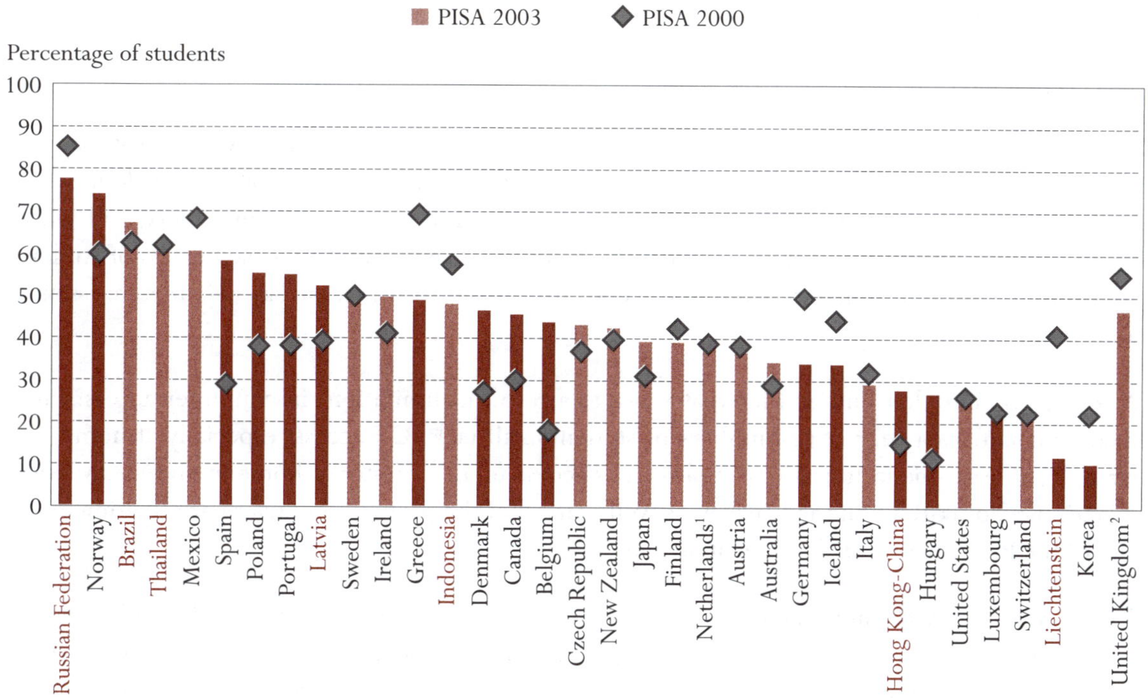

Countries are ranked in descending order of percentage of students hindered by the shortage of computers for instruction in PISA 2003.
Note: Statistically significant differences between 2000 and 2003 are marked in a darker tone.
1. Response rate too low to ensure comparability for PISA 2000.
2. Response rate too low to ensure comparability for PISA 2003.
Source: OECD PISA 2003 database, Table 2.5.

and Korea, and the partner countries Liechtenstein and the Russian Federation. The hindering of instruction was reported more frequently in 2003 than 2000 in Belgium, Canada, Denmark, Hungary, Luxembourg, Norway, Poland, Portugal and Spain, and the partner countries Hong Kong-China and Latvia. In 17 countries, there has been no significant change.

Availability of ICT resources at school and school location

To what extent does access to ICT resources depend on the school's location (rural locations and towns versus cities)? In most countries there are no differences in the number of computers per student between schools in rural locations or towns and schools in cities. But in few countries, such as Austria, Denmark, Iceland, Ireland, Italy, Korea and Norway, and the partner countries Latvia and Serbia, schools in rural locations or towns tend to have more computers per student than city schools, while in countries such as Poland and the Slovak Republic, and the partner country Brazil, it is the reverse (Table 2.6).

There are also differences by school location in some, but not most countries, in terms of the extent to which instruction was reported to be hindered by ICT availability. The effects of computer shortages are more likely to have been reported as hindering instruction in schools in rural locations or towns in Australia, Iceland and Mexico, and the partner countries Brazil and Thailand, but in city schools in Belgium. In the case of shortage of instructional software, the effect is more severe in schools in rural locations or towns in Iceland, Mexico and New Zealand, and the partner counties Brazil and Thailand (Table 2.6).

CONCLUSIONS AND IMPLICATIONS

In most OECD countries and in some partner countries in the PISA 2003 survey, the great majority of 15-year-old students have ready access to computers, at home and at school. In a world in which computer access has become an essential prerequisite for full participation in society, and where computers have an integral role in learning, the main concern is whether some groups of students are being left behind. Students who lack access are unable to use what has become an essential educational tool.

Who then is being left out, and in what ways, as a result of limitations in computer access? First, in some countries a very large numbers of students still lack ICT access, especially at home. For example, at least one in four 15-year-olds lacks access to a computer at home in Greece, Mexico, Poland, the Slovak Republic and Turkey, as well as in all of the partner countries participating in this part of the PISA survey, except Liechtenstein.

Even in countries with much higher access rates overall, people from less advantaged socio-economic backgrounds have less chance of accessing computers than their peers. Among the quarter of students from the least advantaged backgrounds, at least one-third lack home computer access in nearly one-half of OECD countries, and in Hungary, Mexico, Poland, the Slovak Republic and Turkey, the majority of these students have no computer to use at home. Thus, while only a few countries still need to focus on tackling the problem of general computer access, many continue to have serious issues of whether disadvantaged students are able to work on computers at home. Access to computers at other places outside school does not seem to have fully resolved this inequality. Note, however, that there are some countries where even relatively disadvantaged students overwhelmingly have access to computers at home. In Austria, Denmark, Iceland, Korea, Sweden and Switzerland, this applies to over 90% of the least advantaged quarter of students by socio-economic status.

In this context, the disadvantage in terms of differences in resources to support school learning that some students face in their home environments varies in its nature from one country to another. In the past, the presence or absence of books at home to support school learning seemed to play an important role, and has been highly correlated with educational outcomes. Today, in some countries, socio-economic background is a stronger predictor of whether students have computers than whether they have books available to support schoolwork at home, and responses to social inequalities need to be adapted accordingly.

While very few students in most countries lack any access to a computer at school, a third source of inequality of access concerns the number of students per computer available to them. Even among affluent countries, this continues to vary greatly, with, for example, over three times as many students sharing each computer in Germany as in Australia, Korea and the United States. An interesting indicator of whether differences in the quantity of hardware and software affect the ability of schools to fulfil their educational aims using ICT is the extent to which principals say that shortages impede learning. The above analysis (and Annex A2) makes it clear that too much should not be read into differences in principals' views in this respect across countries, but that within each country policy makers can consider the range of principals' views to gauge the impact of localised shortages.

A final potential area of difference, gender, is not one that greatly affects access to ICT today. There are minor differences in some countries, but it is in how much they use computers and are confident in using them that most distinguish male and female experiences of ICT; these are the subjects of the next chapter.

Notes

1. See Table A3.1 in *Learning for Tomorrow's World: First Results from PISA 2003* (OECD, 2004b)
2. Portugal is not included in this trend analysis due to a change in target population between the 2000 and 2003 surveys.
3. Since the data collection for PISA 2000 for Thailand was conducted in 2001, the changes presented here are over two years.
4. This comparison should however be made with caution, since the question was slightly different in the two surveys.

3

Students' Use of and Attitudes towards ICT

KEY POINTS

- Even though access to computers is more universal at school than at home, 15-year-old students use their computers at home more frequently. Nearly three-quarters are using computers at home several times each week.
- Students use computers for a wide range of functions, not just to play games. Various common uses, such as Internet research, have educational potential, but students use specific educational software less frequently.
- The vast majority of students are able to tackle basic ICT tasks and students are generally confident about their Internet abilities. While fewer believe they can perform high-level tasks unaided, most think they could do so with some help.
- Overall, female students use computers less frequently, and are less confident in ICT, than their male counterparts. However, this varies by type of use. Males are more likely to play games and to do programming than females, but there is little gender difference in frequency of word processing and sending e-mails. Females are now about as confident as are males that they can perform basic computer functions, but males remain much more confident in high-level tasks such as programming, suggesting that the male bias in advanced computer studies has persisted.

Figure 3.1 ■ **Student computer use in OECD countries**

Percentage of students on average in OECD countries who:

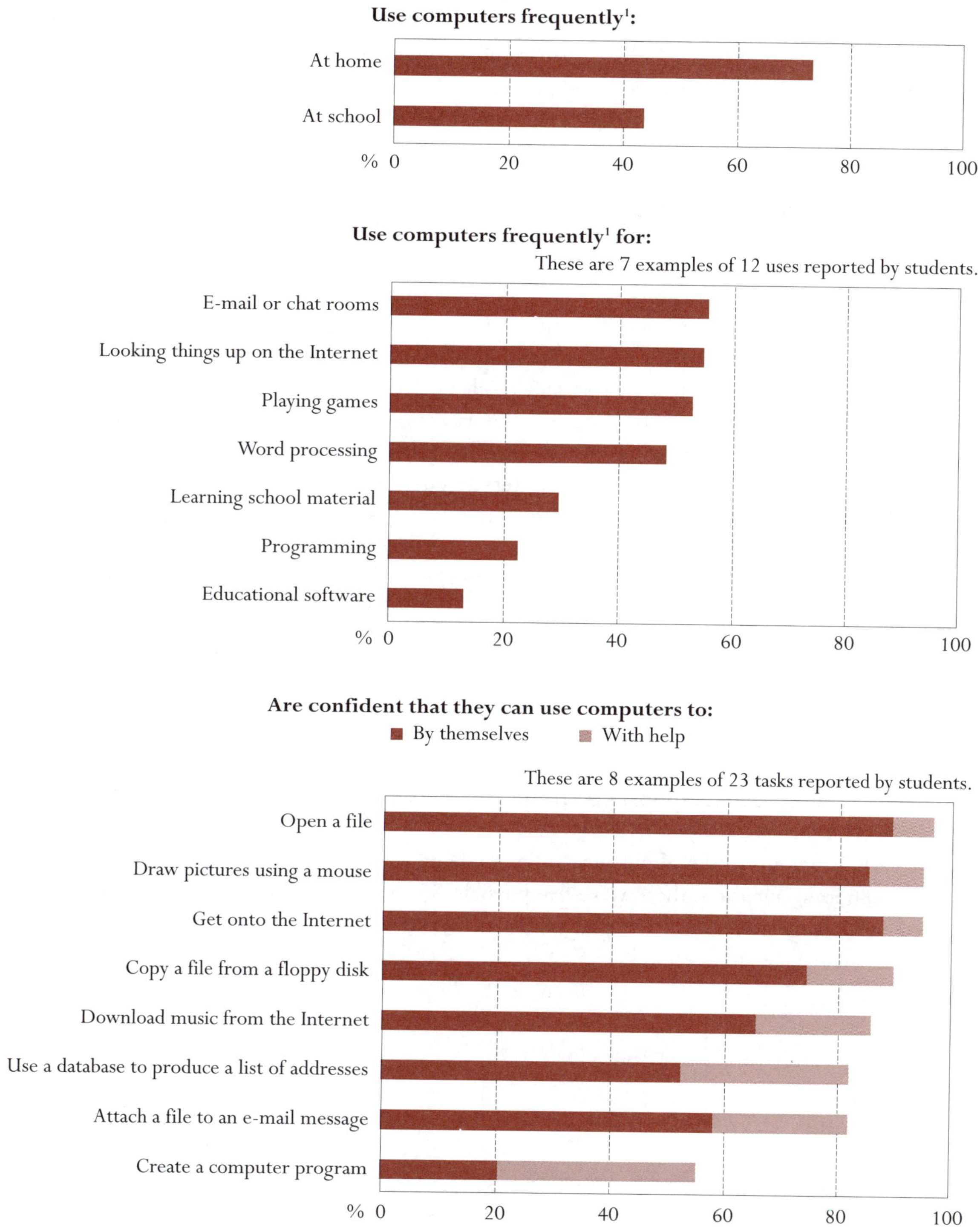

1. Students reported that they use computers "Almost every day" or "A few times each week".

INTRODUCTION

As more and more students gain access to computers and to the Internet, how in practice are they using ICT? This chapter examines how frequently students use their computers overall, at home and at school. It then considers the range of tasks for which they use computers and compares students in different countries in terms of indices showing how widely they use computers. Computer usage can be strongly affected by how positive students feel about computers and by how confident they are in performing particular ICT tasks. This chapter considers each of these in turn and looks at the extent of gender differences for each.

FREQUENCY OF USE BY LOCATION

How often do students use computers and how does this vary by location? PISA 2003 asked students how often they used a computer at home, at school or at other places. Figure 3.2 shows the results. If students responded that they used computers almost every day or a few times each week, they are considered to make frequent use of computers (see Box 3.1). In all countries except Hungary, Mexico and the partner countries Serbia and Thailand, students report that they use computers most frequently at home. Over three-quarters report doing so in 17 of the 32 surveyed countries, although in some it is much fewer. In most countries, it appears that most students who have access to computers at home use their home computers frequently. However, this is not true in Japan, where 79% of students have access to computers at home, but where only 37% report using them frequently (Tables 2.2a and 3.1). Typically, much fewer students use computers frequently at school than do at home, and in only ten countries do the majority of students use them frequently at school. However, over two-thirds of students do so in Denmark (68%), Hungary (80%) and the United Kingdom (71%) (Figure 3.2).

Box 3.1 ■ Student responses on frequency of use and how they were classified

For each question in PISA about how often students used computers in different locations or for different purposes, there were five possible responses, but the answers were grouped into three categories:

Frequent use:

"Almost every day" or "A few times each week"

Moderate use:

"Between once a week and once a month"

Rare or no use:

"Less than once a month" or "Never"

Figure 3.2 ■ **Students frequently using a computer at home, school or other places**

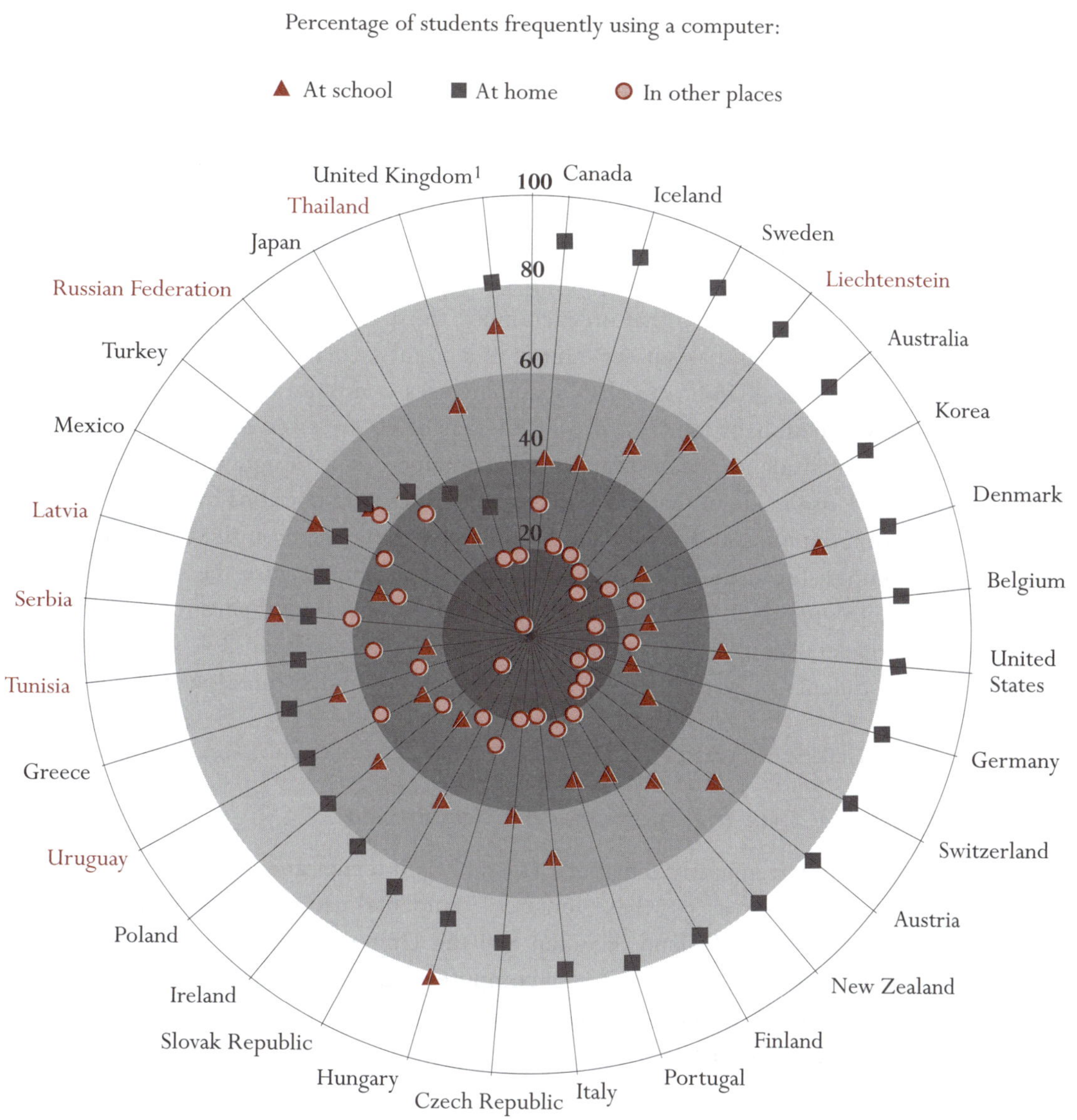

Moving clockwise, countries are ranked in descending order of percentage of students frequently using computers at home.
1. Response rate too low to ensure comparability.
Source: OECD PISA 2003 database, Table 3.1.

FREQUENCY OF USE BY TYPE OF USE

Having asked students how much they used computers overall at home and at school, the survey went on to pose 12 questions about how frequently they used computers to perform various types of functions. In order to summarise the results, an index of frequency was constructed for each of two groups of usage, each representing six types of ICT functions. The first index is for Internet and entertainment tasks, which incorporates both educational uses such as looking up information and leisure uses such as playing games. The second index is for the use of programs such as word processing or spreadsheets and the use of educational software. These indices can be grouped into two main types: use of ICT for Internet and entertainment and use of ICT for programs and software.

Box 3.2 ■ Interpreting the indices of frequency of ICT usage

Each index comparing how much use different students make of a range of ICT functions combines their responses to several questions into a composite score. These scores are represented as index numbers so that on each index the average score for all students in all OECD countries is zero, and about two-thirds of students score between +1 and -1. Thus, for example, a score of -1 indicates that a student uses computers more than about one-sixth students internationally, and a score of +1 that he or she uses computers more than about five-sixths of students. Each index is self-contained: it is designed only to show the relative amount of use made of that particular set of computer functions by different groups of students. Comparing a country's mean on one index to its mean on the other index does not allow a comparison to the effect that students in that country use the set of computer functions more frequently in the index with the higher score. To compare frequency of use of each index readers should refer to the first panel in Figures 3.3 and 3.4, which show the percentage of students reporting frequent use of each computer function included in the index.

Frequency of use of ICT for the Internet and entertainment

Students were asked how frequently they perform various Internet and entertainment tasks using ICT. Looking first at an index across these functions, students' use of ICT is highest in Australia, Canada, Iceland, Korea, New Zealand, Sweden and the United States, and the partner country Liechtenstein (Figure 3.3). The lowest usage of computers for the Internet and entertainment is in Ireland, Japan and the Slovak Republic, and the partner countries Latvia, the Russian Federation, Serbia, Thailand, Tunisia and Uruguay.

It is also possible to compare across countries how wide a gap there is between those who use ICT the most and the least. This is shown in Figure 3.3 by the symbols representing the usage made by the quarter of students with the greatest use of ICT for the Internet and entertainment and the quarter with the lowest usage. The widest gaps between the most and least frequent users (of 2.6 index points or more) are in Belgium, Mexico and Turkey, and the partner countries Serbia and Uruguay, while the smallest gaps (2 points or less), representing the most even usage across the population, are in Finland, Hungary, Japan, Korea and the Slovak Republic (Figure 3.3).

Within this index, there are some tasks that could include both entertainment and educational elements: for example, using the Internet to look up information could comprise both educational research and leisure use. Familiarity with e-mail and the Internet, even if not always used directly for educational purposes, can have a wide range of spin-off benefits in an information-oriented society.

Figure 3.3 ■ **Students' use of ICT for Internet and entertainment**

Percentage of students reporting frequent use[1] of:

	The Internet to look up information about people, things or ideas	Games on a computer	The Internet to collaborate with a group or team	The Internet to download software (including games)	The Internet to download music	A computer for electronic communication (*e.g.* e-mail or chat rooms)
Canada	75	59	49	58	77	83
United States	74	62	42	52	64	71
Korea	59	57	49	47	79	73
Liechtenstein	66	47	32	52	62	76
Sweden	62	57	28	44	62	75
Australia	74	50	43	47	58	69
Iceland	73	53	25	43	58	71
New Zealand	65	56	39	47	58	69
Belgium	60	50	33	44	58	71
Denmark	68	58	34	38	43	63
Portugal	58	60	44	41	50	53
Austria	62	43	26	38	50	58
Switzerland	57	43	26	37	47	58
Germany	53	52	21	37	48	54
Poland	44	56	38	32	40	45
Czech Republic	54	53	30	27	33	48
Greece	45	61	26	46	50	36
Finland	40	53	13	30	38	59
Italy	54	57	25	44	47	41
Mexico	50	45	40	36	46	47
Turkey	38	56	29	40	47	43
Hungary	42	61	33	24	33	48
Uruguay	45	55	29	33	39	44
Latvia	37	50	22	28	36	40
Ireland	38	47	17	24	33	34
Slovak Republic	36	57	26	19	23	29
Tunisia	38	50	24	29	33	30
Serbia	28	65	22	27	36	29
Thailand	30	46	24	25	27	24
Russian Federation	18	55	13	22	21	18
Japan	26	19	7	9	12	22
OECD average	**55**	**53**	**31**	**38**	**49**	**56**
United Kingdom[2]	65	58	41	49	58	69

Index of ICT Internet and entertainment use

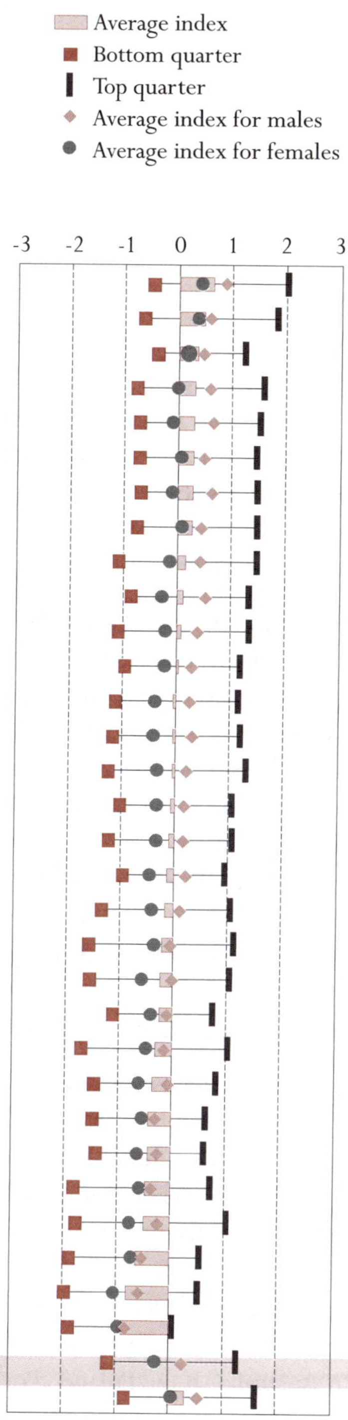

1. Students reported that they use computers "Almost every day" or "A few times each week".
2. Response rate too low to ensure comparability.
Source: OECD PISA 2003 database, Table 3.2.

Specific types of Internet and entertainment use

On average across OECD countries, a small majority of students frequently use their computers for each of three of the purposes classified here as Internet and entertainment use: 56% use them for e-mail or chat rooms, 55% to look up information about people, things or ideas on the Internet and 53% to play games. Nearly as many (49%) frequently use them to download music but only about one-third to download software (38%) or to collaborate with a group or team (31%).

The results for individual countries for each activity are listed in Figure 3.3. In some countries more than two-thirds of students use computers for certain purposes. This is true in the largest number of countries for e-mail and chat rooms, which at least two-thirds of students report doing frequently in Australia, Belgium, Canada, Iceland, Korea, New Zealand, Sweden, the United Kingdom and the United States, and the partner country Liechtenstein. Two-thirds or more use the Internet to look things up in Australia, Canada, Denmark, Iceland and the United States, and the partner country Liechtenstein, and this many frequently download music in Canada and Korea. In comparison, Canada stands out as the place with the most active student use of the Internet, with at least three-quarters frequently engaging in each of the above three activities. Interestingly, even though on average similar numbers play games as use the Internet for each of these purposes, no one country stands out as having a much higher than average percentage of games users: nowhere do more than two-thirds of students do so frequently, even though over one-half do on average across countries.

Gender differences in frequency of use of ICT for the Internet and entertainment

In all countries participating in PISA 2003, males use ICT more than females for Internet and entertainment (Table 3.2). The most pronounced gender differences are in reported use of computer games. On average in the OECD, males are twice as likely as females to play such games frequently (70 and 35%, respectively). In Denmark and Sweden, the gap is even wider, with more than 80% of males frequently playing computer games. In the United States, where the gender gap is narrower, over one-half of females aged 15 frequently use computers for games. On average across the OECD, males are also twice as likely to download games and other software frequently (51% of males and 25% of females) (Table 3.3). However, males and females make similar use of computers for electronic communication, with an average of 56% of males and 55% of females reporting frequent use of computers for this purpose.

Frequency of use of ICT for programs and software

Students were also asked how frequently they use ICT for different programs and software. There were five possible answers (see Box 3.1). Figure 3.4 compares the average student usage for these purposes on an index. Overall, considerably fewer students report a frequent use of programs and software when compared to their reported use of ICT for the Internet and entertainment: only a minority of students on average say that they use computers frequently for any one of these purposes (see the first panel of Figure 3.4). However, note that the index values are adjusted so that on each index the OECD country average is zero, so a given score on the programs and software index represents a lower average frequency than on the Internet and entertainment index. In Australia, Italy, Poland, Portugal, the United Kingdom and the United States, and the partner country Uruguay, students report comparatively high use of programs and software. Students in Finland, Ireland, Japan and Korea, and the partner countries Latvia and the Russian Federation, report comparatively low use.

Figure 3.4 ■ **Students' use of ICT for programs and software**

Percentage of students reporting frequent use[1] of:

	The computer for programming	The computer to help learn school material	Educational software such as mathematics programs	Drawing, painting or graphics programs on a computer	Spreadsheets (*e.g.* <Lotus 123®> or Microsoft Excel®>)	Word processing (*e.g.* <Word® or WordPerfect®>)
United States	33	36	18	41	22	62
Uruguay	23	54	46	36	34	51
Italy	31	44	20	41	31	59
Australia	25	32	10	32	22	70
Portugal	34	57	15	29	28	53
Poland	28	26	25	40	32	47
Mexico	32	45	25	48	32	38
Denmark	20	51	15	22	18	65
New Zealand	25	30	12	33	22	54
Canada	29	29	9	35	17	62
Liechtenstein	23	21	10	32	24	59
Austria	23	31	9	28	25	60
Greece	28	23	22	45	27	45
Iceland	22	38	11	23	14	44
Turkey	37	32	26	45	32	43
Czech Republic	19	26	15	28	22	46
Serbia	28	28	18	56	21	52
Hungary	17	31	10	30	32	53
Slovak Republic	20	32	18	33	23	44
Tunisia	32	40	34	34	24	34
Germany	23	27	11	24	19	49
Thailand	23	37	17	39	19	36
Switzerland	21	20	8	22	19	45
Sweden	18	23	5	25	8	47
Belgium	23	24	7	19	17	49
Latvia	16	25	14	29	20	33
Finland	11	18	3	18	6	27
Russian Federation	21	22	18	30	21	35
Korea	8	19	6	15	7	32
Ireland	13	16	9	26	15	34
Japan	3	5	1	9	8	17
OECD average	**23**	**30**	**13**	**30**	**21**	**48**
United Kingdom[2]	27	34	19	36	31	66

Index of ICT program and software use

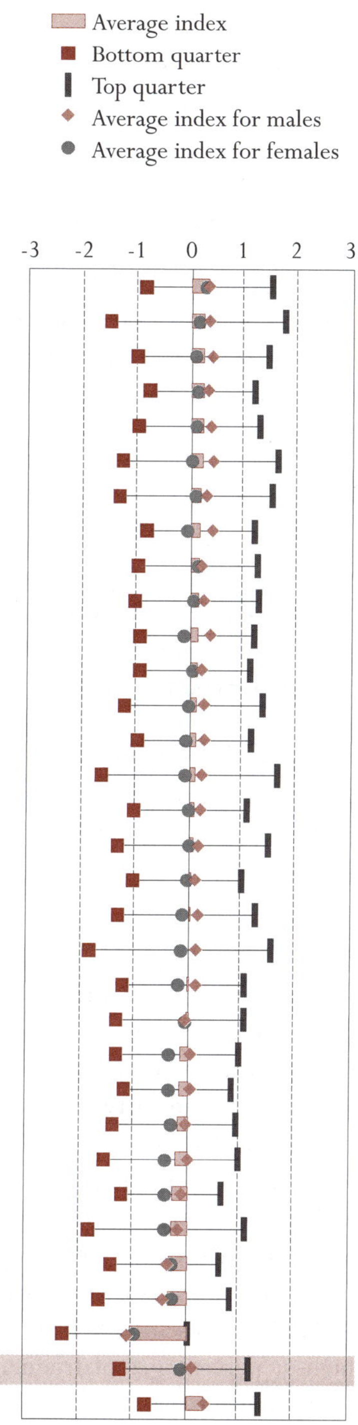

1. Students reported that they use computers "Almost every day" or "A few times each week".
2. Response rate too low to ensure comparability.
Source: OECD PISA 2003 database, Table 3.4.

Also, the range in reported use of ICT for programs and software within countries varies. For example, there is a range of at least 2.8 index points between students in the top and bottom quarters of the index of ICT programs and software use in Mexico, Poland and Turkey, and the partner countries the Russian Federation, Serbia, Tunisia and Uruguay. However, there is a range of 2.0 index points or less between the top and bottom quarters in Australia, Denmark, Finland, Korea and Sweden (Figure 3.4).

Of the programs students were asked about using on a computer, word processing (*e.g.* <Microsoft® Word®> or <WordPerfect®>) was frequently used by the highest percentage of students on average in the OECD (48%). This ranges from below 20% of students in Japan to 70% in Australia, but in 18 of the 32 countries with available data between 40 and 60% of students reported frequent use of word processing software (Figure 3.4).

Thirty per cent of students on average in the OECD report frequent use of drawing, painting or graphics programs on a computer, as well as frequent use of the computer to learn school material. Notably, over 50% of students report frequent use of the computer to learn school material in Denmark and Portugal, and the partner country Uruguay, and the figure is around 45% in Italy and Mexico.

Twenty-three per cent and 21% of students on average in OECD countries report frequent use of the computer for programming and spreadsheets (*e.g.* <Lotus 123® or Microsoft® Excel®>) respectively. Over 30% of students report frequent use of the computer for programming in Italy, Mexico, Portugal, Turkey and the United States, and the partner country Tunisia, and over 30% frequently use spreadsheets in Hungary, Italy, Mexico, Poland, Turkey and the United Kingdom, and the partner country Uruguay (Figure 3.4).

Out of all 12 ICT uses that students were asked about in the survey, the one that fewest reported using frequently was educational software, such as mathematics programs (13%). However, in the partner countries Tunisia and Uruguay, 34 and 46% of students, respectively, report frequent use of educational software.

Gender differences in frequent use of ICT for programs and software

In the majority of countries, males report the most frequent use of ICT for programs and software. However, the gender gap here is on average less than half as wide as for Internet and entertainment uses, and in Ireland, Japan and Korea a higher percentage of females report more frequent use (Table 3.4). Almost twice as many males report frequent use of computers for programming (30% of males and 16% of females on average in the OECD). This gender difference is particularly large in the Czech Republic, Denmark and Sweden, and the partner country Liechtenstein, where males are three to four times more likely to frequently use computers for programming than are females, and in Finland males are nearly six times as likely to do so. However, gender differences for other program and software uses are not very pronounced. For example, on average in OECD countries 49% of females and 48% of males report frequent use of word processing. Indeed, the cases of the highest percentages of frequent word-processing users by country and gender are mainly those where females use them more. In OECD countries, the proportion of students using computers for word processing at least several times a week rises above two thirds only for females and males in Australia (73 and 67%, respectively), and for females in Austria (67%), the United Kingdom (72%)

and the United States (67%). The partner country Liechtenstein provides the sole exception to this rule, with 69% of males, but only 49% of females, using word processing frequently (Table 3.5).

ATTITUDES TOWARDS ICT

How positive are students' experiences using computers? Students were asked whether they strongly agree, agree, disagree or strongly disagree with four positive statements about working with computers. These covered whether students think computer use is important, whether they enjoy using them, whether they are motivated by an interest in computers and whether they lose track of time when they use computers. These responses were used to create an index of attitudes towards computers. The results are shown on an index constructed in the same way as those described in Box 3.2 above. Note that a negative score on this index does not necessarily signify a negative attitude to computers, but an attitude less positive than the average for students in OECD countries. It is important to bear in mind that each index combines information reported by students and not information that is directly measured or observed. Students across countries may vary with respect to how they perceive and respond to the questionnaire items on which the constructs are based.

Comparatively, students in Austria, Canada, Germany, Iceland, Korea, Poland and Portugal, and the partner countries Liechtenstein, Serbia and Tunisia, express more positive attitudes towards computers, whereas students in Denmark, Finland, Hungary, Ireland and Japan, and the partner country Latvia report slightly less positive attitudes (Table 3.6). In all countries except Japan and the partner countries Thailand and Tunisia males report more positive attitudes towards computers than do females.

To what extent can students' gender be used to predict their attitudes to computers, compared to other factors such as the availability of computers at home, how frequently students use computers or whether students have taught themselves to use computers? Figure 3.5 shows how much of the variation in students' attitudes towards computers is accounted for by each of these factors, but this does not show that the factors are causes, rather it shows that there is an association that would allow a student's attitude to be predicted according to these other characteristics. Altogether, these factors only explain 6% or less of the variance in students' attitudes towards computers in Ireland, Korea and the United States, and the partner countries Tunisia and Uruguay. However, they explain more than twice this amount – between 13 and 22% of variation in attitudes – in the Czech Republic, Denmark, Finland, Germany, Hungary, Iceland, Portugal, the Slovak Republic and Sweden. In 13 of the 32 countries with available data, gender has the largest explanatory value on students' attitudes towards computers among these factors. On the other hand, the strongest factor in this respect is whether students taught themselves to use computers in a number of other countries: Australia, Austria, Belgium, Canada, Ireland, Japan, Korea, the United Kingdom and the United States, and the partner country Tunisia. A third factor plays the biggest role in another set of countries: whether students have access to a computer at home. Not surprisingly, the countries where this is the most important - Mexico, Portugal and Turkey, and the partner countries the Russian Federation, Serbia, Thailand and Uruguay – are ones where relatively large numbers of students still lack home access.

In other words, while students' attitudes to computers are associated with their gender to some extent (more so in some countries than others), their attitudes are mainly determined by other factors. In some countries students who are self-taught have particularly positive attitudes,

Figure 3.5 ■ **Factors influencing students' attitudes towards computers**

Percentage of explained variance in students' attitudes towards computers

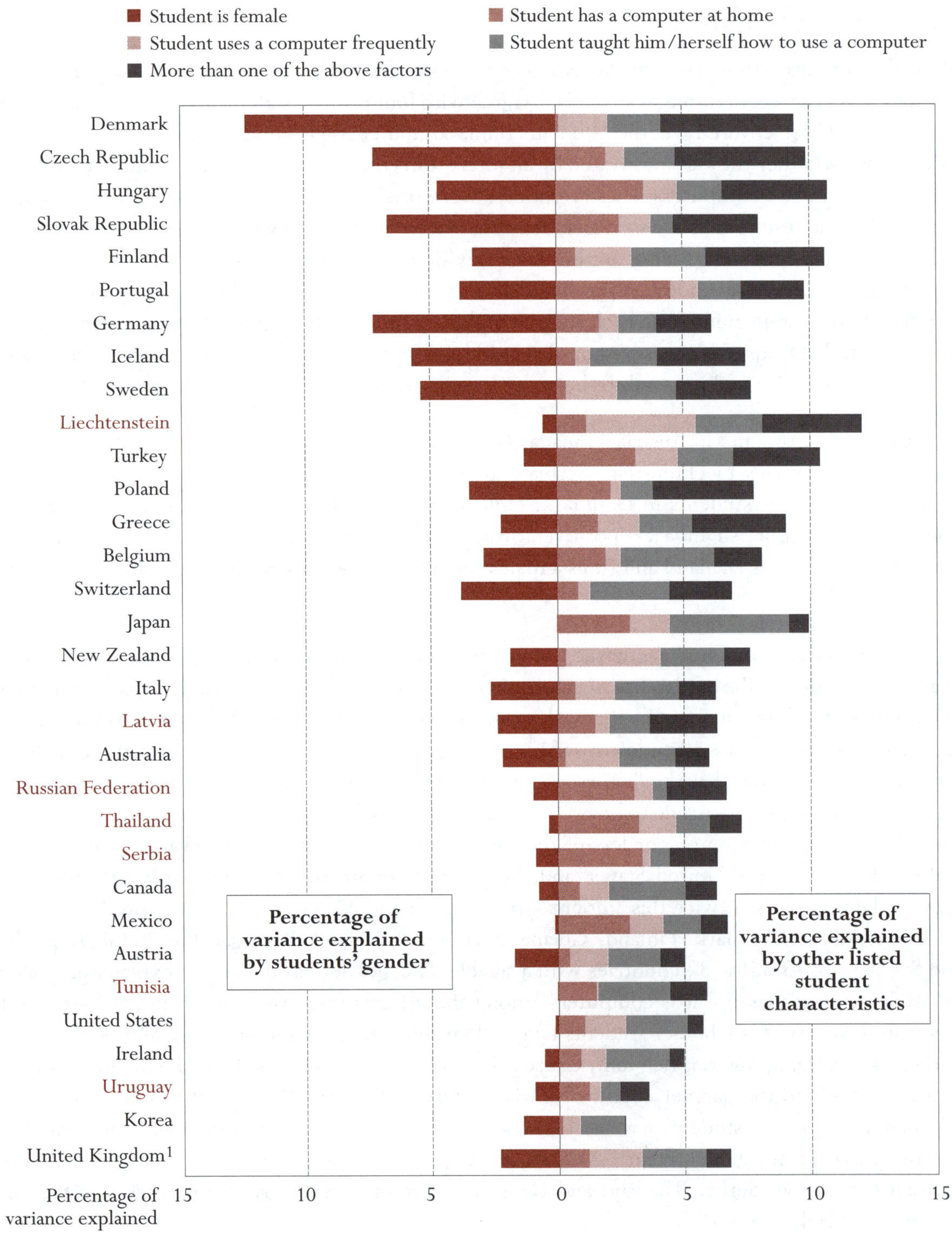

Countries are ranked in descending order of variance explained.

1. Response rate too low to ensure comparability.

Source: OECD PISA 2003 database, Table 3.7.

and in some an important criterion is the obvious one of whether they have a computer available at home. Nevertheless, all these factors put together explain only a small part of varying student attitudes.

STUDENTS' CONFIDENCE IN USING ICT

In PISA 2003 students provided information on how well they felt they could perform various tasks using a computer. These tasks fell into three broad categories: routine tasks on a computer, such as opening, saving, deleting or copying files; Internet tasks, such as downloading files or music from the Internet; and high-level tasks, such as creating presentations, multi-media presentations or computer programs. The tasks included in each of the three categories and the percentage of students on average in the OECD reporting how well they could perform each task are presented in Box 3.3. When interpreting these results it is important to bear in mind that the indices of confidence in using ICT are based on students' subjective assessments and students in different countries may perceive and respond to questions differently.

This report considers students to be at least somewhat confident in performing a task if they answered "I can do this with help from someone" and to have high level of confidence if they answered "I can do this very well by myself".

Generally, students in all participating countries report high confidence in using ICT, with the majority saying they are able to perform 17 of the 23 tasks specified very well by themselves. Students are relatively more confident performing routine tasks than Internet tasks or high-level tasks on a computer, although even in the case of the latter, most students thought that they could do each task at least if they had some help.

On all three indices of confidence in ICT tasks, students in Australia, Canada and the United States, and the partner country Liechtenstein are among the most confident on average, although students in Korea have greatest confidence when using the Internet. Conversely, students in Japan and the partner countries the Russian Federation, Serbia, Thailand and Tunisia have among the lowest mean levels of reported confidence on all three indices (Figure 3.6). This appears to reflect lower rates of access to computers at home reported in the partner countries the Russian Federation, Serbia, Thailand and Tunisia, and also at school, where, despite the fact that 76% of students in the Russian Federation, 95% of students in Serbia and 96% of students in Thailand report having access to computers at school, these countries have among the lowest numbers of computers per student (0.03, 0.03 and 0.05 respectively) (Tables 2.2a and 2.4). In Japan, access to computers is higher, but as noted in Chapter 2, fewer than half of students in Japan say that they can use home computers for school work, and as noted earlier in the present chapter, only just over one-third used their home computers frequently (Tables 2.3a and 3.1).

Routine tasks

On average in OECD countries, students are particularly confident performing routine tasks such as opening a file or playing a computer game, but are slightly less confident moving or copying files on a computer (although on average around 75% of students report they can do this by themselves). The most confident students in these tasks are in Australia, Austria, Canada, the Czech Republic, Iceland, Portugal, Sweden and the United States, and the partner country Liechtenstein.

Box 3.3 ■ Students' confidence in performing different computing tasks

What can students do with a computer? PISA 2003 asked students how well they could perform 23 different ICT tasks. There were four possible answers, shown in the table below. The questions identified three broad groups of tasks: routine tasks, Internet tasks and high-level tasks. Three indices were derived from these and are presented in Tables 3.8, 3.10 and 3.12.

Percentage of students reporting how well they can perform routine tasks, Internet tasks and high-level tasks on a computer (OECD average)

	I can do this very well by myself	I can do this with help from someone	I know what this means but I cannot do it	I don't know what this means
Routine tasks				
Open a file	90	7	2	1
Play computer games	90	7	2	1
Start a computer game	86	10	3	1
Save a computer document or file	88	8	3	2
Delete a computer document or file	88	8	3	2
Draw pictures using a mouse	85	10	3	1
Print a computer document or file	86	9	3	2
Scroll a document up and down a screen	87	8	3	3
Create/edit a document	80	13	4	2
Move files from one place to another on a computer	76	17	6	2
Copy a file from a floppy disk	75	16	7	3
Internet tasks				
Get onto the Internet	88	7	3	1
Write and send e-mails	79	12	6	3
Copy or download files from the Internet	70	19	8	3
Download music from the Internet	66	21	11	3
Attach a file to an e-mail message	58	24	13	5
High-level tasks				
Use a database to produce a list of addresses	52	30	11	7
Create a presentation (*e.g.* using <Microsoft® PowerPoint® >	47	27	15	10
Use a spreadsheet to plot a graph	44	31	17	9
Create a multi-media presentation (with sound, pictures, video)	35	35	23	7
Construct a Web page	28	39	27	6
Use software to find and get rid of computer viruses	37	29	26	7
Create a computer program (*e.g.* in Logo, Pascal, Basic)	21	35	31	14

Note: Each group of tasks is listed in descending order of the percentage of students responding "I can do this very well by myself" or "I can do this with help from someone", *i.e.* students on average are more confident performing tasks at the top of each list.

In 27 of the 32 countries with available data significantly more males than females report being confident performing routine tasks on a computer (Table 3.8). In fact, in all countries except the partner country Tunisia, at least 75% of students report feeling confident about each of the routine tasks listed in Box 3.1, and in 17 countries this is at least 90% of students (Table 3.9). Thus, across the OECD the majority of students are comfortable and familiar enough with ICT to be confident in their ability to perform its essential tasks.

Figure 3.6 ■ Indices of students' confidence with routine tasks, Internet tasks and high-level tasks

1. Response rate too low to ensure comparability.
Source: OECD PISA 2003 database, Tables 3.8, 3.10 and 3.12.

Internet tasks

As can been seen in Figure 3.6, students are most confident in performing Internet tasks in Australia, Canada, Iceland, Korea, New Zealand, Sweden and the United States, and the partner country Liechtenstein. In fact, in these countries at least 90% of students report being confident on each of the 5 Internet tasks (Table 3.11). The mean on the index of confidence in ICT Internet tasks for students in Korea is particularly high (0.77) and contrasts starkly with reported means on the indices of routine and high-level tasks which are just above and just below the OECD average, respectively. Within this category, students report the most confidence on average in getting on to the Internet and writing and sending e-mails, but slightly less confidence in downloading files or music from the Internet and in attaching files to an e-mail message (Box 3.3).

High-level tasks

In all participating countries students are, as expected, comparatively less confident in performing high-level tasks on a computer. On average the task that students are least confident performing is creating a computer program. However, over one-half of students in OECD countries (56%) still report that they can do this either by themselves or with help from someone (Box 3.3). Comparatively more students in Australia, Austria, Canada, Iceland, New Zealand, Poland and the United States, and the partner country Liechtenstein report being confident performing high-level tasks on a computer (Figure 3.6).

Gender differences

There are quite clear gender differences on the indices of confidence in routine tasks, Internet tasks and high-level tasks. In the majority of countries, males report far higher confidence in all three categories of ICT tasks (Figure 3.6). However, the largest differences in favour of males are found with regard to confidence in performing high-level tasks, and these exist in all countries except Thailand. In particular, far fewer females in the Czech Republic, Denmark, Finland, Germany, Iceland, Poland, Sweden and Switzerland, as well as in the partner countries Latvia and Liechtenstein, report being confident in performing high-level tasks on a computer, with a difference of at least 0.60 index points in favour of male students (Table 3.12).

A closer look at students' self-reports on level of confidence in high-level tasks on a computer reveals some insights into where gender differences are most and least important. On average in the OECD a higher percentage of males report being confident in all seven of the tasks in this category. The smallest gender differences (less than 10 percentage points) are found for the high-level tasks in which most students are confident: using a database to produce a list of addresses, creating a presentation and using a spreadsheet to plot a graph (Table 3.14). Conceivably these tasks are more likely to be used in an academic context than the remaining four tasks in the high-level tasks category. Males are 10 percentage points more likely to report confidence in constructing a Web page. The relatively low averages for the three remaining tasks are in part explained by the large gender differences: 15 percentage points fewer females are confident in creating a computer program, 16 percentage points fewer females are confident in creating a multi-media presentation, and 25 percentage points fewer females are confident in using software to find and get rid of computer viruses.

To the extent that students' confidence at age 15 is predictive of their future educational choices, students' reports of confidence in PISA 2003 give policy makers an indication that among the PISA 2003 cohort of 15-year-olds, there are still likely to be significantly fewer females following and completing higher academic studies in computing. Figure 3.7 shows the proportion of all higher academic qualifications (ISCED 5A/6) awarded to females in 2003 (dark bar), and this provides a snapshot picture of educational choices of previous cohorts of school students. This picture mirrors the gender difference in the reports of confidence among today's 15-year-olds. On average only 24% of university-level and advanced research qualifications in computing were awarded to females. In contrast, when considering all fields of study, 56% of higher academic qualifications were awarded to females (light bar). Some countries have much lower gender gaps in terms of computing qualifications, however. Between 39 and 42% of higher academic qualifications in computing are awarded to females in Finland, Korea, Mexico and Sweden. Yet these four countries show a striking contrast in gender gaps in the confidence of 15-year-olds in ICT use, as shown in PISA. The gap is quite moderate in Korea and Mexico. In Finland and Sweden, on the other hand, students' self-reports in PISA 2003

Figure 3.7 ■ **Proportion of higher academic qualifications[1] in computing and all fields of education awarded to females (2003)**

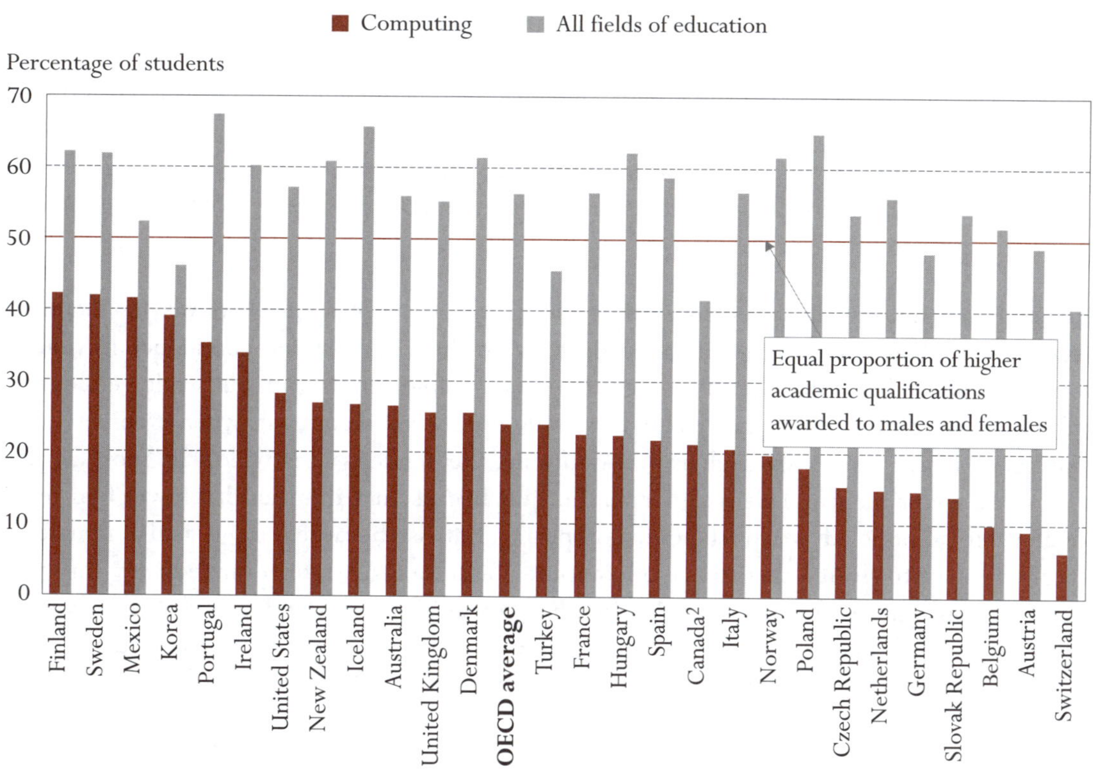

Countries are ranked in descending order of proportion of computing qualifications awarded to females.
1. Includes qualifications from theoretically oriented university-level programmes (ISCED 5A) and advanced research programmes such as Ph.D.s (ISCED 6). Excludes vocationally-oriented tertiary programmes (ISCED 5B).
2. Data are for the year 2001.
Source: OECD Education database, Table 3.15.

reveal very large differences in levels of confidence between males and females, despite the relatively high participation of females in advanced computer studies. In contrast, only 15% or fewer of the higher academic qualifications in computing were awarded to females in Austria, Belgium, the Czech Republic, Germany, the Netherlands, the Slovak Republic and Switzerland (Figure 3.7).

CONCLUSIONS AND IMPLICATIONS

Overall, students are more likely to use computers frequently at home than at school, and the educational value of computers needs to be considered in a range of settings, not just in terms of the classroom. This chapter has shown that students do employ computers for many functions that may entertain them, educate them and help them communicate with others. It is noteworthy that the usage most readily identified as entertainment – playing games – while common among 15-year-old students, is not dominant. About half play games frequently, about the same number as use computers to look things up on the Internet and to do word processing. However, only a small minority of students engage frequently in the most purely "educational" type of usage, employing educational software. Furthermore, many of the educational benefits of computers seem to occur when students use ICT tools that are not designed purely for learning, like Internet search engines, spreadsheet programs or e-mail.

In this respect, it is a good sign when students are observed using a wide range of ICT tools with confidence and are therefore able to harness them for learning as appropriate. The indices of usage give some idea of the extent to which different students in different countries are using ICT. While this does vary considerably across and within countries, it is encouraging that when asked about their confidence in performing ICT tasks, the vast majority of 15-year-olds said they were comfortable with the basic computer functions. This suggests that there is not today a general problem with young people's ability and willingness to use a computer as a basic learning tool to find information or to write up a project, for example.

Yet even those students who have mastered the basic tools of the computer have varying inclinations to use these tools to their full potential, depending on their interest and confidence in venturing into more advanced or unfamiliar uses. Here there is a visible gender gap, but while gender makes a difference here, it is not the principal determining influence. In contrast, when it comes to using computers for high-level tasks such as programming, the gender gap is wide. The more advanced the task, the wider the gap. This is important not just because it will mean that fewer females may be inclined to go on to advanced studies in computing, but also because it suggests that females may be more hesitant to stretch their usage of computers as a tool. A strategy for reducing this gender difference would need to concentrate on building females' interest and confidence in computer usage itself, helping them to see how ICT can be used flexibly as a learning tool, rather than coaching females in the use of familiar functions, which they have generally already mastered.

4

Students' Access to and Use of ICT and Their Performance in PISA 2003

KEY POINTS

- The minority of students who still have only limited access to computers performed below the OECD average in PISA 2003. In particular, those without access to computers at home are, on average, one proficiency level below the OECD average. In most countries this effect remains even after accounting for socio-economic background of students.
- Students with the shortest experience of using computers scored poorly on average in PISA 2003. Those with less than a year's experience can typically perform only the simplest mathematics tasks.
- Students who use computers least frequently at home also performed below average in PISA 2003. However, students using computers most frequently at school do not in all countries perform better than others. Looking at the frequency with which students use computers for a range of purposes, the highest performances in PISA 2003 were seen among those students with a medium level of computer use rather than among those using computers the most.
- Students with low confidence in their ability to undertake routine tasks on the computer or to use the Internet performed much lower in mathematics in PISA 2003 than did the most confident students.

Figure 4.1 ■ **Students' mathematics scores on average in OECD countries and access to and familiarity with ICT**

OECD average scores in mathematics according to :

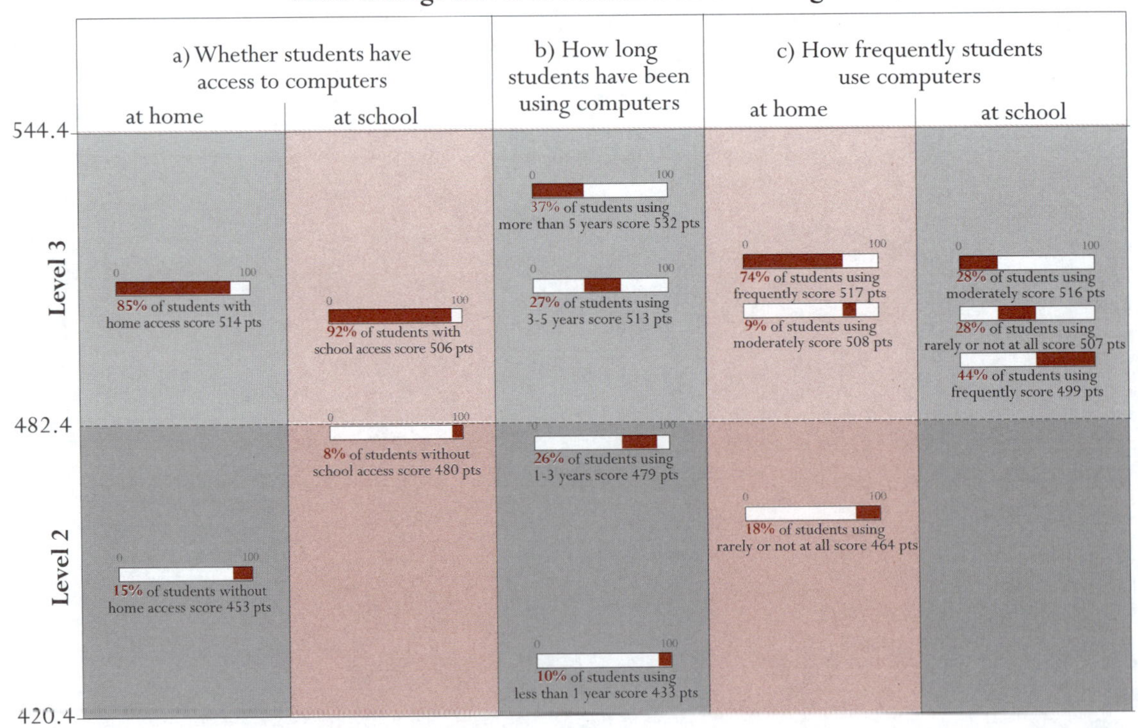

INTRODUCTION

How is the way that students use computers associated with their performance in mathematics and other subject areas measured by PISA? The inclusion of an optional ICT questionnaire in the PISA 2003 survey enabled the comparison of data on student performance in mathematics with data on student access to and use of computers. Associating computer access and usage with performance cannot provide evidence of the impact of computers on learning, since the PISA data do not demonstrate causation. The data do, however, raise important issues for closer investigation. In particular, the following evidence shows that the minority of students who still lack access to computers, or who use them little, underperform at school, but also shows that there is no simple relationship demonstrating that the more students use computers, the better they will perform.

This analysis makes an important distinction between the use of computers in the home and at school. Previous studies have demonstrated that home use of computers is most strongly correlated with higher academic achievement (Ravitz *et al.,* 2002; Harrison *et al.,* 2003). However, the relationship between use of computers in school and achievement is more ambiguous and some early correlational studies found a negative association (Ravitz *et al.,* 2002; Papanastasiou *et al.,* 2003; Wenglinsky, 1998). A complication in making such comparisons, at school in particular, is that weaker students may be more likely to be given computer-aided instruction, so a negative association with performance when looking at the whole student population is not inconsistent with a positive effect of such instruction for individuals.

This chapter looks first at how students perform according to two aspects of computer access – whether they have computers available to use today and for how long they have been using them. It goes on to consider the relationship between computer usage and performance, in terms both of overall usage at home and at school and of how much they use computers for particular purposes. A third part of the analysis looks at how student attitudes to computers relate to their performance.

EQUITY OF ACCESS TO TECHNOLOGY AND STUDENT PERFORMANCE

As was seen in Chapter 2, in many countries schools play an important role in providing more equitable access to technology. While in six OECD countries at least one in five students still lack access to computers at home, in only one country, Turkey, do more than one in five lack access at school. But to what extent might school access reduce any performance differences associated with inequitable home access?

Table 4.1 looks at the relationship between students' access to a computer in various settings and their mathematics performance in PISA. It shows that the largest performance differences are seen between students who have access to a computer at home and those who do not (Table 4.1). What these differences mean in terms of the levels of proficiency of students with and without a computer available for use at home is shown in Figure 4.2. The diamonds, showing mean performance for all students, allow these results to be benchmarked against each country's average. In most countries, given that the great majority of students do now have access to a computer, the biggest difference from the country average is seen among those who lack access, whose scores are everywhere below average.[1] In other words, the key issue raised here is the comparatively low performance among those without home computers.

Box 4.1 ■ ICT and educational achievement: what the research says

What's School Got to Do With It? Cautionary Tales about Correlations between Student Computer Use and Academic Achievement, J. Ravitz, J. Mergendoller and W. Rush (2002)

This American study is based on student achievement data taken from the Iowa Test of Basic Skills and the Test of Academic Proficiency (ITBS/TAP), given to 31,000 students from over 300 schools, and school data from the School Technology Inventory completed by school or district-level administrators in the state of Iowa. The researchers demonstrate an overall positive relationship between student achievement and computer proficiency, as well as between use of computers at home and student achievement. However, generally there is an inverse relationship between in-school computer use and student achievement. This latter finding is explained by a greater percentage of students in smaller, lower-performing schools using computers and a smaller percentage of students in larger, higher-performing schools using computers. Additionally, the researchers use mean family incomes in the school area as a proxy to control for the students' socio-economic status (SES), and results hold for both low-SES and high-SES students. The researchers conclude that lack of access to computing at home is a more substantial barrier to achievement than lack of access to computers at school.

Children and Young People's Home Use of ICT for Educational Purposes: The Impact on Attainment at Key Stages 1-4, G. Valentine, J. Marsh, C. Pattie and BMRD (2005)

This British study conducted research in 12 schools in England to establish the types and amount of home use of ICT by students aged 11, 14 and 16 (school years 6, 9 and 11). Students completed questionnaires on their use of ICT outside school in general, for educational purposes and for specific curriculum subjects. This information was linked to students' attainment in national tests and lower secondary qualifications (GCSEs). Results showed that students aged 11 and 14 years using ICT at home for educational purposes performed statistically significantly better in mathematics. ICT was perceived to increase pupils' confidence and motivation by making school work more enjoyable. However, the study found a negative association between students' use of ICT out of school for leisure purposes and attainment.

On average in OECD countries, students with computers available to use at home have a mean score in mathematics of 514 score points, whereas those without computers available score only 453 points. This is a substantial difference in terms of mathematics proficiency, equal to one full proficiency level on PISA's six-level proficiency scale for mathematics. Students who do have a computer at home perform on average at Level 3; those without perform at Level 2. These are the average levels reached in most OECD countries. The exceptions are that students with access to computers reach, on average, Level 4 in Belgium, Finland and Japan, but only Level 2 in Greece, Italy, Mexico and Portugal; those without access to computers reach Level 3 in Canada, Finland and Japan, but only Level 1 in Mexico, Turkey and the United States. Box 4.2 explains what these proficiency levels

Figure 4.2 ■ **Availability of a computer at home and student performance in mathematics**

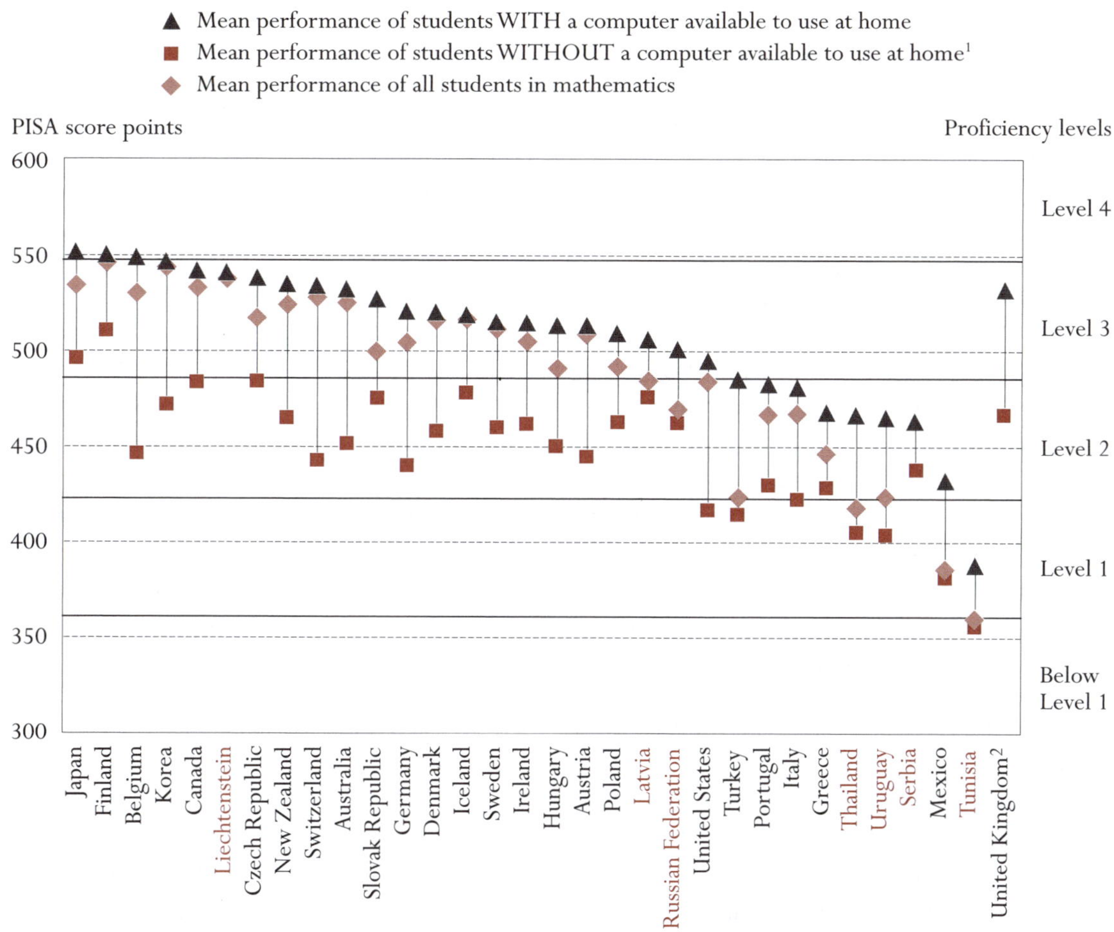

Countries are ranked in descending order of performance of students who report that a computer is available to use at home.
1. Results based on less than 3% of students in Denmark, Iceland, Korea and Sweden (see Table 2.2a).
2. Response rate too low to ensure comparability.
Source: OECD PISA 2003 database, Table 4.1.

mean in terms of what students are typically able to do, showing that these comparisons demonstrate serious differences in the capabilities of students with and without computer access.

In every country, this gap is significant (Table 4.2). It is greatest in Belgium and Switzerland, where students with access to computers at home are about one and a half proficiency levels ahead of those without. In Belgium, the 94% of students with home computer access can on average perform at least some of the relatively complex tasks at Level 4, whereas the 6% without access can on average perform only the basic tasks at Level 2. In the nine countries with the widest gaps in performance, except Turkey, only 10% or less of students lack home access to a computer; this minority is at a substantial disadvantage. However, in Finland and Iceland where access is near universal, the performance disadvantage of students without a computer available to use at home is only about half the OECD average (Table 4.2).

Box 4.2 ■ **Performance differences:**
The PISA proficiency levels and what students can typically do

How large is the performance gap?

A performance difference of 62 score points represents one proficiency level on the PISA mathematics scale. This can be considered a comparatively large difference in student performance in substantive terms. Below there are descriptions of what students can typically do at each mathematics proficiency level in PISA 2003. Note that the mean student performance for students in OECD countries is set at 500 points, with about two-thirds scoring between 400 and 600.

Level 6 (above 668 score points): Students can conceptualise, generalise and utilise information based on their investigations into and modelling of complex problem situations. They can link different information sources and representations and flexibly translate among them. Students at this level are capable of advanced mathematical thinking and reasoning. These students can apply insight and understanding, along with a mastery of symbolic and formal mathematical operations and relationships, in order to develop new approaches and strategies for attacking novel situations. Student at this level can formulate and precisely communicate their actions and reflections regarding their findings, interpretations and arguments, and the appropriateness of these to the original situations.

Level 5 (from 607 to 668 score points): Students can develop and work with models for complex situations, identifying constraints and specifying assumptions. They can select, compare and evaluate appropriate problem-solving strategies for dealing with complex problems related to these models. Students at this level can work strategically using broad, well-developed thinking and reasoning skills, appropriate linked representations, symbolic and formal characterisations, and insight pertaining to these situations. They can reflect on their actions and formulate and can communicate their interpretations and reasoning.

Level 4 (from 545 to 606 score points): Students can work effectively with explicit models for complex concrete situations that may involve constraints or call for making assumptions. They can select and integrate different representations, including symbolic ones, and can linking them directly to aspects of real-world situations. Students at this level can utilise well-developed skills and reason flexibly, with some insight, in these contexts. They can construct and communicate explanations and arguments based on their interpretations, arguments and actions.

Level 3 (from 483 to 544 score points): Students can execute clearly described procedures, including those that require sequential decisions. They can select and apply simple problem-solving strategies. Students at this level can interpret and use representations based on different information sources and reason directly from them. They can develop short communications reporting their interpretations, results and reasoning.

Level 2 (from 421 to 482 score points): Students can interpret and recognise situations in contexts that require no more than direct inference. They can extract relevant information from a single source and make use of a single representational mode.

Students at this level can employ basic algorithms, formulae, procedures or conventions. They are capable of direct reasoning and making literal interpretations of the results.

Level 1 (from 358 to 420 score points): Students can answer questions involving familiar contexts where all relevant information is present and the questions are clearly defined. They are able to identify information and to carry out routine procedures according to direct instructions in explicit situations. They can perform actions that are obvious and that follow immediately from the given stimuli.

To what extent can these performance differences be interpreted as merely reflecting the fact that students without computers at home tend to be disadvantaged in other ways, in particular by their socio-economic background? In all countries with data, the use of either a computer or the Internet is significantly and positively correlated with the head of household's educational attainment (OECD, 2004a), while parental education background correlates strongly with performance. Do performance differences associated with computer access disappear when accounting for such socio-economic background characteristics? This can be calculated in PISA using its index of economic, social and cultural status (ESCS), based on student reports of their parents' occupational status, educational level and cultural possessions at home. In fact, once accounting for socio-economic background the performance advantage associated with home computer access remains in 23 of the 31 countries with data available. These performance differences, which are typically between one-third and one-half as great as before controlling for ESCS, remain above 30 score points (around one-half a proficiency level) in Australia, Belgium, Germany, Korea, Switzerland and the United States, and the partner country Thailand (Figure 4.3).

The performance difference associated with student access to a computer at school is less clear-cut than in the case of access at home. In 15 out of 29 countries with available data students with a computer available to use at school perform better than students who lack school computer access (Figure 4.3). In this case the performance advantage is particularly prominent in the United States (98 score points) and is also high in Canada and the Czech Republic (64 and 62 score points respectively – or about one proficiency level). These three countries are the only ones where access to a computer at school has a greater impact on performance than access to a computer at home does. This also holds when socio-economic background is accounted for. Again, only a minority of students (less than 5%) in these countries lack access to a computer at school (Table 2.2a). After accounting for student background, a performance advantage associated with school access to computers remains in 14 countries. In contrast, students with access to a computer in school in Greece and the partner country Tunisia perform lower than other students once socio-economic background has been accounted for (Figure 4.3).

Thus, even though more students have access to computers at school than at home in most countries (Table 2.2a), it is not clear that this school-based access has an effect strong enough to compensate for the effect of lacking a computer at home. If it did, larger performance differences between those with and without access at school might be observed, although such an effect could be hard to measure if lower-ability students had greater access to computers for some purposes.

Figure 4.3 ■ **Differences in mathematics performance associated with students' access to a computer at home or at school**

Countries are ranked in descending order of the performance difference between students with a computer at home and students without a computer at home.

1. Results based on less than 3% of students in Denmark, Iceland, Korea and Sweden (see Table 2.2a).
2. Results based on less than 3% of students in Australia, Canada, Hungary, Iceland, New Zealand and Sweden (see Table 2.2a).
3. Response rate too low to ensure comparability.

Source: OECD PISA 2003 database, Table 4.2.

This picture is not the same, however, in all countries. In the United States in particular, where 10% of students lack computers at home, only 3% lack them at school and the remaining 97% perform more than one proficiency level higher than those without school access, even after socio-economic background has been taken into account. PISA data do not provide direct evidence of causation, but this finding could be consistent with the hypothesis that using computers at school helps compensate for the disadvantage of not having them at home.

Are there other settings, other than home and school, where access to a computer might contribute to students' performance? When asked about whether they used computers in places other than home or school, many students did not answer the question, perhaps because they were not aware of opportunities for accessing computers in these other settings. In around one-half of the countries with available data between 22 and 34% of students did not answer this question. Among those who did answer, Table 4.2 shows the performance differences in mathematics between those reporting that they do and do not access a computer in places other than home or school. These results should be interpreted with caution in the countries where over 20% of students did not respond: Austria, Germany, Greece, Italy, Korea, Mexico, Portugal, the Slovak Republic, Switzerland and Turkey, and the partner countries Liechtenstein, Thailand, Tunisia and Uruguay. Nevertheless, the results are still of interest, since they show a significant positive association in 19 countries, and in 15 after accounting for socio-economic background. While these differences are in most cases smaller than for school or home-based access, the gap exceeds 20 score points after correcting for socio-economic background in: Greece, Mexico, Poland and the United States, and the partner countries Latvia and Thailand.

Length of time students have been using computers and their performance

Both schools and families have invested rapidly in acquiring ICT in recent years. Governments have pursued policies to increase equity of access to computers at school, while the proportion of homes with computers has also grown. This helps to explain why a number of students have only relatively recently started to use computers, whereas others have been using them for several years. PISA 2003 asked students how long they had been using a computer (see Chapter 2). In most OECD countries between 60 and 90% have been using them for three years or more, but in no country is there a clear pattern showing that the great majority of 15-year-olds were introduced to computers at about the same age. It is therefore useful to examine whether students who have been using a computer longer and are therefore more familiar with computers perform differently from students who are not so familiar with computers and are just starting to use them. Figure 4.4 shows a clear progression in student performance in mathematics the longer students have been using a computer. Those who have been using a computer for more than five years, and are therefore most familiar with computers, perform at the higher end of Level 3, whereas students who have used a computer for less than one year perform on average at the lower end of Level 2. This gap is particularly large in Belgium, Korea, New Zealand, Switzerland and the United States. In the United States, for example, those who have used a computer for less than one year are likely to struggle with even the simplest PISA mathematics questions – they are near the bottom of Level 1 – whereas those with at least five years' experience perform above average for the OECD, being on average proficient at Level 3.

The results therefore indicate that there is some type of association between the length of time that students have been using computers and their performance in PISA mathematics. Looking more closely at these results shows that the majority of countries fall into a similar pattern:

Figure 4.4 ■ **Length of time students have been using a computer and mean performance in mathematics**

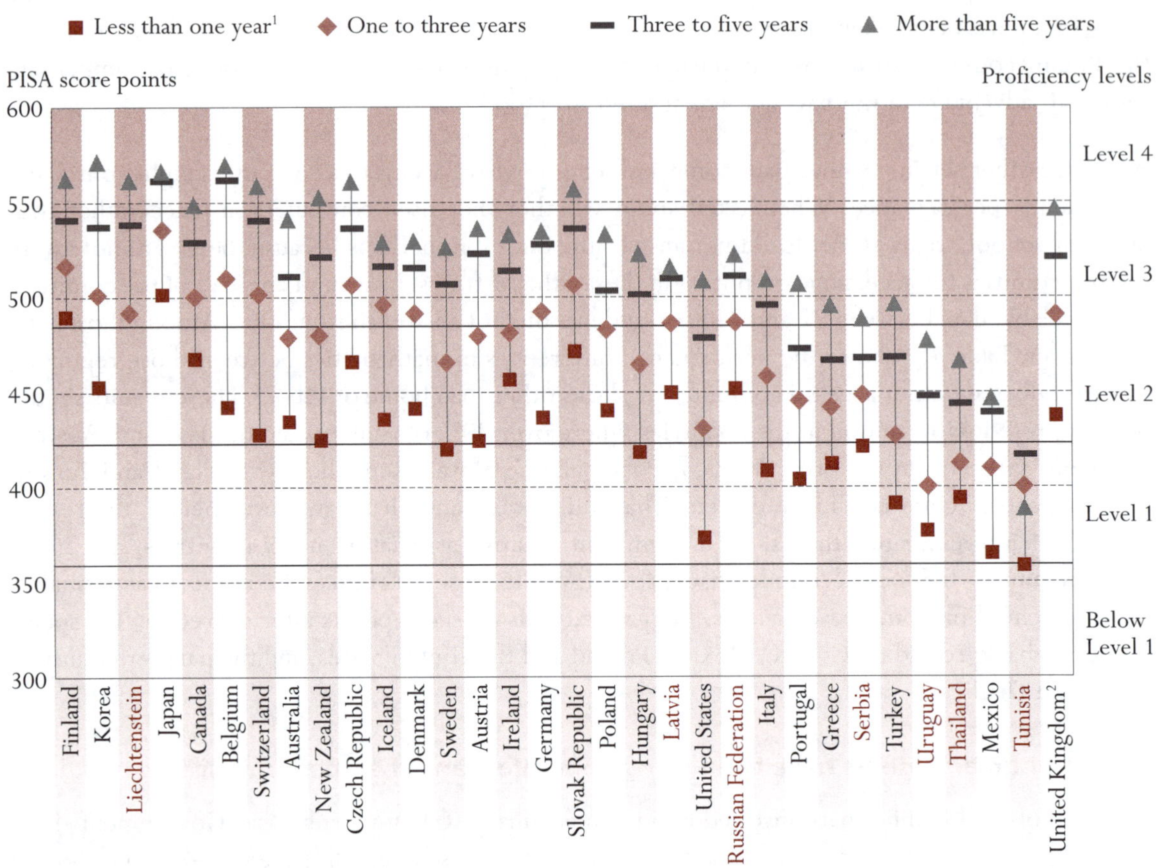

Countries are ranked in descending order of mean performance in mathematics.
1. Results based on less than 3% of students in Australia, Canada, Denmark, Finland, Iceland, Sweden and the United Kingdom (see Table 2.1).
2. Response rate too low to ensure comparability.
Source: OECD PISA 2003 database, Table 4.3.

the biggest performance gaps are between students in categories indicating the least amount of computer experience. For example, students who have used computers for one to three years perform 46 score points above those with below one year's experience, on average in OECD countries, but students with above five years of experience are only 20 score points ahead of those with three to five years' experience. Particularly large performance gaps between the two groups of students least familiar with computers, of around one proficiency level, are observed in Austria, Belgium, Germany, Iceland, New Zealand, Switzerland and the United States (Figure 4.4). Those with below a year's experience are almost everywhere capable on average of only basic mathematics tasks at Levels 1 or 2; only in Finland and Japan do they reach Level 3. In contrast, in 21 of the 32 countries with available data students who have been using computers for from three to five years perform at Level 3, around or slightly above the OECD average, and in Belgium and Japan these students perform at Level 4. These figures show that higher performing students are more familiar with computers, even though they cannot demonstrate that computer familiarity leads to high performance.

Again to what extent can these performance differences be interpreted as merely reflecting the fact that students who have been using computers for the longest time tend to be those coming from a more advantaged socio-economic background? Table 4.3 shows performance differences associated with the length of time students have been using a computer once socio-economic background is accounted for using the PISA index of economic, social and cultural status (ESCS). Results show that performance differences hold once accounting for socio-economic background and that the biggest differences remain between students who have just started using computers (less than a year before the survey) and those who have used computers for at least one year. Compared to students who have only been using a computer for less than a year, on average in the OECD countries there is a 34 score points advantage for students who have used computers for one to three years, a 56 score points advantage for students who have used computers for 3 to 5 years and a 64 score points advantage for students who have used computers for more than 5 years. In fact, once accounting for socio-economic background the performance differences between students who have used a computer for more than 5 years and students who have used a computer for less than one year remain the equivalent of one proficiency level or more in Australia, Austria, Belgium, Iceland, Italy, Korea, New Zealand, Portugal, Sweden, Switzerland, the United Kingdom and the United States, and the partner country Uruguay (Table 4.3).

The clear picture that emerges from the PISA results is that students who have never used a computer or who do not have access to computers at home or at school are low performing. The benchmark is the average performance in PISA mathematics for the OECD: 500 score points. Students who have never used a computer perform significantly lower than average, with an average performance of 380 score points. Students without access to a computer at home score 453 points on average, meaning that they perform one proficiency level lower than the OECD average. Students without access to a computer at school perform one-half of a proficiency level lower than the OECD average, scoring 480 points (Table 4.1). Similarly, students who have only recently started to use computers (less than one year before the survey) perform below the OECD average, scoring 433 points on average. It is encouraging to see that students who have been using computers between one and three years perform significantly better than those students just starting to use computers, although at 479 score points, their performance is still below the OECD average. The picture is equally clear for students who have access to computers. Students reporting that they have access to computers at home, school or other places perform above the OECD average, with students having access to computers at home performing comparatively better and scoring 514 points. The highest score point advantage can be seen on average for those students who are most familiar with computers (having used them for more than five years), who achieve 532 score points.

STUDENTS' USE OF COMPUTERS AND STUDENT PERFORMANCE

The relationship between frequency of computer use and student performance in mathematics

Having access to a computer is only a first step, and Chapter 3 discussed variations in the frequency and type of use that students make of computers at home and at school. In comparing this to performance, it is possible to look first at how much students use their computers overall in each of these two settings.

Figures 4.5a and 4.5b show that the relationship between frequency of use and performance differs substantially depending on whether students are frequently using computers at home or at school. The more clear-cut effect appears with home use: in every country, students reporting rare or no use of computers at home (on average 18% of students) score much lower than their counterparts

Box 4.3 ■ **Frequency of use of computers**

As in Chapter 3, this chapter uses the following definitions for frequency of use of computers, based on student responses:

Frequent use: "Almost every day" or "A few times each week"

Moderate use: "Between once a week and once a month"

Rare/No use: "Less than once a month" or "Never"

Figure 4.5a ■ **Frequency of use of computers at home and student performance in mathematics**

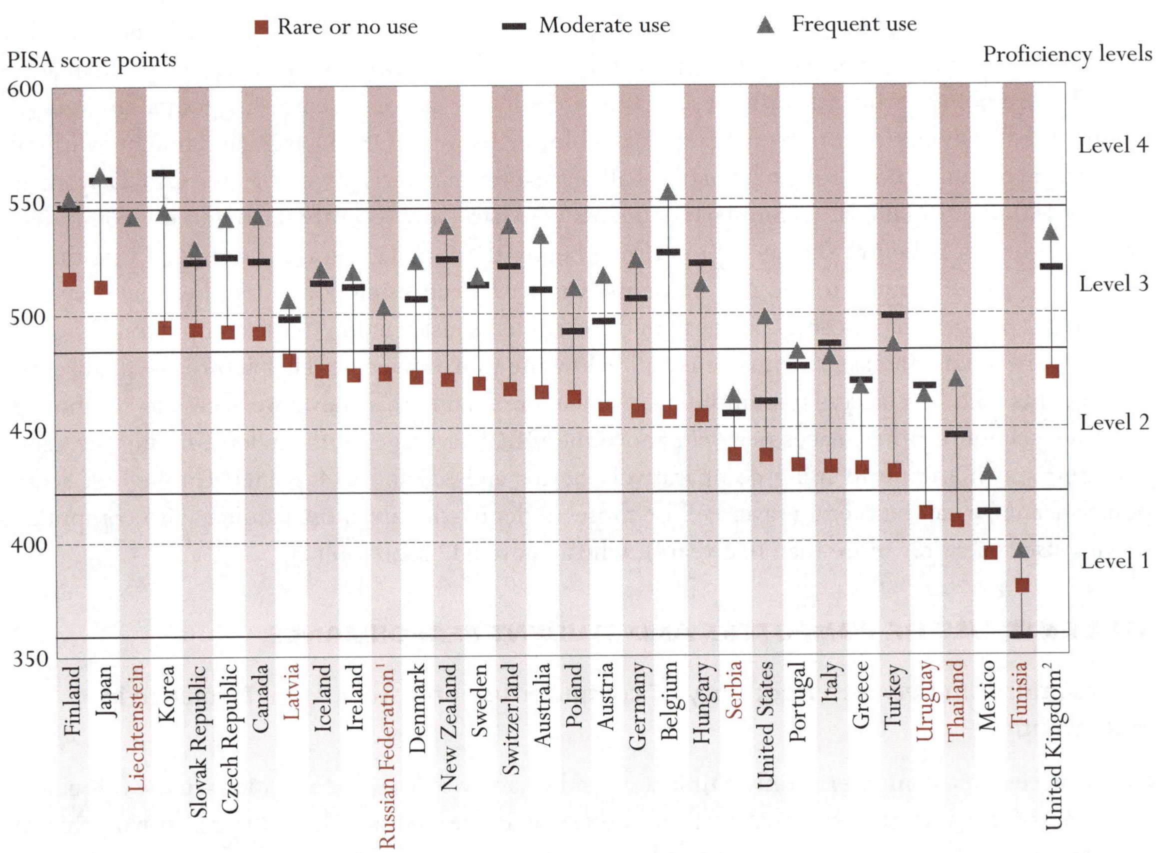

Countries are ranked in descending order of performance of students with rare or no use of computers at home.
1. Results for moderate use based on less than 3% of students.
2. Response rate too low to ensure comparability.
Source: OECD PISA 2003 database, Table 4.4.

reporting moderate use or frequent use (Table 3.1 and Figure 4.5a). In the majority of countries, students using computers rarely at home perform at Level 2 and, in some cases, at Level 1 on the mathematics proficiency scale.

However, when it comes to frequency of use at school, there is less consistent association with performance. In some countries such as the Czech Republic and the Slovak Republic, rare users perform substantially worse than their peers, but in Germany, Greece, Japan and Korea, and the partner country Tunisia, it is the other way around. In around one-half of the countries with available data, lower-performing students, school tracks or schools make more frequent use of computers at school. There may be several factors that contribute to the negative association between school computer use and performance in some countries, and/or obscure any performance benefit that one might expect to see. It is possible that instructional strategies involve some lower performing students in a greater than average amount of work on computers. Another possibility is that the minority of students who do not have access to computers at home spend more time on computers at school in order to master missing computer skills. Also, lower performing students may not be using computers at school effectively, taking longer to complete tasks set on the computer.

Figure 4.5b ■ **Frequency of use of computers at school and student performance in mathematics**

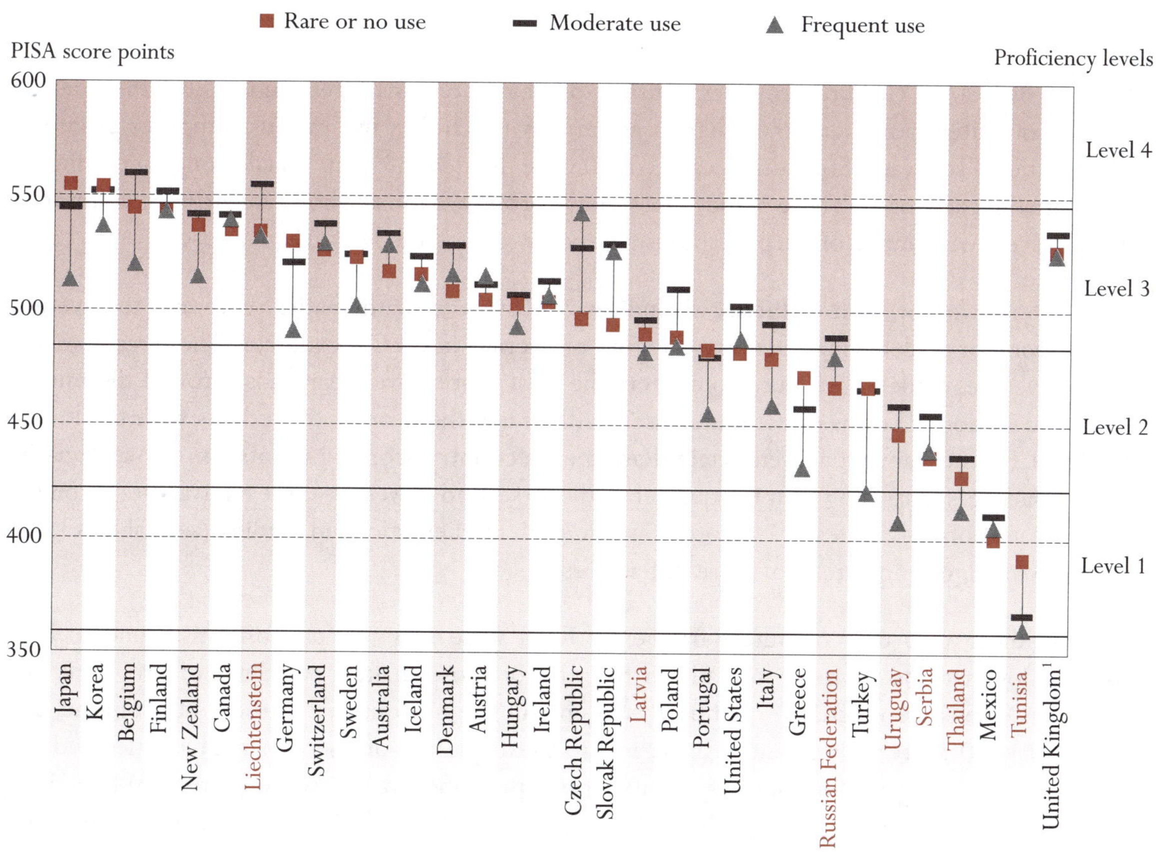

Countries are ranked in descending order of performance of students with rare or no use of computers at school.
1. Response rate too low to ensure comparability.
Source: OECD PISA 2003 database, Table 4.4.

These kinds of explanations could account for an association between low performance and more frequent computer use, regardless of any effect that such usage has on performance itself.

There could also however be ways in which greater computer use adversely affects performance. For example, spending too much time on computers at school could be a distraction from learning. This possibility would be consistent with the observation that the amount of usage most commonly associated with the best performance is "moderate" – between once a week and once a month. In 23 of the countries shown in Figure 4.5b, this category of students performs better than either more frequent or less frequent users. If high amounts of computer usage at school are not associated with the better performing students, teachers may need to look more closely at the manner of this usage. Stronger supervision and structured lessons, involving the setting of concrete tasks to be achieved using computers, may improve their impact on performance.

Overall usage and performance in mathematics and reading

Chapter 3 developed indices measuring students' overall ICT usage on a continuous scale. By comparing these usage levels to performance, the extent to which students using computers more across a range of functions tend to do better or worse in the PISA assessment can be analysed. The answers cannot show whether certain kinds of ICT use help students to perform better at school, but do indicate the extent to which those students who do well are also those students who use ICT for certain purposes.

This analysis looks at two broad indices of usage, one based on how often students use the Internet and play computer games, and the other based on how much they use various computer programs and educational software. Students in each country are divided into four equal groups according to their scores on each index. Those in the highest usage group are those who frequently use computers for a relatively wide range of purposes; those in the lowest are the least frequent users.

Figure 4.6 shows, for each of these two indices, the average mathematics score and the average reading score for students in each usage category on average in OECD countries. These results show that, on average, students who use computers the least score lower than those around the middle of the distribution in terms of computer use. On average, the quarter of students with the lowest use of ICT for the Internet and entertainment in each country score 12 points less in mathematics and 11 points less in reading than the quarter with the second-lowest use; the equivalent gap on the programs and software index is 14 score points in both mathematics and reading (see Table A3.1 in Annex A3 for significance tests of these differences).

However, those who use computers frequently for a wide range of purposes also tend to have relatively low average scores, especially in the case of those making wide use of programs and software. On average in OECD countries, students in the top quarter of users of programs and software are 20 score points below those in the third quarter of users in mathematics and the difference in reading performance is slightly more pronounced (25 score points). While these differences are not as great as the performance differences observed earlier between students with and without computer access, they are significant in nearly all OECD countries (see Table A3.1 in Annex A3).

Figure 4.6 ■ **Students' use of ICT and OECD average performance in mathematics and reading, by quarter of the indices**

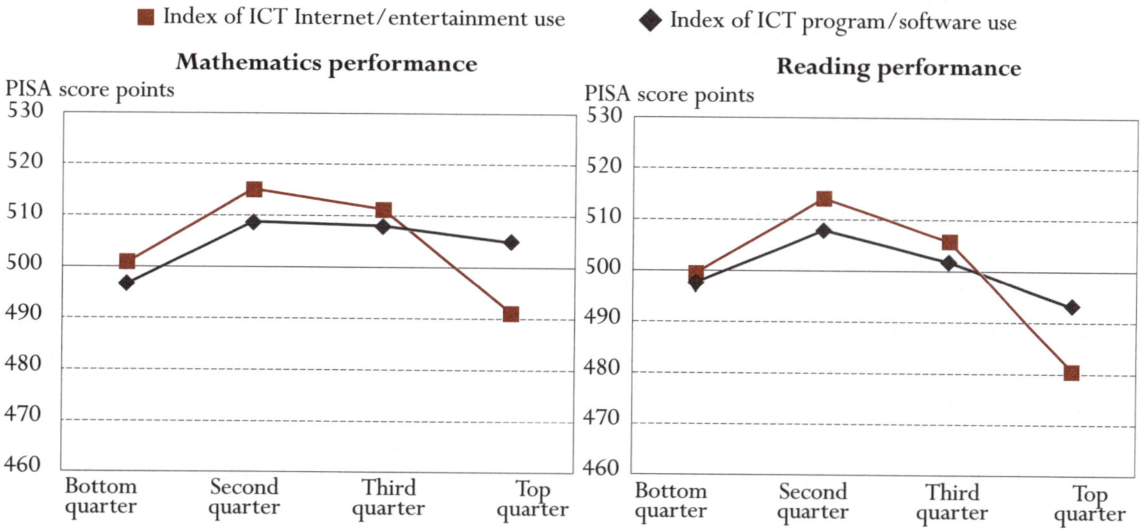

Source: OECD PISA 2003 database, Tables 4.5, 4.6 and 4.7.

A closer examination of mathematics performance shows that in 16 countries – Belgium, Canada, the Czech Republic, Denmark, Germany, Hungary, Ireland, Korea, Poland, Portugal, the Slovak Republic, Sweden and Switzerland, and the partner countries Latvia, Thailand and Uruguay – the second and third quarters of users of programs and software performed at a similar level, which was significantly higher than the bottom and the top quarters.[2] In Australia, Iceland, Italy and the United States, the second quarter of users performed highest in mathematics among the quarters. In the partner country the Russian Federation, the third quarter of users performed highest in mathematics among the quarters. In the Czech Republic, Japan, Korea, and the Slovak Republic and the partner countries the Russian Federation and Uruguay, the bottom quarter of users had a lower mean performance in mathematics than the other three quarters, which performed at the same level. In Austria, Greece, New Zealand, Mexico, Turkey and the United Kingdom, and the partner countries Liechtenstein and Serbia, the bottom quarter of users did not perform significantly lower in mathematics than the second quarter, but the top quarter performed significantly lower than the third quarter (see Table A3.1 in Annex A3).

These results reflect those described above, which show that for school usage, the most frequent users tend to perform a bit below those who use computers moderately often. Weaker students tend, for example, to report using educational software programs more frequently. Although PISA did not ask students how often they used computers to learn particular subjects, the fact that the most frequent computer users perform lower in both mathematics and reading reinforces the message that one cannot readily assume that more computer usage is bound to be beneficial for students in all cases. Note that this particular part of the analysis considers the breadth of frequent computer use. Students who are the most computer literate and ready to use computers in many parts of their lives might be expected to have certain advantages as a result. But this evidence suggests that it may be risky to assume that in every case it is associated with improved school performance.

ATTITUDES TOWARDS COMPUTERS, CONFIDENCE IN PERFORMING TASKS ON A COMPUTER AND STUDENT PERFORMANCE IN MATHEMATICS

A final part of the analysis concerns the relationship between how students regard computers and how well they perform in mathematics. Students were first asked how strongly they agreed or disagreed with each of four declarations of positive attitudes towards computers. Their combined responses to the four questions were scored on an index, and performance was compared to scores on this index. In 15 countries, more positive attitudes towards computers are associated with improved performance in mathematics (Figure 4.7). However, even in these countries the association is not large (Table 4.11).

The relationship between student confidence in ICT and performance is more clear-cut. In particular, the quarter of students with the greatest confidence in performing routine ICT tasks such as opening and saving files score on average more than one proficiency level (67 score points) higher than those with the least confidence (see Box 3.3 in Chapter 3 for a complete list of routine tasks). This comparison does not tell us that feeling confident of basic ICT ability leads to good mathematics skills, or vice versa, but that the two attributes tend to go together. The quarter of students with the lowest confidence in these skills are, in most countries, at least twice as likely as average to be among the lowest quarter of performers in mathematics. Indeed, students' confidence in performing routine tasks on a computer is a relatively strong predictor of student performance, explaining 10% of the variance in mathematics performance on average across OECD countries and between 15 and 19% in Hungary, Mexico, Portugal and the Slovak Republic (Table 4.8).

Confidence in their ability to perform Internet tasks is associated with students' performance almost as strongly as ability to perform routine tasks. It is strongest, with a difference of over 50 score points between the quarter of students with highest and lowest confidence, in Belgium, Greece, Hungary, Italy, Japan, Mexico, Poland, Portugal, the Slovak Republic, Switzerland and Turkey, and the partner countries Thailand and Uruguay. Students' confidence in performing high-level tasks is also positively associated with performance in mathematics (9 score points on average), although this relationship is less than half as strong as for routine and Internet tasks and is not observed in five of the countries with available data (Figure 4.7). However, the relationship in Hungary and Japan is stronger, with a gap of around 50 score points between the least confident and most confident students in these tasks (Table 4.10).

CONCLUSION AND IMPLICATIONS

These results show that some features of ICT availability and use are strongly associated with student performance, but that this is not true of all such features.

One thing that is now clear is that in an age in which computers feature strongly in everyday life and in education, the minority of students who have little access to them, who use them little and who are not confident in using ICT are not performing well. This is partly because students with low home access are more likely to come from disadvantaged backgrounds, but the observed gap cannot nearly be explained by socio-economic status. Thus, the disadvantages faced by students whose parents have low educational or occupational status are likely to be exacerbated where they also do not have access to computers. The PISA evidence confirms previous studies showing the particularly strong association of performance with home access and usage.

Figure 4.7 ■ **Students' confidence in ICT tasks, attitudes towards ICT and changes in mathematics performance**

Change in mathematics performance per unit increase of the index of attitudes towards computers, confidence in high-level ICT tasks, confidence in Internet ICT tasks and confidence in routine ICT tasks

Countries are ranked in descending order of score points difference per unit increase on each of the indices.
Note: Statistically significant differences are marked in darker tone.
1. Response rate too low to ensure comparability.
Source: OECD PISA 2003 database, Tables 4.8, 4.9, 4.10 and 4.11.

Figure 4.7 ■ Students' confidence in ICT tasks, attitudes towards ICT and changes in mathematics performance (*continued*)

Change in mathematics performance per unit increase of the index of attitudes towards computers, confidence in high-level ICT tasks, confidence in Internet ICT tasks and confidence in routine ICT tasks

Countries are ranked in descending order of score points difference per unit increase on each of the indices.
Note: Statistically significant differences are marked in darker tone.
1. Response rate too low to ensure comparability.
Source: OECD PISA 2003 database, Tables 4.8, 4.9, 4.10 and 4.11.

Usage at school may help to compensate for this disadvantage, although the relatively weaker association between school access/usage and performance raises questions over the extent to which it can fully compensate.

While this evidence therefore underlines the importance of bridging a digital divide that still leaves some students marginalised in terms of computer usage, a harder question is to what extent extending the usage of computers within schools can contribute to higher standards and greater equity in student performance. Students in PISA who used computers most widely tended to perform slightly worse on average than those with moderate usage. This can partly be explained by the fact that when we look at individual uses, there are certain kinds of software used more by weaker students. But even with a function such as looking up information on the Internet, where there appears to be a positive correlation with performance, the advantage of greater usage does not appear to be continuous: there is little to distinguish students who do this occasionally from those doing it frequently, even if those who do it rarely or never perform worse than those who use either computers on occasion or often. This raises the issue of whether students who are using computers more are necessarily using them to best effect.

More micro-studies are needed within countries to explore the extent to which for individual students, certain kinds of computer usage raise performance, and which kinds are most effective. At the same time, in countries where basic computer access is approaching universal, policy needs to turn its attention from providing the technology to ensuring that its usage is effective. This means ensuring that teachers are appropriately trained and that ICT usage is well integrated in the timetable and curriculum. Surveys such as the OECD's survey of upper secondary schools (OECD, 2004c) have shown severe weaknesses in this respect, with a lack of teacher know-how and time, along with scheduling difficulties, hindering the achievement by schools of their ICT development goals. The apparent negative association between performance and some kinds of computer usage, shown by PISA, also carries a warning not to assume that more means better. Above all, it is the quality of ICT usage, rather than necessarily the quantity, that will determine the contribution that these technologies make to student outcomes.

Notes

1. Note that the country means displayed here are taken from *Learning for Tomorrow's World – First Results from PISA 2003*. Other means are calculated based on responses students provided via the ICT familiarity questionnaire. In cases where there is a high percentage of non-responses to the relevant ICT question mean scores are only calculated for the student population having responded. Therefore, in countries where there are high non-response rates the means are not strictly comparable to the overall country mean reported. This is the case for Mexico.
2. All comparisons made between performance of students in the second and third quarters as well as in the third and top quarters are tested for statistical significance and are presented in Table A3.1 of Annex A3. Table 4.6 in Annex B1 only presents information on statistical significance of performance differences between the top and bottom quarters of the index ICT use for programs and software.

REFERENCES

Ganzeboom, H.B.G., P.M. De Graaf and D.J. Treiman (1992), "A Standard International Socio-Economic Index of Occupational Status," *Social Science Research,* Vol. 21, Issue 1, Elsevier Ltd.

Harrison, C., C. Comber, T. Fisher, K. Haw, C. Lewin, E. Lunzer, A. McFarlane, D. Mavers, P. Scrimshaw, B. Somekh and **R. Watling** (2003), *ImpaCT2: The Impact of Information and Communication Technologies on Pupil Learning and Attainment,* DfES: London.

OECD (2004a), *Science, Technology and Industry: Outlook 2004,* OECD: Paris.

OECD (2004b), *Learning for Tomorrow's World – First Results from PISA 2003,* OECD: Paris.

OECD (2004c) *Completing the Foundations for Lifelong Learning: An OECD Survey of Upper Secondary Schools*

OECD (2005a), *PISA 2003 Technical Report,* OECD: Paris.

OECD (2005b), *PISA 2003 Data Analysis Manual: SAS® Users,* OECD: Paris.

OECD (2005c), *PISA 2003 Data Analysis Manual: SPSS® Users,* OECD: Paris.

Papanastasiou, E., M. Zembylas and V. Charalambos (2003), "Can Computer Use Hurt Science Achievement? The USA Results from PISA," *Journal of Science and Technology,* Vol. 12, No. 3, Plenum Publishing Corporation: New York.

Ravitz, J., J. Mergendoller and **W. Rush** (2002), *What's School Got to Do With It? Cautionary Tales about Correlations between Student Computer Use and Academic Achievement,* AERA: New Orleans.

Valentine, G., J. Marsh, C. Pattie and **BMRB** (2005), *Children and Young People's Home Use of ICT for Educational Purposes: The Impact on Attainment at Key Stages 1-4,* DfES: London.

Wenglinsky, H. (1998), *Does it Compute? The Relationship Between Educational Technology and Student Achievement in Mathematics,* ETS Policy Information Center – Research Division: Princeton, NJ.

Annex A

TECHNICAL BACKGROUND

Annex A1: Questionnaire indices

This section explains the indices derived from the student questionnaires that are used in this report. For a description of other PISA 2003 indices and details on the methods see the *PISA 2003 Technical Report* (OECD, 2005a). For further information on the coding used in PISA 2003 indices, see the *PISA 2003 Data Analysis Manual* (OECD, 2005b and 2005c), available for SAS® and SPSS® users.

Economic, Social and Cultural Status (ESCS)

The PISA 2003 index of economic, social and cultural status (ESCS) is derived from three variables related to family background: the index of highest level of parental education in number of years of education according to the ISCED classification (PARED), the index of highest parental occupation status (HISEI) and the index of home possessions (HOMEPOS). Missing values for these three variables are imputed and then transformed to an international metric with OECD averages of 0 and OECD standard deviations of 1. These OECD-standardised variables were used for a principal component analysis in order to obtain ESCS scores applying an OECD population weight giving each OECD country a weight of 1,000. The PISA index of economic, social and cultural status (ESCS) is computed for PISA 2003 and also re-computed for the PISA 2000 data, but items and the wording of items are slightly different between PISA 2000 and PISA 2003. Further details on constructing ESCS are found in *PISA 2003 Technical Report* (OECD, 2005a).

Highest occupational status of parents (HISEI)

The occupational data for both the student's father and student's mother were obtained by asking open-ended questions ST07Q01 and Q8 in the student questionnaire for mothers' occupational status and ST09Q01 and Q10 in the student questionnaire for fathers' occupational status. The responses were coded in accordance with the four-digit International Standard Classification of Occupation (ISCO 1988) (ILO, 1990) and then mapped to the SEI index (Ganzeboom *et al.*, 1992). The PISA 2003 index of the highest occupational level of parents (HISEI) corresponds to the higher SEI score of either parent or to the only available parent's SEI score. Higher values on these indices indicate higher level of occupational status.

Educational level of parents (PARED)

The PISA 2003 indices of parents' educational level are derived from students' responses to the items ST11RQ01 and ST12Q01-ST12Q03 for mothers' educational level and ST13RQ01 and ST14Q01-ST14Q03 for fathers' educational level. The students' responses to these items are coded in accordance with the International Standard Classification of Education (ISCED 1997) (OECD 1999) in order to obtain internationally comparable categories of educational attainment. The highest level of educational attainment of parents is converted into an index of years of schooling (PARED) using the conversion coefficients shown in Table A1.1.

Home possessions (HOMEPOS)

The PISA 2003 index of home possessions (HOMEPOS) is derived from students' responses to the 14 items listed below. These variables are binary and the scale construction is done through IRT scaling. Positive values on this index indicate higher levels of home possessions.

Table A1.1 Levels of parental education converted into years of schooling

		Did not go to school	Completed ISCED Level 1 (primary education)	Completed ISCED Level 2 (lower secondary education)	Completed ISCED Levels 3B or 3C (upper secondary education providing direct access to the labour market or to ISCED 5B programmes)	Completed ISCED Level 3A (upper secondary education providing access to ISCED 5A and 5B programmes)	Completed ISCED Level 5A (university level tertiary education)	Completed ISCED Level 5B (non-university tertiary education)
OECD countries	Australia	0.0	6.5	10.0	11.5	12.0	15.0	14.0
	Austria	0.0	4.0	8.0	11.0	13.0	17.0	15.0
	Belgium	0.0	6.0	8.0	12.0	12.0	16.0	15.0
	Canada	0.0	6.0	9.0	12.0	12.0	17.0	15.0
	Czech Republic	0.0	5.0	9.0	12.0	13.0	17.0	16.0
	Denmark	0.0	6.0	9.5	12.5	12.5	16.5	15.5
	Finland	0.0	6.0	9.0	12.0	12.0	15.5	14.5
	France	0.0	5.0	9.0	11.0	12.0	15.0	14.0
	Germany	0.0	4.0	10.0	12.0	12.5	17.0	15.0
	Greece	0.0	6.0	9.0	11.5	12.0	17.0	15.5
	Hungary	0.0	4.0	8.0	10.5	12.0	16.5	13.5
	Iceland	0.0	7.0	10.0	13.0	14.0	17.0	16.5
	Ireland	0.0	6.0	9.0	a	12.0	16.0	14.0
	Italy	0.0	5.0	8.0	11.0	13.0	17.0	16.0
	Japan	0.0	6.0	9.0	12.0	12.0	16.0	14.0
	Korea	0.0	6.0	9.0	12.0	12.0	16.0	15.0
	Luxembourg	0.0	6.0	9.0	12.0	13.0	17.0	17.0
	Mexico	0.0	6.0	9.0	12.0	12.0	16.0	14.0
	Netherlands	0.0	6.0	10.0	a	12.0	15.0	a
	New Zealand	0.0	6.0	10.0	12.0	13.0	16.0	16.0
	Norway	0.0	7.0	10.0	13.0	13.0	17.0	15.0
	Poland	0.0	a	8.0	11.0	12.0	16.0	15.0
	Portugal	0.0	6.0	9.0	12.0	12.0	17.0	15.0
	Slovak Republic	0.0	4.0	9.0	12.0	12.5	17.0	15.0
	Spain	0.0	6.0	10.0	12.0	12.0	15.0	14.0
	Sweden	0.0	6.0	9.0	12.0	12.0	15.5	14.0
	Switzerland	0.0	6.0	9.0	12.0	12.5	15.0	14.0
	Turkey	0.0	5.0	8.0	11.0	11.0	16.0	14.0
	United States	0.0	6.0	9.0	a	12.0	16.0	15.0
Partner countries	Brazil	0.0	4.0	8.0	11.0	11.0	16.0	14.5
	Hong Kong-China	0.0	6.0	9.0	11.0	13.0	16.0	14.0
	Indonesia	0.0	6.0	9.0	12.0	12.0	16.0	15.0
	Latvia	0.0	4.0	9.0	12.0	12.0	16.0	16.0
	Liechtenstein	0.0	5.0	9.0	11.0	12.0	15.0	14.0
	Macao-China	0.0	6.0	9.0	11.0	13.0	16.0	14.0
	Russian Federation	0.0	4.0	9.0	11.5	12.0	15.0	a
	Serbia	0.0	4.0	8.0	11.0	12.0	16.0	14.0
	Thailand	0.0	6.0	9.0	12.0	12.0	16.0	14.0
	Tunisia	0.0	6.0	9.0	12.0	13.0	17.0	16.0
	Uruguay	0.0	6.0	9.0	11.0	12.0	16.0	15.0
	United Kingdom	0.0	6.0	9.0	11.0	12.0	16.0	15.0

Q17	WHICH OF THE FOLLOWING DO YOU HAVE IN YOUR HOME?
ST17Q01	*a) A desk for study*
ST17Q02	*b) A room of your own*
ST17Q03	*c) A quiet place to study*
ST17Q04	*d) A computer you can use for school work*
ST17Q05	*e) Educational software*
ST17Q06	*f) A link to the Internet*
ST17Q07	*g) Your own calculator*
ST17Q08	*h) Classic literature (e.g. <author>)*
ST17Q09	*i) Books of poetry*
ST17Q10	*j) Works of art (e.g. paintings)*
ST17Q11	*k) Books to help with your school work*
ST17Q12	*l) A dictionary*
ST17Q13	*m) A dishwasher*
Q19	**IN YOUR HOME, DO YOU HAVE:**
ST19Q01	*More than 100 books (recoded)*

ICT Internet/entertainment use (INTUSE)

The PISA 2003 index of ICT internet/entertainment use (INTUSE) is derived from students' responses to the six items measuring the frequency of different types ICT use as listed below. A five-point scale with the response categories recoded as "almost every day" (=0), "a few times each week" (=1), "between once a week and once a month" (=2), "less than once a month" (=3) and "never" (=4) is used. All items are inverted for IRT scaling and positive values on this index indicate high frequencies of ICT internet/entertainment use.

Q5 HOW OFTEN DO YOU USE:

ALMOST EVERY DAY	A FEW TIMES EACH WEEK	BETWEEN ONCE A WEEK AND ONCE A MONTH	LESS THAN ONCE A MONTH	NEVER

IC05Q01	*a) The Internet to look up information about people, things, or ideas? (+)*
IC05Q02	*b) Games on a computer? (+)*
IC05Q04	*d) The Internet to collaborate with a group or team? (+)*
IC05Q06	*f) The Internet to download software? (+)*
IC05Q10	*j) The Internet to down-load music? (+)*
IC05Q12	*l) A computer for electronic communication (e.g. e-mail or "chat rooms")? (+)*

(+) Item inverted for IRT scaling.

ICT program/software use (PRGUSE)

The PISA 2003 index of ICT program/software use (PRGUSE) is derived from students' responses to the six items listed below. A five-point scale with the response categories recoded as "almost every day" (=0), "a few times each week" (=1), "between once a week and once a month" (=2), "less than once a month" (=3) and "never" (=4) is used. All items are inverted for IRT scaling and positive values on this index indicate high frequencies of ICT program/software use.

Q5 HOW OFTEN DO YOU USE:

		ALMOST EVERY DAY	A FEW TIMES EACH WEEK	BETWEEN ONCE A WEEK AND ONCE A MONTH	LESS THAN ONCE A MONTH	NEVER
IC05Q03	*c) Word processing (e.g. Word® or Word Perfect®)? (+)*					
IC05Q05	*e) Spreadsheets (e.g. Lotus 1 2 3® or Microsoft Excel®)? (+)*					
IC05Q07	*g) Drawing, painting or graphics programs on a computer? (+)*					
IC05Q08	*h) Educational software such as mathematics programs? (+)*					
IC05Q09	*i) The computer to help you learn school material? (+)*					
IC05Q11	*k) The computer for programming? (+)*					

(+) Item inverted for IRT scaling.

Confidence in routine ICT tasks (ROUTCONF)

The PISA index of confidence in routine ICT tasks (ROUTCONF) is derived from students' responses to the 11 items on self-confidence with ICT tasks. A four-point scale with the response categories recoded as "I can do this very well by myself" (=0), "I can do this with help from someone" (=1), "I know what this means but I cannot do it" (=2) and "I don't know what this means" (=3) is used. All items are inverted for IRT scaling and positive values on this index indicate high self-confidence in routine ICT tasks.

Q6 HOW WELL CAN YOU DO EACH OF THESE TASKS ON A COMPUTER?

		I CAN DO THIS VERY WELL BY MYSELF	I CAN DO THIS WITH HELP FROM SOMEONE	I KNOW WHAT THIS MEANS BUT I CANNOT DO IT	I DON'T KNOW WHAT THIS MEANS
IC06Q01	*a) Start a computer game (+)*				
IC06Q03	*c) Open a file (+)*				
IC06Q04	*d) Create/edit a document (+)*				
IC06Q05	*e) Scroll a document up and down a screen (+)*				
IC06Q07	*g) Copy a file from a floppy disk (+)*				
IC06Q08	*h) Save a computer document or file (+)*				
IC06Q09	*i) Print a computer document or file (+)*				
IC06Q10	*j) Delete a computer document or file (+)*				
IC06Q11	*k) Moves files form one place to another on a computer (+)*				
IC06Q18	*r) Play computer games (+)*				
IC06Q21	*u) Draw pictures using a mouse (+)*				

(+) Item inverted for IRT scaling.

Confidence in Internet ICT tasks (INTCONF)

The PISA 2003 index of confidence in internet ICT tasks is derived from students' responses to the five items listed below. A four-point scale with the response categories recoded as "I can do this very well by myself" (=0), "I can do this with help from someone" (=1), "I know what this means but I cannot do it" (=2), and "I don't know what this means" (=3) is used. All items are inverted for IRT scaling and positive values on this index indicate high self-confidence in internet ICT tasks.

Q6 HOW WELL CAN YOU DO EACH OF THESE TASKS ON A COMPUTER?

		I CAN DO THIS VERY WELL BY MYSELF	I CAN DO THIS WITH HELP FROM SOMEONE	I KNOW WHAT THIS MEANS BUT I CANNOT DO IT	I DON'T KNOW WHAT THIS MEANS
IC06Q12	*l) Get on to the Internet (+)*				
IC06Q13	*m) Copy or download files from the Internet (+)*				
IC06Q14	*n) Attach a file to an e-mail message (+)*				
IC06Q19	*s) Download music from the Internet (+)*				
IC06Q22	*v) Write and send e-mails (+)*				

(+) Item inverted for IRT scaling.

Confidence in high-level ICT tasks (HIGHCONF)

The PISA 2003 index of confidence in high-level ICT asks (HIGHCONF) is derived from students' responses to the seven questions listed below. A four-point scale with the response categories recoded as "I can do this very well by myself" (=0), "I can do this with help from someone" (=1), "I know what this means but I cannot do it" (=2), and "I don't know what this means" (=3) is used. All items are inverted for IRT scaling and positive values on this index indicated high self-confidence in high-level ICT tasks.

Q6 HOW WELL CAN YOU DO EACH OF THESE TASKS ON A COMPUTER?

I CAN DO THIS VERY WELL BY MYSELF	I CAN DO THIS WITH HELP FROM SOMEONE	I KNOW WHAT THIS MEANS BUT I CANNOT DO IT	I DON'T KNOW WHAT THIS MEANS

IC06Q02	*b) Use software to find and get rid of computer viruses (+)*
IC06Q06	*f) Use a database to produce a list of addresses (+)*
IC06Q15	*o) Create a computer program (e.g. in <Logo, Pascal, Basic>) (+)*
IC06Q16	*p) Use a spreadsheet to plot a graph (+)*
IC06Q17	*q) Create a presentation (e.g. using <PowerPoint®>) (+)*
IC06Q20	*t) Create a multi-media presentation (with sound, pictures, video) (+)*
IC06Q23	*w) Construct a Web page (+)*

(+) Item inverted for IRT scaling.

Attitudes toward computers (ATTCOMP)

The PISA 2003 index of attitudes toward computers is derived from students' responses to the four items listed below. A four-point scale with the response categories recoded as "strongly agree" (=0), "agree" (=1), "disagree" (=2), and "strongly agree" (=3) is used. All items are inverted for IRT scaling and positive values on the index indicate positive attitudes toward computers. Due to the modifications in the item format and wording, this PISA 2003 index is not entirely comparable to the PISA 2000 index of interest in computers which was using a dichotomous form (Yes/No).

Q7 THINKING ABOUT YOUR EXPERIENCE WITH COMPUTERS: TO WHAT EXTENT DO YOU AGREE WITH THE FOLLOWING STATEMENTS?

STRONGLY AGREE	AGREE	DISAGREE	STRONGLY AGREE

IC07Q01	*a) It is very important to me to work with a computer. (+)*
IC07Q02	*b) To play or work with a computer is really fun. (+)*
IC07Q03	*c) I use a computer because I am very interested. (+)*
IC07Q04	*d) I lose track of time when I am working with the computer. (+)*

(+) Item inverted for IRT scaling.

Annex A2: Are principals' assessments of the extent to which lack of computers hinders instruction comparable across schools and countries?

The assessment made by principals of whether shortage of ICT resources hindered instruction gives a snapshot indication of the implications for teaching and learning of the quantity of such resources. But are the ways in which principals make such judgements comparable across different contexts, or are they subjectively influenced by the specific cultural or social context? One way to investigate this is to compare the pattern of principals' responses with the actual supply of computers in schools. If judgements were being made on consistent criteria, one would expect the principals on average to identify more serious consequences for instruction in schools where computers were scarcer.

Figure A2.1 looks at this question in terms of comparison between countries. The countries are shown in order of the percentage of students whose principals think that learning has been hindered a lot or to some extent, as shown by the bottom two bars. The white diamonds represent the country mean of computers per student. If countries where principals showed the most concern were also those with the fewest computers per student, the dots would tend to be higher at the right and lower at the left of the graph. The lack of any such pattern suggests that school principals' subjective perceptions of shortage were affected in different countries by factors other than the actual seriousness of the shortage. This means that caution is needed when comparing across countries principals' perceptions of the extent to which instruction is hindered.

Looking within each country, however, there appears much more consistency between perception and reality. Figure A2.2 shows in each country how many computers schools had per student according to whether the school heads reported that instruction was hindered a lot, to some extent, very little or not at all. Within each country, the schools whose principals reported that instruction was hindered the most also had fewer computers per student than other categories, in all countries except Austria, Canada, Japan, Korea, the Netherlands and Switzerland and the partner countries Hong Kong-China and Macao-China. This pattern indicates that within countries, principals seem to be reasonably consistent in how they judge a shortage and its consequences.

Figure A2.1 ■ **Reported computer and computer software shortages and mean number of computers per student**

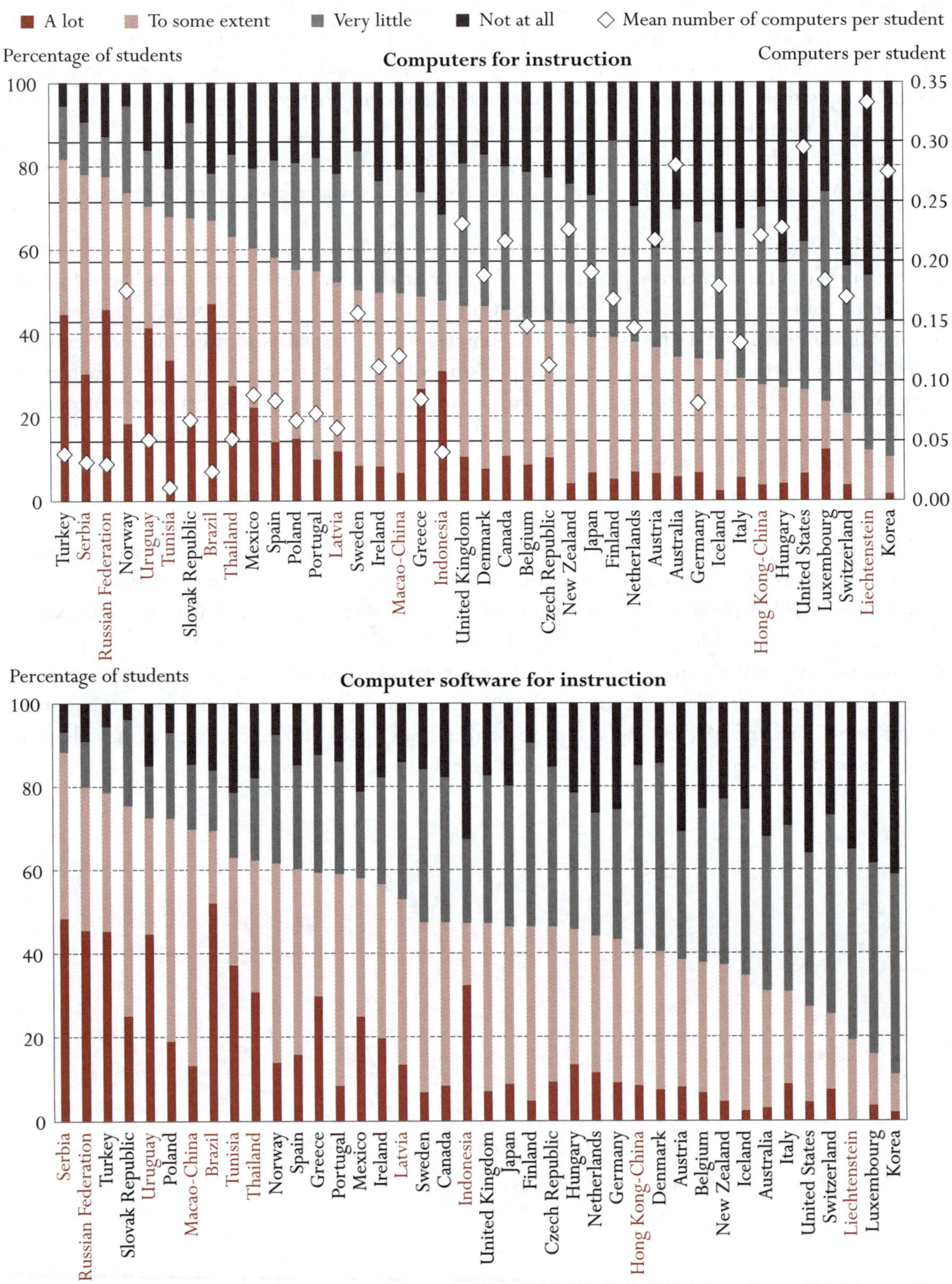

Source: OECD PISA 2003 database, Table 2.5.

Figure A2.2 ■ **Mean number of computers per student in schools, by reported level of computer shortages**

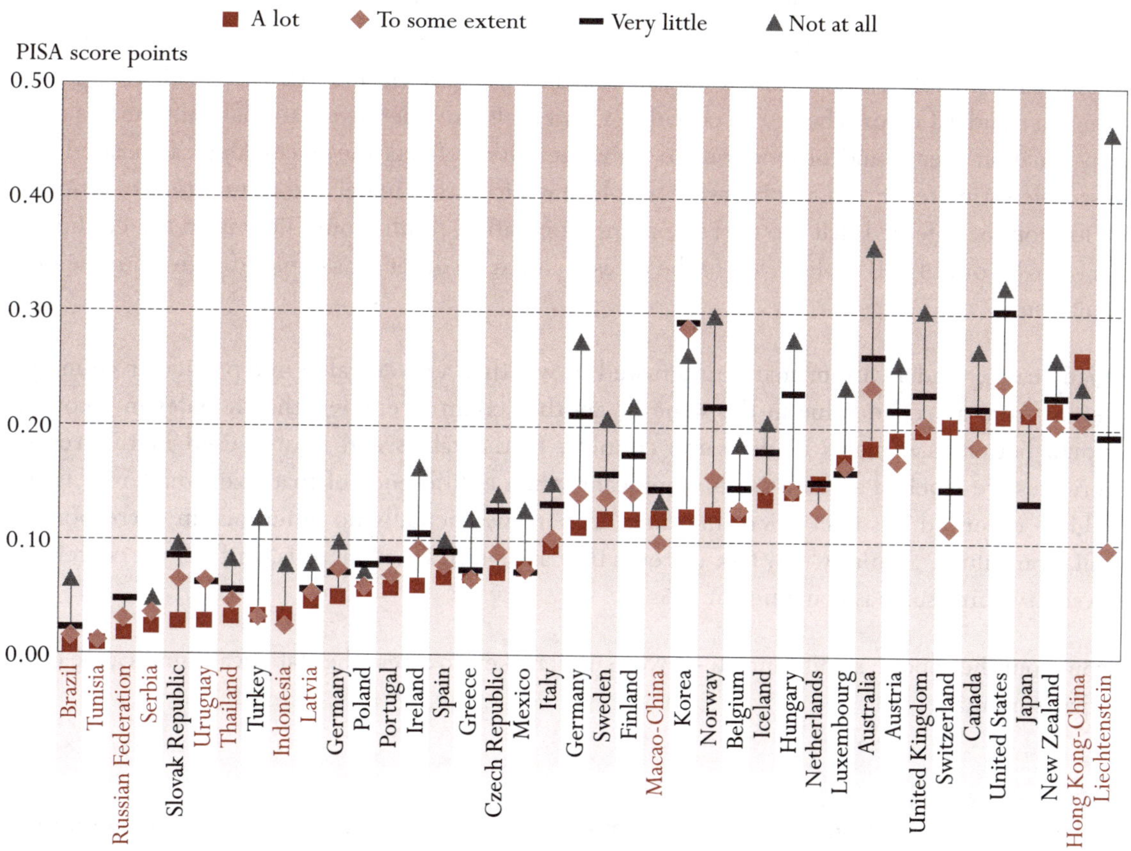

Source: OECD PISA 2003 database, Table 2.5.

Annex A3: Standard errors, significance tests and subgroup comparisons

The statistics in this report represent estimates of national performance based on samples of students rather than values that could be calculated if every student in every country had answered every question. Consequently, it is important to have measures of the degree of uncertainty of the estimates. In PISA, each estimate has an associated degree of uncertainty, which is expressed through a standard error. The use of confidence intervals provides a way to make inferences about the population means and proportions in a manner that reflects the uncertainty associated with the sample estimates. From an observed sample statistic it can, under the assumption of a normal distribution, be inferred that the corresponding population result would lie within the confidence interval in 95 out of 100 replications of the measurement on different samples drawn from the same population.

In many cases, readers are primarily interested in whether a given value in a particular country is different from a second value in the same or another country, e.g. whether females in a country perform better than males in the same country. In the tables and figures used in this report, differences are labelled as statistically significant when a difference of that size, smaller or larger, would be observed less than 5% of the time, if there was actually no difference in corresponding population values. Similarly, the risk of reporting as significant if there is, in fact, no correlation between two measures is contained at 5%.

Throughout the report, significance tests were undertaken to assess the statistical significance of the comparisons made.

Gender differences

Gender differences in means and percentages of some variables were tested for statistical significance. Positive differences indicate higher scores for males while negative differences indicate higher scores for females. Differences marked in bold in the tables in Annexes B1 and B2 are statistically significant at the 95% confidence level.

Differences in means and percentages between top and bottom quartiles

Differences in means and percentages between the top quarter and the bottom quarter on the PISA indices were tested for statistical significance. Figures marked in bold indicate that performance between the top and bottom quarter of students on the respective index is statistically significantly different at the 95% confidence level.

Change in the performance per unit of the index

For many tables in Annex B1, the difference in student performance per unit of the index shown was calculated. Figures in bold indicate that the differences are statistically significantly different from zero at the 95% confidence level.

Differences in means and percentages between 2003 and 2000

Where percentages are compared between the PISA 2003 and PISA 2000 samples, differences were tested for statistical significance. Figures in bold in Annex B1 indicate statistically significantly different percentages at the 95% confidence level. When comparing data between 2003 and 2000, it should be borne in mind that in 2000 school principals were asked to report with regard to the situation of 15-year-olds in their school whereas in 2003 school principals were asked to reflect the situation in the entire school in their responses. Similarly, in 2000 students were asked to reflect the situation in their language classes whereas in 2003 they were asked to reflect the situation in their mathematics classes.

Table A3.1

	Performance differences between national quarters of the index of ICT use for the Internet and entertainment on the:								Performance differences between national quarters of the index of ICT use for programs and software on the:											
	PISA mathematics scale				PISA reading scale				PISA mathematics scale						PISA reading scale					
	Bottom quarter - Second quarter		Third quarter - Top quarter		Bottom quarter - Second quarter		Third quarter - Top quarter		Bottom quarter - Second quarter		Second quarter - Third quarter		Third quarter - Top quarter		Bottom quarter - Second quarter		Third quarter - Top quarter			
	Dif.	S.E.	Dif.	S.E.	Dif.	S.E.	Dif.	S.E.	Dif.	S.E.	Dif.	S.E.	Dif.	S.E.	Dif.	S.E.	Dif.	S.E.		
Australia	-5	(3.1)	3	(3.1)	-3	(3.3)	**9**	(3.3)	**-14**	(3.4)	12	(4.1)	**20**	(3.5)	**-9**	(3.5)	**24**	(3.0)		
Austria	**-17**	(4.8)	1	(4.8)	**-18**	(5.2)	11	(5.6)	**-6**	(4.6)	3	(5.1)	**19**	(5.4)	-10	(5.7)	**26**	(5.6)		
Belgium	**-33**	(4.1)	3	(4.0)	**-31**	(4.3)	**9**	(3.7)	**-26**	(3.6)	-7	(3.9)	**30**	(4.2)	**-26**	(4.0)	**37**	(4.6)		
Canada	**-6**	(2.7)	-2	(3.3)	-4	(3.2)	2	(3.3)	**-9**	(3.0)	1	(2.4)	**14**	(2.9)	**-10**	(2.9)	**19**	(2.8)		
Czech Republic	**-20**	(4.4)	6	(3.9)	**-15**	(4.3)	**12**	(4.0)	**-28**	(4.7)	3	(4.3)	**11**	(4.3)	**-25**	(4.9)	**15**	(4.0)		
Denmark	-1	(4.9)	2	(4.3)	3	(4.7)	**11**	(4.7)	**-20**	(4.5)	4	(4.5)	**19**	(4.6)	**-14**	(4.6)	**23**	(4.8)		
Finland	1	(3.8)	-4	(3.8)	-1	(3.6)	**11**	(3.8)	**-11**	(3.8)	-2	(3.6)	**6**	(4.0)	**-10**	(3.8)	**14**	(3.8)		
Germany	**-17**	(4.5)	-1	(5.8)	**-15**	(5.0)	**13**	(5.4)	**-11**	(5.5)	4	(4.7)	**27**	(4.9)	-8	(5.1)	**35**	(5.6)		
Greece	-1	(4.7)	5	(4.5)	2	(5.1)	4	(5.1)	**3**	(4.8)	5	(4.5)	**18**	(5.0)	-4	(5.7)	**22**	(5.8)		
Hungary	**-22**	(5.1)	2	(5.0)	**-20**	(4.8)	8	(5.0)	**-20**	(4.6)	3	(5.0)	**10**	(4.7)	**-17**	(5.0)	**17**	(5.2)		
Iceland	-8	(4.3)	**10**	(4.7)	-6	(4.6)	**21**	(5.1)	**-20**	(5.0)	11	(5.1)	**17**	(4.6)	**-20**	(5.9)	**25**	(5.3)		
Ireland	**-16**	(4.7)	8	(4.8)	**-15**	(4.8)	**15**	(4.8)	**-10**	(4.3)	1	(4.2)	**27**	(4.8)	**-16**	(3.8)	**30**	(4.6)		
Italy	**-21**	(4.8)	6	(4.1)	**-23**	(4.5)	**17**	(4.6)	**-10**	(3.7)	11	(5.2)	**18**	(4.5)	-4	(4.1)	**33**	(5.2)		
Japan	**-26**	(5.7)	-1	(5.2)	**-29**	(6.5)	-4	(5.1)	**-24**	(6.3)	-11	(4.8)	**7**	(5.9)	**-29**	(6.4)	8	(5.8)		
Korea	-3	(4.2)	**19**	(4.0)	2	(3.5)	**13**	(3.6)	**-17**	(4.1)	-6	(4.4)	**10**	(4.3)	**-21**	(3.9)	**9**	(3.6)		
Mexico	**-17**	(4.4)	-6	(3.9)	**-21**	(5.7)	-4	(4.4)	**-5**	(3.7)	2	(3.8)	**15**	(3.9)	**-10**	(4.7)	**16**	(4.3)		
New Zealand	4	(4.5)	7	(5.1)	9	(5.2)	5	(5.0)	**-7**	(4.3)	20	(4.3)	**31**	(4.6)	**-12**	(5.3)	**33**	(4.8)		
Poland	**-12**	(4.0)	4	(4.1)	**-9**	(4.2)	**10**	(4.5)	**-18**	(4.5)	2	(4.1)	**19**	(4.3)	**-13**	(5.2)	**29**	(4.3)		
Portugal	**-13**	(4.2)	**-10**	(5.0)	**-12**	(4.9)	-5	(5.3)	**-19**	(5.5)	-1	(4.5)	**31**	(5.1)	**-20**	(5.4)	**34**	(5.1)		
Slovak Republic	**-27**	(4.2)	**10**	(4.1)	**-26**	(4.4)	**18**	(4.6)	**-22**	(4.9)	0	(4.8)	**12**	(4.5)	**-28**	(5.5)	**19**	(4.0)		
Sweden	2	(4.7)	8	(4.5)	2	(5.0)	**17**	(3.9)	**-14**	(4.2)	2	(5.3)	**19**	(4.2)	**-11**	(4.4)	**26**	(4.3)		
Switzerland	**-23**	(4.1)	2	(4.9)	**-18**	(5.3)	**13**	(4.9)	**-24**	(4.7)	-1	(4.3)	**30**	(4.1)	**-19**	(3.9)	**37**	(4.5)		
Turkey	**-11**	(5.8)	7	(7.3)	-9	(6.0)	10	(7.3)	**-11**	(7.9)	21	(6.0)	**40**	(9.9)	-13	(7.5)	**36**	(8.5)		
United States	**-12**	(5.0)	-4	(3.8)	-8	(4.9)	-1	(4.9)	**-9**	(4.3)	12	(4.3)	**25**	(3.9)	-8	(4.9)	**32**	(4.5)		
OECD average	*-12*	*(0.9)*	*3*	*(0.9)*	*-11*	*(1.0)*	*9*	*(0.9)*	*-14*	*(0.9)*	*4*	*(0.0)*	*20*	*(1.0)*	*-14*	*(1.0)*	*25*	*(1.0)*		
Latvia	**-21**	(5.7)	2	(4.9)	**-15**	(4.9)	10	(5.7)	**-16**	(4.9)	-7	(5.8)	**15**	(5.6)	**-14**	(4.8)	**21**	(5.3)		
Liechtenstein	-16	(16.7)	10	(17.6)	-5	(16.5)	22	(17.4)	2	(17.7)	-9	(18.1)	**40**	(17.5)	6	(18.4)	25	(17.9)		
Russian Federation	-6	(4.8)	-4	(4.7)	-4	(5.0)	1	(4.2)	**-18**	(4.9)	-22	(4.6)	**14**	(4.2)	**-18**	(4.9)	**17**	(4.7)		
Serbia	-5	(4.2)	5	(4.6)	5	(3.8)	**8**	(4.1)	**-7**	(4.2)	-3	(4.8)	**28**	(4.4)	**-10**	(4.5)	**25**	(4.4)		
Thailand	-7	(4.1)	**-13**	(5.0)	-4	(4.1)	**-11**	(4.3)	**-12**	(4.4)	2	(4.0)	**14**	(4.3)	**-14**	(3.9)	**13**	(3.9)		
Tunisia	-2	(5.7)	0	(5.8)	-6	(6.7)	4	(7.0)	**1**	(6.2)	6	(5.4)	**4**	(6.0)	-2	(6.5)	5	(7.1)		
Uruguay	**-16**	(4.8)	-3	(5.8)	**-23**	(7.8)	1	(7.6)	**-26**	(5.0)	-6	(6.8)	**19**	(5.3)	**-27**	(7.2)	**17**	(6.4)		
United Kingdom[1]	0	(5.6)	2	(4.2)	2	(6.1)	6	(4.5)	**-7**	(4.8)	13	(5.3)	**24**	(5.1)	-5	(5.1)	**34**	(5.0)		

Note: Differences marked in bold are statistically significant.

1. Response rate too low to ensure comparability.

Annex A4: Information and Communication Technology (ICT) Questionnaire

The following questions ask about computers: This does not include calculators or games consoles like a <Sony PlayStation™>.

Q1 IS THERE A COMPUTER AVAILABLE FOR YOU TO USE AT ANY OF THESE PLACES?

(PLEASE <TICK> ONE BOX ON EACH ROW.)			YES	NO
IC01Q01	*a)*	*At home*	☐ 1	☐ 2
IC01Q02	*b)*	*At school*	☐ 1	☐ 2
IC01Q03	*c)*	*At other places*	☐ 1	☐ 2

Q2 HAVE YOU EVER USED A COMPUTER?

	YES	NO
IC02Q01	☐ 1	☐ 2

If you use a computer in any setting, please continue.
If you do not, please stop here. <Instructions>

Q3 HOW LONG HAVE YOU BEEN USING COMPUTERS?

(PLEASE TICK ONLY ONE BOX.)

IC03Q01	*Less than one year*	☐ 1
	One to three years	☐ 2
	Three to five years	☐ 3
	More than five years	☐ 4

Q4 HOW OFTEN DO YOU USE A COMPUTER AT THESE PLACES?

(PLEASE <TICK> ONE BOX ON EACH ROW.)			ALMOST EVERY DAY	A FEW TIMES EACH WEEK	BETWEEN ONCE A WEEK AND ONCE A MONTH	LESS THAN ONCE A MONTH	NEVER
IC04Q01	*a)*	*At home*	☐ 1	☐ 2	☐ 3	☐ 4	☐ 5
IC04Q02	*b)*	*At school*	☐ 1	☐ 2	☐ 3	☐ 4	☐ 5
IC04Q03	*c)*	*At other places*	☐ 1	☐ 2	☐ 3	☐ 4	☐ 5

Q5 HOW OFTEN DO YOU USE:

		(PLEASE <TICK> ONE BOX ON EACH ROW.)	ALMOST EVERY DAY	A FEW TIMES EACH WEEK	BETWEEN ONCE A WEEK AND ONCE A MONTH	LESS THAN ONCE A MONTH	NEVER
IC05Q01	a)	*The Internet to look up information about people, things or ideas?*	☐ 1	☐ 2	☐ 3	☐ 4	☐ 5
IC05Q02	b)	*Games on a computer?*	☐ 1	☐ 2	☐ 3	☐ 4	☐ 5
IC05Q03	c)	*Word processing (e.g. <Word® or WordPerfect®>)?*	☐ 1	☐ 2	☐ 3	☐ 4	☐ 5
IC05Q04	d)	*The Internet to collaborate with a group or team?*	☐ 1	☐ 2	☐ 3	☐ 4	☐ 5
IC05Q05	e)	*Spreadsheets (e.g. <Lotus 1 2 3® or Microsoft Excel®>)?*	☐ 1	☐ 2	☐ 3	☐ 4	☐ 5
IC05Q06	f)	*The Internet to download software (including games)?*	☐ 1	☐ 2	☐ 3	☐ 4	☐ 5
IC05Q07	g)	*Drawing, painting or graphics programs on a computer?*	☐ 1	☐ 2	☐ 3	☐ 4	☐ 5
IC05Q08	h)	*Educational software such as mathematics programs?*	☐ 1	☐ 2	☐ 3	☐ 4	☐ 5
IC05Q09	i)	*The computer to help you learn school material?*	☐ 1	☐ 2	☐ 3	☐ 4	☐ 5
IC05Q10	j)	*The Internet to download music?*	☐ 1	☐ 2	☐ 3	☐ 4	☐ 5
IC05Q11	k)	*The computer for programming?*	☐ 1	☐ 2	☐ 3	☐ 4	☐ 5
IC05Q12	l)	*A computer for electronic communication (e.g. e-mail or "chat rooms")?*	☐ 1	☐ 2	☐ 3	☐ 4	☐ 5

Q6 HOW WELL CAN YOU DO EACH OF THESE TASKS ON A COMPUTER?

(PLEASE <TICK> ONE BOX ON EACH ROW.)			I CAN DO THIS VERY WELL BY MYSELF.	I CAN DO THIS WITH HELP FROM SOMEONE.	I KNOW WHAT THIS MEANS BUT I CANNOT DO IT.	I DON'T KNOW WHAT THIS MEANS.
IC06Q01	a)	*Start a computer game*	☐1	☐2	☐3	☐4
IC06Q02	b)	*Use software to find and get rid of computer viruses*	☐1	☐2	☐3	☐4
IC06Q03	c)	*Open a file*	☐1	☐2	☐3	☐4
IC06Q04	d)	*Create/edit a document*	☐1	☐2	☐3	☐4
IC06Q05	e)	*Scroll a document up and down a screen*	☐1	☐2	☐3	☐4
IC06Q06	f)	*Use a database to produce a list of addresses*	☐1	☐2	☐3	☐4
IC06Q07	g)	*Copy a file from a floppy disk*	☐1	☐2	☐3	☐4
IC06Q08	h)	*Save a computer document or file*	☐1	☐2	☐3	☐4
IC06Q09	i)	*Print a computer document or file*	☐1	☐2	☐3	☐4
IC06Q10	j)	*Delete a computer document or file*	☐1	☐2	☐3	☐4
IC06Q11	k)	*Move files from one place to another on a computer*	☐1	☐2	☐3	☐4
IC06Q12	l)	*Get on to the Internet*	☐1	☐2	☐3	☐4
IC06Q13	m)	*Copy or download files from the Internet*	☐1	☐2	☐3	☐4
IC06Q14	n)	*Attach a file to an e-mail message*	☐1	☐2	☐3	☐4
IC06Q15	o)	*Create a computer program (e.g. in <Logo, Pascal, Basic>)*	☐1	☐2	☐3	☐4
IC06Q16	p)	*Use a spreadsheet to plot a graph*	☐1	☐2	☐3	☐4
IC06Q17	q)	*Create a presentation (e.g. using <PowerPoint®>)*	☐1	☐2	☐3	☐4
IC06Q18	r)	*Play computer games*	☐1	☐2	☐3	☐4
IC06Q19	s)	*Download music from the Internet*	☐1	☐2	☐3	☐4
IC06Q20	t)	*Create a multi-media presentation (with sound, pictures, video)*	☐1	☐2	☐3	☐4
IC06Q21	u)	*Draw pictures using a mouse*	☐1	☐2	☐3	☐4
IC06Q22	v)	*Write and send e-mails*	☐1	☐2	☐3	☐4
IC06Q23	w)	*Construct a Web page*	☐1	☐2	☐3	☐4

Q7 THINKING ABOUT YOUR EXPERIENCE WITH COMPUTERS: TO WHAT EXTENT DO YOU AGREE WITH THE FOLLOWING STATEMENTS?

(PLEASE <TICK> ONE BOX ON EACH ROW.)			STRONGLY AGREE	AGREE	DISAGREE	STRONGLY DISAGREE
IC07Q01	a)	*It is very important to me to work with a computer.*	☐1	☐2	☐3	☐4
IC07Q02	b)	*I think playing or working with a computer is really fun.*	☐1	☐2	☐3	☐4
IC07Q03	c)	*I use a computer because I am very interested.*	☐1	☐2	☐3	☐4
IC07Q04	d)	*I lose track of time when I am working with the computer.*	☐1	☐2	☐3	☐4

Q8 WHO TAUGHT YOU MOST ABOUT HOW TO USE COMPUTERS?
(PLEASE <TICK> ONLY ONE BOX.)

IC08Q01	*My school*	☐ 1
	My friends	☐ 2
	My family	☐ 3
	I taught myself	☐ 4
	Others	☐ 5

Q9 WHO TAUGHT YOU MOST ABOUT HOW TO USE THE INTERNET?
(PLEASE <TICK> ONLY ONE BOX.)

IC09Q01	*I don't know how to use the Internet*	☐ 1
	My school	☐ 2
	My friends	☐ 3
	My family	☐ 4
	I taught myself	☐ 5
	Others	☐ 6

Annex B

DATA TABLES

Table 2.1

Percentage of students having never used a computer, by gender and by national quarters of the index of economic, social and cultural status (ESCS) and percentage of students according to the length of time for which they had been using a computer

Results based on students' self-reports

		Percentage of students having never used a computer							
		All students		Males		Females		Gender difference (M-F)	
		%	S.E.	%	S.E.	%	S.E.	Dif.	S.E.
OECD countries	Australia	0.15	(0.10)	0.27	(0.19)	0.03	(0.03)	0.24	(0.19)
	Austria	0.09	(0.04)	0.14	(0.07)	0.04	(0.04)	0.11	(0.08)
	Belgium	0.53	(0.11)	0.61	(0.20)	0.44	(0.11)	0.16	(0.24)
	Canada	0.47	(0.07)	0.76	(0.13)	0.20	(0.05)	**0.56**	(0.14)
	Czech Republic	0.23	(0.08)	0.15	(0.09)	0.31	(0.14)	-0.17	(0.17)
	Denmark	0.05	(0.04)	0.07	(0.05)	0.03	(0.03)	0.04	(0.04)
	Finland	0.00	(0.00)	0.00	(0.00)	0.00	(0.00)	a	a
	Germany	0.20	(0.05)	0.08	(0.06)	0.32	(0.09)	**-0.24**	(0.11)
	Greece	1.96	(0.25)	1.35	(0.27)	2.53	(0.35)	**-1.18**	(0.38)
	Hungary	0.11	(0.05)	0.09	(0.06)	0.14	(0.09)	-0.05	(0.11)
	Iceland	0.06	(0.04)	0.12	(0.08)	0.00	(0.00)	a	a
	Ireland	0.29	(0.09)	0.30	(0.14)	0.27	(0.13)	0.02	(0.19)
	Italy	1.83	(0.27)	1.54	(0.30)	2.10	(0.36)	-0.56	(0.39)
	Japan	1.44	(0.20)	1.89	(0.34)	1.01	(0.19)	**0.88**	(0.38)
	Korea	0.11	(0.04)	0.16	(0.07)	0.03	(0.03)	0.12	(0.08)
	Mexico	13.12	(1.48)	12.36	(1.69)	13.79	(1.62)	-1.43	(1.47)
	New Zealand	0.25	(0.09)	0.21	(0.10)	0.30	(0.14)	-0.09	(0.17)
	Poland	0.52	(0.13)	0.67	(0.19)	0.37	(0.15)	0.30	(0.22)
	Portugal	0.58	(0.11)	0.59	(0.14)	0.57	(0.17)	0.02	(0.21)
	Slovak Republic	3.82	(0.67)	3.25	(0.81)	4.42	(0.67)	-1.17	(0.64)
	Sweden	0.20	(0.10)	0.27	(0.14)	0.13	(0.08)	0.14	(0.11)
	Switzerland	0.34	(0.12)	0.37	(0.13)	0.31	(0.17)	0.06	(0.19)
	Turkey	14.43	(1.43)	9.06	(1.18)	21.04	(1.97)	**-11.98**	(1.60)
	United States	2.02	(0.36)	2.57	(0.41)	1.46	(0.44)	**1.11**	(0.45)
	OECD average	*1.71*	*(0.09)*	*1.47*	*(0.00)*	*2.00*	*(0.11)*	*-0.60*	*(0.11)*
Partner countries	Latvia	0.59	(0.12)	0.47	(0.17)	0.71	(0.19)	-0.24	(0.25)
	Liechtenstein	0.30	(0.30)	0.59	(0.59)	0.00	(0.00)	a	a
	Russian Federation	6.19	(0.70)	5.23	(0.62)	7.15	(0.90)	**-1.92**	(0.66)
	Serbia	1.39	(0.22)	1.50	(0.27)	1.29	(0.33)	0.21	(0.41)
	Thailand	5.83	(1.00)	5.79	(1.14)	5.86	(1.04)	-0.07	(0.85)
	Tunisia	38.64	(1.62)	34.99	(2.08)	42.13	(1.72)	**-7.14**	(2.00)
	Uruguay	3.89	(0.54)	3.34	(0.44)	4.40	(0.77)	-1.06	(0.66)
	United Kingdom[1]	0.05	(0.05)	0.00	(0.00)	0.09	(0.09)	a	a

		Percentage of students having never used a computer, by national quarters of the index of ESCS							
		Bottom quarter		Second quarter		Third quarter		Top quarter	
		%	S.E.	%	S.E.	%	S.E.	%	S.E.
OECD countries	Australia	0.50	(0.35)	0.04	(0.04)	0.01	(0.01)	0.00	(0.00)
	Austria	0.07	(0.07)	0.05	(0.07)	0.07	(0.07)	0.17	(0.12)
	Belgium	1.02	(0.32)	0.42	(0.16)	0.14	(0.08)	**0.23**	(0.12)
	Canada	**1.20**	(0.25)	0.36	(0.11)	0.15	(0.05)	**0.13**	(0.05)
	Czech Republic	0.52	(0.23)	0.16	(0.16)	0.09	(0.07)	0.05	(0.05)
	Denmark	0.00	(0.00)	0.07	(0.07)	0.15	(0.10)	0.00	(0.00)
	Finland	0.00	(0.00)	0.00	(0.00)	0.00	(0.00)	0.00	(0.00)
	Germany	**0.58**	(0.17)	0.07	(0.07)	0.09	(0.09)	**0.07**	(0.07)
	Greece	**3.25**	(0.41)	1.57	(0.46)	1.47	(0.35)	**1.48**	(0.57)
	Hungary	0.42	(0.21)	0.03	(0.03)	0.00	(0.00)	0.00	(0.00)
	Iceland	0.00	(0.00)	0.00	(0.00)	0.12	(0.12)	0.12	(0.12)
	Ireland	0.90	(0.33)	0.00	(0.00)	0.00	(0.00)	0.14	(0.14)
	Italy	**4.18**	(0.78)	2.07	(0.42)	0.90	(0.31)	**0.19**	(0.08)
	Japan	**2.22**	(0.45)	1.59	(0.46)	1.03	(0.38)	**0.86**	(0.29)
	Korea	0.00	(0.00)	0.00	(0.00)	0.33	(0.16)	0.05	(0.07)
	Mexico	**28.52**	(3.62)	15.38	(1.80)	6.86	(1.00)	**1.63**	(0.37)
	New Zealand	0.30	(0.22)	0.30	(0.17)	0.09	(0.09)	0.00	(0.00)
	Poland	1.05	(0.32)	0.69	(0.34)	0.35	(0.18)	0.00	(0.00)
	Portugal	1.69	(0.41)	0.50	(0.17)	0.14	(0.09)	0.00	(0.00)
	Slovak Republic	**10.83**	(2.15)	2.11	(0.48)	1.23	(0.33)	**0.90**	(0.36)
	Sweden	0.61	(0.32)	0.00	(0.00)	0.00	(0.00)	0.09	(0.09)
	Switzerland	0.46	(0.21)	0.35	(0.21)	0.22	(0.15)	0.14	(0.11)
	Turkey	**24.58**	(2.69)	17.92	(2.06)	11.71	(1.37)	**3.36**	(0.81)
	United States	**3.59**	(0.74)	2.19	(0.60)	1.66	(0.38)	**0.59**	(0.25)
	OECD average	*3.46*	*(0.21)*	*1.84*	*(0.12)*	*1.07*	*(0.08)*	*0.41*	*(0.05)*
Partner countries	Latvia	0.72	(0.25)	0.99	(0.31)	0.46	(0.22)	0.14	(0.14)
	Liechtenstein	0.00	(0.00)	0.00	(0.00)	0.00	(0.00)	1.22	(1.23)
	Russian Federation	**12.44**	(1.44)	6.85	(1.14)	3.63	(0.60)	**1.81**	(0.37)
	Serbia	**2.83**	(0.62)	1.60	(0.39)	0.87	(0.43)	**0.27**	(0.16)
	Thailand	**11.64**	(2.55)	5.43	(1.17)	5.22	(0.94)	**1.10**	(0.33)
	Tunisia	**69.87**	(2.41)	47.50	(1.78)	26.33	(1.62)	**10.62**	(1.19)
	Uruguay	**9.83**	(1.66)	3.19	(0.68)	2.10	(0.44)	**0.39**	(0.18)
	United Kingdom[1]	0.00	(0.00)	0.19	(0.19)	0.00	(0.00)	0.00	(0.00)

Note: Statistically significant differences are marked in bold.

1. Response rate too low to ensure comparability.

Table 2.1 (*continued*)

Percentage of students having never used a computer, by gender and by national quarters of the index of economic, social and cultural status (ESCS) and percentage of students according to the length of time for which they had been using a computer

Results based on students' self-reports

		Length of time using a computer							
		Less than one year		One to three years		Three to five years		More than five years	
		%	S.E.	%	S.E.	%	S.E.	%	S.E.
OECD countries	Australia	2	(0.1)	8	(0.4)	21	(0.4)	69	(0.5)
	Austria	5	(0.4)	30	(1.0)	36	(0.9)	30	(0.7)
	Belgium	8	(0.4)	30	(0.7)	28	(0.6)	34	(0.7)
	Canada	2	(0.1)	10	(0.3)	22	(0.4)	66	(0.5)
	Czech Republic	9	(0.6)	32	(0.8)	29	(0.7)	29	(0.9)
	Denmark	2	(0.2)	18	(0.6)	28	(0.8)	52	(0.9)
	Finland	2	(0.2)	17	(0.6)	30	(0.7)	51	(0.9)
	Germany	5	(0.4)	30	(0.9)	32	(0.8)	33	(0.9)
	Greece	22	(1.0)	41	(1.0)	24	(0.9)	14	(1.0)
	Hungary	6	(0.5)	25	(0.7)	32	(0.8)	36	(0.7)
	Iceland	2	(0.3)	19	(0.7)	30	(0.7)	50	(0.9)
	Ireland	8	(0.6)	28	(0.9)	33	(0.7)	31	(1.1)
	Italy	14	(0.6)	41	(0.7)	23	(0.6)	21	(0.6)
	Japan	18	(0.9)	41	(0.9)	25	(0.8)	15	(0.6)
	Korea	2	(0.2)	18	(0.7)	35	(0.8)	45	(1.1)
	Mexico	39	(1.8)	33	(1.0)	14	(0.8)	14	(1.8)
	New Zealand	4	(0.4)	16	(0.7)	24	(0.7)	55	(0.9)
	Poland	11	(0.7)	44	(1.0)	25	(0.9)	21	(1.0)
	Portugal	10	(0.6)	26	(0.8)	33	(0.8)	32	(1.0)
	Slovak Republic	27	(1.0)	36	(0.7)	19	(0.5)	18	(0.7)
	Sweden	1	(0.2)	12	(0.6)	30	(0.9)	57	(1.0)
	Switzerland	5	(0.4)	29	(0.7)	32	(0.7)	34	(0.7)
	Turkey	29	(1.8)	38	(1.4)	19	(0.9)	15	(1.3)
	United States	3	(0.3)	13	(0.5)	22	(0.6)	62	(1.0)
	OECD average	***10***	***(0.1)***	***26***	***(0.2)***	***27***	***(0.1)***	***37***	***(0.2)***
Partner countries	Latvia	21	(1.2)	44	(1.3)	23	(1.2)	12	(0.7)
	Liechtenstein	1	(0.6)	21	(2.3)	38	(2.9)	40	(2.8)
	Russian Federation	47	(2.0)	33	(1.2)	11	(0.8)	9	(0.7)
	Serbia	43	(1.1)	36	(0.9)	11	(0.6)	10	(0.7)
	Thailand	28	(1.5)	38	(1.3)	17	(0.8)	17	(1.0)
	Tunisia	50	(1.7)	27	(1.0)	9	(0.6)	14	(1.0)
	Uruguay	15	(0.8)	32	(1.2)	22	(0.7)	31	(1.2)
	United Kingdom[1]	2	(0.3)	18	(0.9)	33	(0.9)	48	(1.0)

Note: Statistically significant differences are marked in bold.

1. Response rate too low to ensure comparability.

Table 2.2a

Percentage of students having access to a computer at home, school or other places in PISA 2003 and PISA 2000

Results based on students' self-reports

		PISA 2003													PISA 2000					
	At home		At school		Other places		Computer available at home and at school		Computer available at home but not available at school		Computer not available at home but available at school		Computer not available at home nor at school		At home		At school		Other places	
	%	S.E.	%	S.E.	%	S.E.	%	S.E.	%	S.E.	%	S.E.	%	S.E.	%	S.E.	%	S.E.	%	S.E.
OECD countries																				
Australia	**97**	(0.2)	**100**	(0.1)	**93**	(0.3)	96	(0.2)	0	(0.1)	3	(0.2)	0	(0.0)	**91**	(0.5)	**98**	(0.3)	**96**	(0.4)
Austria	97	(0.3)	97	(0.5)	76	(0.9)	94	(0.6)	3	(0.5)	3	(0.3)	0	(0.1)	a	a	a	a	a	a
Belgium	**94**	(0.3)	**91**	(0.8)	**85**	(0.5)	86	(0.8)	7	(0.7)	5	(0.3)	2	(0.2)	**85**	(0.7)	**80**	(1.2)	**74**	(0.7)
Canada	**95**	(0.2)	**99**	(0.1)	**98**	(0.2)	95	(0.3)	1	(0.1)	4	(0.2)	0	(0.1)	**88**	(0.3)	**95**	(0.2)	**94**	(0.2)
Czech Republic	**82**	(0.7)	**95**	(0.8)	**86**	(0.6)	78	(1.0)	4	(0.7)	17	(0.7)	1	(0.2)	**58**	(1.1)	**79**	(1.9)	**74**	(0.9)
Denmark	**97**	(0.3)	**100**	(0.1)	**85**	(0.8)	97	(0.3)	0	(0.1)	3	(0.3)	0	(0.0)	**92**	(0.5)	**99**	(0.3)	**91**	(0.8)
Finland	**91**	(0.5)	**97**	(0.7)	**89**	(0.4)	88	(0.9)	3	(0.7)	9	(0.4)	1	(0.1)	**82**	(0.6)	**96**	(0.7)	**93**	(0.4)
Germany	**96**	(0.4)	**93**	(0.6)	72	(0.9)	89	(0.7)	7	(0.5)	4	(0.3)	1	(0.1)	**87**	(0.5)	**69**	(1.5)	73	(0.8)
Greece	67	(1.3)	93	(0.7)	81	(0.7)	60	(1.5)	4	(0.6)	32	(1.4)	3	(0.3)	a	a	a	a	a	a
Hungary	**75**	(0.8)	**98**	(0.5)	**84**	(0.7)	73	(0.9)	2	(0.3)	24	(0.8)	1	(0.3)	**55**	(1.3)	**93**	(1.0)	**66**	(0.9)
Iceland	98	(0.2)	98	(0.2)	88	(0.6)	96	(0.3)	2	(0.2)	2	(0.2)	0	(0.1)	a	a	a	a	a	a
Ireland	**87**	(0.7)	**89**	(0.9)	**84**	(0.7)	78	(1.2)	9	(0.8)	11	(0.7)	2	(0.3)	**71**	(1.1)	**75**	(1.3)	**72**	(1.0)
Italy	87	(0.7)	86	(1.4)	62	(0.7)	74	(1.5)	12	(1.3)	11	(0.6)	2	(0.4)	a	a	a	a	a	a
Japan	79	(0.9)	89	(1.5)	55	(1.2)	69	(1.5)	9	(1.3)	20	(0.9)	2	(0.4)	a	a	a	a	a	a
Korea	98	(0.2)	85	(1.4)	88	(0.6)	84	(1.4)	14	(1.3)	2	(0.2)	1	(0.2)	a	a	a	a	a	a
Mexico	**51**	(1.9)	**83**	(1.6)	**85**	(1.1)	42	(2.3)	5	(0.5)	37	(2.0)	15	(1.7)	**29**	(2.0)	**61**	(2.3)	**72**	(1.2)
New Zealand	**91**	(0.5)	**98**	(0.3)	**92**	(0.4)	90	(0.6)	1	(0.3)	8	(0.5)	0	(0.1)	**82**	(0.7)	**95**	(0.4)	**96**	(0.4)
Poland	64	(1.1)	91	(1.2)	80	(0.9)	58	(1.2)	6	(0.8)	33	(1.2)	3	(0.5)	a	a	a	a	a	a
Portugal	84	(0.9)	98	(0.3)	87	(0.8)	81	(0.9)	1	(0.3)	17	(0.9)	0	(0.1)	a	a	a	a	a	a
Slovak Republic	72	(1.2)	82	(1.6)	84	(1.0)	60	(1.7)	9	(0.8)	20	(0.9)	10	(1.1)	a	a	a	a	a	a
Sweden	**98**	(0.2)	**97**	(0.6)	91	(0.5)	95	(0.6)	2	(0.5)	2	(0.2)	0	(0.1)	**95**	(0.4)	**95**	(0.7)	90	(0.7)
Switzerland	**97**	(0.3)	**94**	(0.7)	**70**	(0.7)	92	(0.8)	5	(0.7)	3	(0.2)	1	(0.2)	**90**	(0.7)	**88**	(1.1)	**73**	(0.8)
Turkey	37	(2.2)	54	(3.5)	73	(1.5)	17	(2.3)	12	(1.4)	26	(2.3)	45	(3.1)	a	a	a	a	a	a
United States	**90**	(0.7)	**97**	(0.4)	**90**	(0.5)	88	(0.7)	1	(0.2)	8	(0.5)	2	(0.3)	**86**	(1.5)	**92**	(0.8)	**95**	(0.6)
OECD average	*85*		*92*	*(0.2)*	*83*	*(0.2)*	*79*	*(0.2)*	*5*	*(0.1)*	*12*	*(0.2)*	*4*	*(0.2)*	*78*	*(0.3)*	*87*	*(0.3)*	*84*	*(0.2)*
Partner countries																				
Latvia	**55**	(1.7)	**90**	(1.2)	**89**	(1.1)	48	(1.8)	5	(0.7)	41	(1.6)	0	(0.8)	**31**	(1.0)	**82**	(1.4)	**66**	(1.4)
Liechtenstein	**98**	(0.7)	**100**	(0.3)	81	(2.2)	98	(0.7)	0	(0.0)	2	(0.7)	0	(0.0)	**88**	(1.6)	**95**	(1.1)	77	(2.4)
Russian Federation	**37**	(2.0)	**76**	(1.7)	**70**	(1.2)	27	(2.0)	7	(0.7)	46	(1.8)	20	(1.6)	**20**	(1.1)	**60**	(2.4)	**44**	(1.6)
Serbia	**57**	(1.5)	**95**	(1.0)	**76**	(1.2)	47	(1.7)	3	(1.0)	47	(1.6)	3	(0.5)	a	a	a	a	a	a
Thailand	**31**	(1.4)	**96**	(1.4)	67	(1.6)	30	(1.3)	0	(0.1)	65	(2.0)	4	(1.4)	**24**	(1.7)	**81**	(1.6)	64	(2.1)
Tunisia	38	(1.7)	35	(2.0)	56	(1.5)	15	(1.4)	16	(1.2)	14	(1.3)	55	(2.0)	a	a	a	a	a	a
Uruguay	63	(1.3)	72	(1.9)	84	(0.9)	44	(1.9)	13	(1.3)	24	(1.4)	19	(1.2)	a	a	a	a	a	a
United Kingdom[1]	93	(0.5)	99	(0.2)	90	(0.8)	93	(0.5)	1	(0.2)	6	(0.5)	0	(0.1)	79	(1.1)	96	(0.6)	94	(0.7)

Note: Statistically significant differences are marked in bold.

1. Response rate too low to ensure comparability.

Table 2.2b

Percentage of students having access to a computer at home, school or other places, by gender in PISA 2003

Results based on students' self-reports

		Percentage of students having access to a computer:																	
		At home						At school						Other places					
		Males		Females		Gender difference (M-F)		Males		Females		Gender difference (M-F)		Males		Females		Gender difference (M-F)	
		%	S.E.	%	S.E.	Dif.	S.E.	%	S.E.	%	S.E.	Dif.	S.E.	%	S.E.	%	S.E.	Dif.	S.E.
OECD countries	Australia	97	(0.5)	96	(0.4)	0	(0.8)	99	(0.1)	100	(0.1)	**0**	(0.1)	93	(0.4)	93	(0.4)	0	(0.5)
	Austria	98	(0.4)	96	(0.4)	**1**	(0.5)	95	(0.8)	98	(0.6)	**-4**	(1.0)	79	(1.3)	73	(1.1)	**5**	(1.6)
	Belgium	94	(0.5)	93	(0.6)	1	(0.8)	89	(1.0)	94	(0.9)	**-5**	(1.1)	85	(0.8)	84	(0.7)	1	(1.0)
	Canada	96	(0.3)	95	(0.3)	1	(0.4)	99	(0.1)	99	(0.2)	0	(0.2)	98	(0.3)	99	(0.2)	-1	(0.3)
	Czech Republic	85	(1.0)	78	(0.9)	**7**	(1.3)	94	(0.9)	96	(0.7)	**-2**	(0.7)	90	(0.7)	83	(1.0)	**6**	(1.3)
	Denmark	98	(0.3)	96	(0.5)	**2**	(0.6)	100	(0.1)	100	(0.1)	0	(0.2)	89	(0.8)	82	(1.2)	**7**	(1.2)
	Finland	92	(0.6)	89	(0.6)	**3**	(0.7)	98	(0.6)	96	(1.0)	**2**	(0.6)	90	(0.6)	89	(0.6)	1	(0.9)
	Germany	97	(0.4)	95	(0.5)	**1**	(0.5)	92	(0.8)	93	(0.7)	-1	(0.9)	75	(1.2)	70	(1.3)	**6**	(1.7)
	Greece	73	(1.5)	62	(1.4)	**11**	(1.4)	93	(0.9)	93	(0.8)	-1	(1.0)	83	(0.9)	79	(1.2)	**4**	(1.6)
	Hungary	79	(1.1)	70	(1.3)	**9**	(1.9)	97	(0.7)	98	(0.5)	0	(0.8)	87	(0.8)	80	(1.1)	**7**	(1.4)
	Iceland	99	(0.3)	98	(0.4)	1	(0.5)	98	(0.3)	97	(0.3)	0	(0.5)	90	(0.8)	86	(0.9)	**4**	(1.3)
	Ireland	88	(0.9)	87	(1.0)	1	(1.3)	87	(1.2)	92	(1.1)	**-5**	(1.4)	81	(0.9)	88	(1.0)	**-7**	(1.3)
	Italy	88	(0.9)	85	(0.9)	**3**	(1.1)	86	(1.4)	85	(1.8)	1	(1.5)	67	(1.1)	57	(1.0)	**10**	(1.6)
	Japan	77	(1.1)	80	(1.2)	-2	(1.5)	88	(1.5)	89	(1.7)	-1	(1.5)	55	(1.5)	55	(1.6)	0	(2.0)
	Korea	98	(0.3)	98	(0.3)	0	(0.4)	82	(1.6)	90	(1.5)	**-8**	(1.7)	88	(0.6)	88	(1.1)	0	(1.2)
	Mexico	53	(2.1)	49	(2.2)	**4**	(2.0)	83	(2.0)	84	(1.6)	-1	(1.5)	84	(1.6)	86	(1.1)	-1	(1.7)
	New Zealand	93	(0.6)	90	(0.8)	**3**	(1.1)	98	(0.4)	99	(0.3)	-1	(0.5)	93	(0.6)	91	(0.6)	**2**	(0.8)
	Poland	70	(1.3)	58	(1.3)	**12**	(1.5)	89	(1.3)	92	(1.3)	**-3**	(0.9)	83	(0.9)	78	(1.2)	**5**	(1.3)
	Portugal	86	(1.1)	82	(1.1)	**4**	(1.4)	98	(0.4)	99	(0.3)	**-1**	(0.4)	89	(1.0)	85	(1.1)	**4**	(1.2)
	Slovak Republic	76	(1.4)	69	(1.4)	**7**	(1.6)	80	(2.0)	84	(1.6)	**-4**	(1.7)	87	(1.0)	81	(1.3)	**6**	(1.3)
	Sweden	98	(0.3)	97	(0.3)	**1**	(0.4)	97	(0.7)	98	(0.5)	-1	(0.5)	91	(0.6)	90	(0.7)	1	(0.9)
	Switzerland	97	(0.4)	96	(0.4)	1	(0.5)	94	(0.7)	94	(0.9)	0	(0.7)	74	(1.3)	66	(1.0)	**8**	(1.8)
	Turkey	39	(2.8)	33	(2.2)	**6**	(2.5)	54	(4.1)	54	(3.6)	0	(3.3)	82	(1.2)	62	(2.2)	**20**	(2.2)
	United States	90	(0.8)	89	(0.8)	1	(0.8)	96	(0.5)	98	(0.5)	**-1**	(0.6)	89	(0.7)	92	(0.6)	**-4**	(0.9)
	OECD average	*86*	*(0.0)*	*83*	*(0.2)*	*3*	*(0.2)*	*91*	*(0.2)*	*93*	*(0.2)*	*-1*	*(0.2)*	*84*	*(0.2)*	*81*	*(0.0)*	*3*	*(0.3)*
Partner countries	Latvia	62	(1.9)	48	(2.0)	**14**	(2.1)	90	(1.3)	90	(1.4)	-1	(1.1)	92	(1.1)	86	(1.4)	**6**	(1.2)
	Liechtenstein	99	(0.9)	98	(1.1)	1	(1.4)	100	(0.0)	99	(0.6)	1	(0.6)	83	(3.5)	79	(3.1)	3	(4.9)
	Russian Federation	44	(2.5)	31	(1.9)	**13**	(1.8)	74	(1.7)	78	(2.0)	**-4**	(1.6)	78	(1.2)	62	(1.6)	***15***	(1.6)
	Serbia	60	(1.8)	53	(1.8)	**7**	(2.1)	95	(0.7)	95	(1.4)	0	(1.1)	81	(1.2)	71	(1.8)	***11***	(2.2)
	Thailand	32	(1.6)	31	(2.0)	0	(2.5)	96	(1.6)	96	(1.3)	0	(0.8)	64	(2.2)	69	(1.8)	-4	(2.3)
	Tunisia	41	(2.0)	34	(1.9)	**7**	(1.9)	35	(2.3)	35	(2.2)	0	(2.0)	58	(2.1)	54	(1.7)	4	(2.3)
	Uruguay	65	(1.6)	60	(1.6)	**5**	(1.8)	73	(2.3)	72	(2.0)	2	(1.9)	85	(1.2)	83	(1.2)	2	(1.6)
	United Kingdom[1]	94	(0.8)	93	(0.8)	1	(1.2)	99	(0.4)	99	(0.3)	-1	(0.4)	89	(1.1)	90	(0.8)	-1	(1.2)

Note: Statistically significant differences are marked in bold.

1. Response rate too low to ensure comparability.

Table 2.2c

Percentage of students having access to a computer at home, school or other places, by national quarters of the index of economic, social and cultural status (ESCS) in PISA 2003

Results based on students' self-reports

		Percentage of students having access to a computer, by national quarters of the index of ESCS																							
		At home								At school								Other places							
		Bottom quarter		Second quarter		Third quarter		Top quarter		Bottom quarter		Second quarter		Third quarter		Top quarter		Bottom quarter		Second quarter		Third quarter		Top quarter	
		%	S.E.	%	S.E.	%	S.E.	%	S.E.	%	S.E.	%	S.E.	%	S.E.	%	S.E.	%	S.E.	%	S.E.	%	S.E.	%	S.E.
OECD countries	Australia	**89**	(0.8)	98	(0.3)	99	(0.2)	**100**	(0.0)	**100**	(0.1)	99	(0.2)	100	(0.2)	**100**	(0.1)	**90**	(0.7)	92	(0.8)	94	(0.6)	**95**	(0.4)
	Austria	**91**	(0.9)	97	(0.5)	99	(0.4)	**100**	(0.2)	**95**	(1.2)	96	(1.0)	98	(0.6)	**98**	(0.5)	**74**	(1.7)	76	(1.5)	77	(1.5)	**78**	(1.5)
	Belgium	**83**	(0.8)	95	(0.5)	98	(0.4)	**100**	(0.1)	**89**	(1.2)	92	(0.8)	92	(1.1)	**93**	(1.1)	83	(1.0)	85	(1.0)	86	(0.9)	86	(1.1)
	Canada	**86**	(0.7)	97	(0.3)	99	(0.2)	**100**	(0.1)	**98**	(0.4)	99	(0.2)	99	(0.2)	**100**	(0.2)	**97**	(0.4)	99	(0.2)	99	(0.3)	**99**	(0.2)
	Czech Republic	**55**	(1.5)	82	(1.5)	93	(0.7)	**96**	(0.8)	**92**	(1.3)	94	(1.1)	97	(0.7)	**98**	(0.5)	85	(1.2)	85	(1.0)	88	(1.0)	88	(1.1)
	Denmark	**92**	(0.9)	98	(0.4)	99	(0.3)	**100**	(0.1)	99	(0.2)	100	(0.1)	100	(0.2)	100	(0.2)	**82**	(1.5)	85	(1.3)	86	(1.5)	**87**	(1.2)
	Finland	**76**	(1.3)	91	(0.9)	97	(0.6)	**99**	(0.3)	97	(0.6)	97	(0.7)	97	(1.0)	97	(1.3)	89	(0.9)	88	(0.9)	91	(0.9)	90	(0.9)
	Germany	**89**	(1.1)	97	(0.5)	99	(0.3)	**100**	(0.1)	**90**	(1.0)	92	(1.2)	94	(0.8)	**94**	(1.0)	73	(1.6)	72	(1.7)	73	(1.6)	72	(1.5)
	Greece	**38**	(1.7)	60	(1.9)	80	(1.4)	**90**	(1.7)	94	(0.9)	93	(1.0)	93	(1.1)	93	(1.6)	**76**	(1.5)	82	(1.2)	82	(1.6)	**86**	(1.4)
	Hungary	**42**	(1.7)	73	(1.2)	89	(0.9)	**96**	(0.5)	97	(0.9)	98	(0.6)	98	(0.6)	98	(0.6)	**76**	(1.5)	84	(1.4)	88	(1.2)	**87**	(1.1)
	Iceland	**96**	(0.7)	99	(0.4)	99	(0.3)	**100**	(0.1)	98	(0.6)	97	(0.6)	98	(0.4)	97	(0.5)	**84**	(1.3)	88	(1.0)	90	(1.1)	**89**	(1.0)
	Ireland	**67**	(2.0)	89	(1.0)	95	(0.7)	**99**	(0.4)	89	(1.3)	90	(1.2)	91	(1.3)	88	(1.5)	**79**	(1.4)	85	(1.4)	86	(1.3)	**89**	(1.1)
	Italy	**67**	(1.7)	87	(1.0)	95	(0.6)	**98**	(0.3)	**88**	(1.7)	87	(1.6)	87	(1.7)	**81**	(2.3)	**54**	(1.5)	59	(1.4)	63	(1.5)	**73**	(1.1)
	Japan	**54**	(2.0)	77	(1.3)	89	(1.1)	**94**	(0.9)	89	(1.8)	90	(1.6)	87	(1.9)	89	(1.9)	**48**	(1.8)	52	(1.8)	56	(1.9)	**63**	(2.0)
	Korea	**94**	(0.8)	98	(0.4)	100	(0.2)	**100**	(0.0)	86	(1.9)	85	(1.4)	84	(1.9)	86	(1.9)	**86**	(1.2)	86	(1.0)	89	(1.1)	**91**	(1.1)
	Mexico	**11**	(1.2)	35	(1.4)	66	(1.8)	**91**	(1.0)	**76**	(3.6)	83	(1.7)	86	(1.8)	**88**	(1.6)	**70**	(2.8)	86	(1.2)	91	(1.1)	**93**	(1.0)
	New Zealand	**75**	(1.4)	94	(0.7)	97	(0.5)	**100**	(0.2)	**98**	(0.5)	98	(0.6)	99	(0.4)	**99**	(0.3)	**90**	(1.0)	90	(1.0)	93	(0.7)	**95**	(0.7)
	Poland	**25**	(1.5)	54	(1.8)	84	(1.3)	**95**	(0.7)	91	(1.5)	90	(1.5)	90	(1.4)	91	(1.5)	**63**	(1.7)	80	(1.2)	88	(1.1)	**90**	(1.1)
	Portugal	**60**	(1.7)	83	(1.2)	94	(0.9)	**99**	(0.3)	98	(0.6)	99	(0.3)	98	(0.5)	99	(0.4)	**81**	(1.7)	87	(1.5)	89	(1.3)	**89**	(1.0)
	Slovak Republic	**41**	(2.3)	69	(1.7)	84	(1.5)	**95**	(0.7)	**71**	(3.1)	83	(2.0)	85	(1.6)	**90**	(1.4)	**75**	(2.4)	85	(1.4)	87	(1.3)	**91**	(0.9)
	Sweden	**93**	(0.7)	98	(0.4)	100	(0.2)	**100**	(0.2)	97	(0.6)	98	(0.6)	97	(1.1)	98	(0.6)	88	(1.2)	93	(0.8)	91	(0.8)	91	(1.2)
	Switzerland	**91**	(0.8)	98	(0.4)	99	(0.4)	**100**	(0.2)	94	(1.0)	95	(0.9)	94	(1.0)	94	(1.1)	**64**	(1.9)	70	(1.5)	72	(1.4)	**73**	(1.9)
	Turkey	**9**	(1.1)	19	(1.8)	42	(2.5)	**77**	(2.1)	54	(4.4)	53	(3.4)	49	(3.9)	59	(5.0)	**59**	(2.4)	70	(2.0)	79	(2.0)	**85**	(1.6)
	United States	**72**	(1.6)	92	(0.9)	96	(0.5)	**99**	(0.3)	**94**	(0.9)	97	(0.5)	97	(0.5)	**99**	(0.3)	**83**	(1.2)	92	(0.8)	92	(0.8)	**95**	(0.7)
	OECD average	***67***	*(0.3)*	*83*	*(0.2)*	*91*	*(0.2)*	***97***	*(0.1)*	*91*	*(0.3)*	*92*	*(0.2)*	*92*	*(0.3)*	*93*	*(0.3)*	***77***	*(0.3)*	*82*	*(0.3)*	*85*	*(0.2)*	***87***	*(0.2)*
Partner countries	Latvia	**25**	(2.0)	46	(2.1)	66	(2.0)	**83**	(2.3)	91	(1.4)	89	(1.4)	89	(1.6)	92	(1.5)	**81**	(2.1)	90	(1.1)	93	(1.4)	**94**	(1.3)
	Liechtenstein	**94**	(2.8)	99	(1.2)	100	(0.0)	**100**	(0.0)	100	(0.0)	100	(0.0)	99	(1.2)	100	(0.0)	76	(5.2)	81	(4.6)	82	(4.5)	85	(4.7)
	Russian Federation	**9**	(1.2)	25	(2.3)	45	(2.7)	**70**	(2.1)	**70**	(2.4)	74	(2.2)	78	(1.8)	**82**	(1.9)	**58**	(2.2)	69	(1.8)	76	(1.9)	**78**	(1.5)
	Serbia	**28**	(1.7)	45	(2.2)	67	(1.9)	**86**	(1.4)	96	(0.8)	95	(1.1)	95	(1.5)	95	(2.0)	**68**	(2.2)	75	(2.4)	80	(1.4)	**81**	(2.1)
	Thailand	**6**	(1.0)	11	(1.0)	31	(1.7)	**78**	(1.8)	**92**	(3.0)	95	(1.7)	97	(1.1)	**100**	(0.2)	**46**	(2.5)	63	(2.4)	75	(2.4)	**81**	(1.9)
	Tunisia	**13**	(1.5)	22	(1.5)	42	(1.9)	**74**	(2.0)	**27**	(2.8)	34	(2.4)	38	(2.4)	**41**	(3.7)	**28**	(2.1)	50	(1.9)	67	(2.0)	**81**	(1.4)
	Uruguay	**24**	(1.6)	51	(2.3)	82	(1.7)	**94**	(1.1)	**69**	(2.4)	66	(3.4)	72	(3.2)	**82**	(1.9)	**71**	(2.1)	83	(1.6)	88	(1.1)	**92**	(1.0)
	United Kingdom[1]	**83**	(1.5)	92	(1.0)	98	(0.6)	**100**	(0.2)	99	(0.5)	99	(0.4)	100	(0.2)	99	(0.3)	87	(1.7)	91	(1.2)	91	(1.3)	90	(1.4)

Note: Statistically significant differences are marked in bold.

1. Response rate too low to ensure comparability.

Table 2.3a
Percentage of students having access to various ICT and educational resources at home
Results based on students' self-reports

		Percentage of students having the following resources at home:							
		A computer you can use for schoolwork		Educational software		Your own calculator		Books to help with you schoolwork	
		%	S.E.	%	S.E.	%	S.E.	%	S.E.
OECD countries	Australia	94	(0.3)	67	(0.6)	97	(0.2)	80	(0.6)
	Austria	93	(0.5)	42	(0.9)	99	(0.2)	71	(0.7)
	Belgium	87	(0.5)	52	(0.7)	97	(0.3)	76	(0.8)
	Canada	93	(0.3)	62	(0.6)	98	(0.2)	75	(0.5)
	Czech Republic	77	(0.8)	53	(0.9)	98	(0.3)	84	(0.8)
	Denmark	93	(0.5)	34	(0.9)	97	(0.3)	77	(0.9)
	Finland	88	(0.6)	37	(0.8)	97	(0.3)	79	(0.7)
	France	79	(0.9)	44	(0.9)	98	(0.3)	85	(0.7)
	Germany	91	(0.6)	53	(0.9)	98	(0.3)	85	(0.6)
	Greece	53	(1.4)	16	(0.9)	74	(0.9)	72	(1.2)
	Hungary	68	(0.9)	28	(0.8)	91	(0.5)	87	(0.6)
	Iceland	97	(0.3)	57	(0.8)	99	(0.2)	89	(0.6)
	Ireland	80	(0.9)	48	(0.8)	97	(0.3)	79	(0.9)
	Italy	78	(0.8)	30	(0.8)	94	(0.4)	84	(0.5)
	Japan	46	(1.0)	11	(0.6)	69	(1.0)	77	(0.9)
	Korea	95	(0.4)	46	(0.9)	60	(0.9)	85	(0.6)
	Luxembourg	90	(0.4)	47	(0.8)	98	(0.2)	86	(0.5)
	Mexico	33	(1.8)	20	(1.2)	80	(0.9)	63	(1.3)
	Netherlands	96	(0.4)	63	(1.0)	98	(0.3)	42	(1.2)
	New Zealand	87	(0.6)	58	(0.9)	96	(0.3)	82	(0.7)
	Norway	94	(0.4)	58	(0.8)	97	(0.3)	86	(0.7)
	Poland	60	(1.2)	48	(1.1)	97	(0.3)	92	(0.6)
	Portugal	75	(1.2)	37	(1.2)	96	(0.4)	83	(0.8)
	Slovak Republic	57	(1.3)	25	(0.8)	97	(0.5)	83	(0.8)
	Spain	79	(0.9)	41	(1.0)	96	(0.2)	83	(0.5)
	Sweden	95	(0.4)	51	(1.0)	92	(0.5)	81	(0.8)
	Switzerland	87	(0.6)	38	(0.8)	98	(0.2)	73	(1.0)
	Turkey	23	(1.9)	13	(1.0)	75	(1.4)	75	(1.5)
	United States	87	(0.7)	60	(0.9)	93	(0.4)	73	(0.7)
	OECD average	***79***	***(0.2)***	***43***	***(0.2)***	***92***	***(0.1)***	***79***	***(0.1)***
Partner countries	Brazil	27	(1.6)	9	(0.7)	71	(1.2)	82	(0.8)
	Hong Kong-China	93	(0.5)	46	(1.0)	95	(0.3)	68	(1.0)
	Indonesia	8	(0.9)	11	(0.7)	60	(1.1)	81	(0.9)
	Latvia	44	(1.6)	29	(1.2)	93	(0.6)	88	(0.7)
	Liechtenstein	94	(1.3)	45	(2.4)	99	(0.7)	73	(2.1)
	Macao-China	89	(1.0)	38	(1.7)	87	(1.1)	55	(1.7)
	Russian Federation	29	(1.7)	21	(1.3)	91	(0.5)	87	(0.7)
	Serbia	38	(1.3)	15	(0.7)	86	(1.0)	77	(0.9)
	Thailand	26	(1.0)	16	(0.8)	82	(1.0)	70	(1.0)
	Tunisia	20	(1.2)	10	(0.7)	54	(1.2)	53	(1.2)
	Uruguay	46	(1.1)	30	(1.0)	87	(0.7)	89	(0.5)
	United Kingdom[1]	91	(0.5)	67	(0.8)	97	(0.3)	90	(0.4)

1. Response rate too low to ensure comparability.

Table 2.3b

Percentage of students having access to various ICT and educational resources at home, by national quarters of the index of economic, social and cultural status (ESCS)

Results based on students' self-reports

		A computer you can use for schoolwork								Educational software							
		Bottom quarter		Second quarter		Third quarter		Top quarter		Bottom quarter		Second quarter		Third quarter		Top quarter	
		%	S.E.	%	S.E.	%	S.E.	%	S.E.	%	S.E.	%	S.E.	%	S.E.	%	S.E.
OECD countries	Australia	**82**	(0.9)	97	(0.3)	98	(0.3)	**100**	(0.1)	**43**	(1.3)	65	(1.1)	74	(0.8)	**87**	(0.6)
	Austria	**83**	(1.6)	93	(0.8)	97	(0.6)	**98**	(0.4)	**22**	(1.2)	37	(1.4)	47	(1.6)	**61**	(1.8)
	Belgium	**67**	(1.3)	89	(0.7)	96	(0.5)	**99**	(0.3)	**28**	(1.2)	48	(1.2)	57	(1.4)	**76**	(1.2)
	Canada	**81**	(0.8)	95	(0.5)	98	(0.3)	**100**	(0.2)	**36**	(1.0)	59	(1.1)	68	(1.0)	**84**	(0.9)
	Czech Republic	**45**	(1.5)	75	(1.6)	91	(0.9)	**95**	(0.9)	**23**	(1.3)	48	(1.5)	68	(1.3)	**73**	(1.2)
	Denmark	**81**	(1.4)	95	(0.7)	97	(0.5)	**100**	(0.2)	**16**	(1.3)	26	(1.4)	35	(1.6)	**58**	(1.9)
	Finland	**69**	(1.5)	89	(1.1)	95	(0.6)	**99**	(0.3)	**18**	(1.2)	32	(1.4)	41	(1.4)	**59**	(1.4)
	France	**51**	(1.8)	76	(1.3)	92	(0.9)	**96**	(0.7)	**21**	(1.5)	38	(1.7)	52	(1.5)	**65**	(1.7)
	Germany	**76**	(1.6)	93	(0.8)	98	(0.5)	**99**	(0.4)	**33**	(1.5)	48	(1.5)	61	(1.7)	**70**	(1.5)
	Greece	**22**	(1.3)	43	(1.9)	66	(1.3)	**81**	(1.7)	**3**	(0.5)	8	(0.8)	17	(1.5)	**37**	(1.8)
	Hungary	**30**	(1.4)	63	(1.5)	83	(1.2)	**94**	(0.6)	**4**	(0.7)	19	(1.2)	38	(1.5)	**51**	(1.8)
	Iceland	**91**	(0.9)	98	(0.5)	99	(0.4)	**100**	(0.0)	**33**	(1.6)	50	(1.7)	64	(1.6)	**81**	(1.3)
	Ireland	**53**	(2.1)	80	(1.4)	91	(1.0)	**97**	(0.7)	**20**	(1.4)	41	(1.7)	58	(1.4)	**72**	(1.2)
	Italy	**51**	(1.7)	77	(1.3)	89	(0.9)	**96**	(0.6)	**11**	(1.0)	24	(1.4)	34	(1.4)	**52**	(1.2)
	Japan	**20**	(1.4)	40	(1.7)	55	(1.6)	**69**	(1.5)	**3**	(0.4)	7	(0.7)	11	(1.0)	**22**	(1.7)
	Korea	**89**	(1.0)	95	(0.5)	97	(0.5)	**99**	(0.3)	**22**	(1.1)	38	(1.4)	51	(1.4)	**73**	(1.3)
	Luxembourg	**76**	(1.2)	90	(1.0)	97	(0.6)	**98**	(0.4)	**29**	(1.4)	39	(1.7)	52	(1.7)	**68**	(1.4)
	Mexico	**3**	(0.4)	13	(0.9)	38	(1.6)	**79**	(1.6)	**1**	(0.2)	6	(0.6)	19	(0.9)	**54**	(1.6)
	Netherlands	**88**	(1.2)	97	(0.6)	99	(0.4)	**100**	(0.2)	**40**	(1.8)	62	(1.9)	70	(1.4)	**80**	(1.5)
	New Zealand	**64**	(1.6)	91	(1.0)	96	(0.6)	**99**	(0.3)	**30**	(1.4)	53	(1.6)	65	(1.6)	**82**	(1.3)
	Norway	**84**	(1.3)	95	(0.7)	97	(0.5)	**99**	(0.4)	**40**	(1.8)	56	(1.4)	60	(1.7)	**76**	(1.4)
	Poland	**18**	(1.3)	49	(1.8)	80	(1.5)	**94**	(0.7)	**9**	(0.8)	34	(1.5)	65	(1.6)	**82**	(1.3)
	Portugal	**44**	(1.7)	71	(1.5)	86	(1.5)	**97**	(0.5)	**10**	(1.2)	26	(1.5)	44	(1.8)	**67**	(1.6)
	Slovak Republic	**21**	(1.6)	47	(1.5)	73	(1.5)	**87**	(1.0)	**3**	(0.6)	14	(1.0)	32	(1.3)	**49**	(1.8)
	Spain	**56**	(1.1)	75	(1.4)	89	(0.8)	**96**	(0.5)	**23**	(1.3)	35	(1.4)	45	(1.5)	**63**	(1.6)
	Sweden	**85**	(1.1)	97	(0.5)	99	(0.3)	**100**	(0.1)	**26**	(1.3)	45	(1.6)	57	(1.7)	**76**	(1.3)
	Switzerland	**71**	(1.4)	88	(1.1)	93	(0.6)	**95**	(0.7)	**22**	(1.2)	33	(1.4)	42	(1.6)	**58**	(1.8)
	Turkey	**3**	(0.5)	10	(1.1)	21	(1.7)	**60**	(2.5)	**3**	(0.5)	5	(0.6)	11	(1.2)	**34**	(1.8)
	United States	**64**	(1.6)	91	(0.9)	96	(0.5)	**100**	(0.2)	**28**	(1.2)	54	(1.5)	71	(1.2)	**88**	(1.1)
	OECD average	*58*	*(0.2)*	*77*	*(0.2)*	*87*	*(0.2)*	*94*	*(0.2)*	*21*	*(0.2)*	*37*	*(0.3)*	*50*	*(0.3)*	*66*	*(0.3)*
Partner countries	Brazil	**3**	(0.5)	15	(1.5)	25	(1.8)	**66**	(2.1)	**1**	(0.3)	4	(0.8)	7	(0.9)	**25**	(1.7)
	Hong Kong-China	**84**	(1.2)	94	(0.8)	95	(0.7)	**98**	(0.5)	**25**	(1.2)	41	(1.9)	51	(1.7)	**69**	(1.3)
	Indonesia	**1**	(0.2)	1	(0.3)	6	(0.8)	**23**	(2.4)	**4**	(0.5)	7	(0.8)	10	(0.9)	**24**	(1.7)
	Latvia	**14**	(1.3)	33	(1.9)	54	(1.9)	**76**	(2.5)	**6**	(0.9)	20	(1.6)	35	(1.5)	**56**	(2.2)
	Liechtenstein	**90**	(3.7)	92	(2.7)	96	(2.1)	**100**	(0.0)	**28**	(4.5)	29	(4.9)	51	(5.9)	**70**	(5.1)
	Macao-China	**74**	(3.0)	93	(1.7)	93	(1.6)	**97**	(1.3)	**19**	(2.4)	32	(3.6)	41	(3.7)	**60**	(3.0)
	Russian Federation	**5**	(0.6)	16	(1.6)	36	(2.1)	**60**	(2.2)	**2**	(0.4)	10	(1.1)	26	(1.7)	**48**	(1.8)
	Serbia	**10**	(0.9)	25	(1.4)	43	(1.7)	**75**	(1.7)	**2**	(0.5)	6	(0.7)	14	(1.1)	**38**	(1.6)
	Thailand	**6**	(0.9)	9	(1.0)	24	(1.3)	**66**	(1.6)	**2**	(0.5)	4	(0.8)	13	(0.9)	**46**	(1.4)
	Tunisia	**2**	(0.4)	5	(0.6)	17	(1.0)	**56**	(2.0)	**2**	(0.4)	3	(0.5)	9	(1.0)	**26**	(1.8)
	Uruguay	**10**	(1.0)	30	(1.8)	56	(1.5)	**87**	(1.3)	**5**	(0.7)	17	(1.3)	36	(1.6)	**61**	(1.6)
	United Kingdom[1]	77	(1.3)	94	(0.8)	97	(0.4)	100	(0.2)	39	(1.4)	67	(1.5)	77	(1.3)	86	(0.9)

Note: Statistically significant differences are marked in bold.

1. Response rate too low to ensure comparability.

Table 2.3b *(continued)*

Percentage of students having access to various ICT and educational resources at home, by national quarters of the index of economic, social and cultural status (ESCS)

Results based on students' self-reports

		Calculator								Books to help with your schoolwork							
		Bottom quarter		Second quarter		Third quarter		Top quarter		Bottom quarter		Second quarter		Third quarter		Top quarter	
		%	S.E.	%	S.E.	%	S.E.	%	S.E.	%	S.E.	%	S.E.	%	S.E.	%	S.E.
OECD countries	Australia	**93**	(0.5)	98	(0.3)	98	(0.4)	**100**	(0.1)	**60**	(1.3)	78	(0.8)	87	(0.8)	**96**	(0.4)
	Austria	**96**	(0.7)	99	(0.3)	99	(0.2)	**100**	(0.2)	**50**	(1.8)	68	(1.4)	80	(1.1)	**89**	(1.0)
	Belgium	**93**	(0.8)	98	(0.3)	99	(0.2)	**100**	(0.1)	**54**	(1.6)	74	(1.2)	82	(0.9)	**94**	(0.5)
	Canada	**96**	(0.5)	98	(0.3)	99	(0.2)	**100**	(0.1)	**55**	(0.9)	71	(0.9)	81	(0.9)	**94**	(0.5)
	Czech Republic	**95**	(0.8)	98	(0.4)	99	(0.3)	**99**	(0.1)	**57**	(1.7)	86	(1.1)	93	(0.7)	**98**	(0.4)
	Denmark	**92**	(1.0)	98	(0.5)	99	(0.3)	**99**	(0.3)	**55**	(1.8)	72	(1.2)	86	(1.3)	**96**	(0.7)
	Finland	**92**	(0.7)	97	(0.5)	98	(0.4)	**99**	(0.3)	**60**	(1.4)	77	(1.4)	84	(1.1)	**96**	(0.6)
	France	**95**	(0.7)	98	(0.4)	99	(0.4)	**100**	(0.2)	**72**	(1.6)	81	(1.5)	91	(1.0)	**96**	(0.5)
	Germany	**96**	(0.9)	99	(0.3)	99	(0.2)	**100**	(0.2)	**70**	(1.5)	84	(1.1)	92	(1.0)	**97**	(0.6)
	Greece	**58**	(1.6)	72	(1.3)	79	(1.4)	**89**	(1.2)	**55**	(2.0)	68	(1.5)	79	(1.3)	**87**	(1.3)
	Hungary	**80**	(1.4)	94	(0.8)	96	(0.7)	**95**	(0.7)	**65**	(1.4)	89	(1.0)	97	(0.5)	**98**	(0.4)
	Iceland	**98**	(0.5)	99	(0.3)	99	(0.3)	**100**	(0.2)	**73**	(1.6)	90	(1.2)	96	(0.6)	**99**	(0.3)
	Ireland	**94**	(0.8)	97	(0.5)	99	(0.4)	**99**	(0.2)	**63**	(1.9)	74	(1.7)	87	(1.2)	**93**	(1.0)
	Italy	**89**	(1.1)	95	(0.7)	96	(0.5)	**98**	(0.4)	**70**	(1.3)	83	(0.8)	87	(1.0)	**95**	(0.5)
	Japan	**55**	(1.7)	69	(1.5)	71	(1.3)	**79**	(1.5)	**55**	(1.7)	76	(1.2)	86	(1.0)	**92**	(0.9)
	Korea	**40**	(1.6)	53	(1.5)	66	(1.5)	**82**	(1.2)	**64**	(1.6)	84	(1.1)	93	(0.7)	**98**	(0.4)
	Luxembourg	**95**	(0.6)	98	(0.5)	99	(0.4)	**100**	(0.2)	**77**	(1.4)	84	(1.2)	88	(1.1)	**96**	(0.7)
	Mexico	**64**	(1.9)	81	(1.1)	83	(1.1)	**93**	(0.7)	**29**	(2.0)	58	(1.4)	74	(1.4)	**90**	(0.8)
	Netherlands	**95**	(0.9)	98	(0.4)	100	(0.1)	**100**	(0.2)	**18**	(1.3)	32	(1.8)	45	(2.0)	**75**	(2.2)
	New Zealand	**91**	(0.8)	97	(0.5)	98	(0.4)	**99**	(0.2)	**64**	(1.6)	78	(1.4)	89	(1.0)	**97**	(0.6)
	Norway	**93**	(1.0)	98	(0.4)	99	(0.4)	**100**	(0.2)	**64**	(1.6)	87	(0.9)	94	(0.8)	**99**	(0.4)
	Poland	**94**	(0.8)	98	(0.5)	99	(0.4)	**99**	(0.4)	**76**	(1.6)	95	(0.6)	98	(0.4)	**99**	(0.2)
	Portugal	**91**	(1.0)	96	(0.5)	96	(0.7)	**99**	(0.4)	**67**	(1.5)	81	(1.5)	88	(1.0)	**96**	(0.8)
	Slovak Republic	**90**	(1.4)	98	(0.3)	99	(0.3)	**98**	(0.5)	**58**	(1.6)	86	(0.8)	92	(0.7)	**97**	(0.5)
	Spain	**91**	(0.8)	96	(0.4)	98	(0.4)	**99**	(0.3)	**70**	(1.2)	81	(1.5)	87	(0.9)	**93**	(0.7)
	Sweden	**80**	(1.5)	93	(0.9)	95	(0.7)	**98**	(0.3)	**56**	(1.9)	81	(1.3)	90	(0.9)	**98**	(0.4)
	Switzerland	**96**	(0.6)	98	(0.4)	99	(0.3)	**100**	(0.1)	**49**	(1.6)	68	(2.1)	82	(1.1)	**93**	(0.7)
	Turkey	**54**	(2.5)	72	(1.9)	83	(1.4)	**92**	(0.9)	**53**	(2.4)	71	(1.8)	82	(1.7)	**95**	(0.8)
	United States	**81**	(1.2)	95	(0.6)	98	(0.4)	**99**	(0.3)	**51**	(1.3)	67	(1.3)	80	(1.2)	**95**	(0.6)
	OECD average	***86***	***(0.2)***	***93***	***(0.1)***	***95***	***(0.1)***	***97***	***(0.1)***	***60***	***(0.3)***	***77***	***(0.2)***	***86***	***(0.2)***	***95***	***(0.1)***
Partner countries	Brazil	**55**	(2.3)	66	(1.6)	76	(1.6)	**86**	(1.2)	**68**	(1.7)	81	(1.3)	85	(1.5)	**93**	(0.9)
	Hong Kong-China	**90**	(0.9)	95	(0.7)	98	(0.5)	**99**	(0.4)	**42**	(1.6)	65	(1.5)	76	(1.3)	**88**	(1.0)
	Indonesia	**32**	(1.7)	58	(1.6)	70	(1.4)	**81**	(1.3)	**67**	(1.8)	80	(1.3)	84	(1.0)	**94**	(0.6)
	Latvia	**86**	(1.3)	94	(0.8)	96	(0.7)	**97**	(1.0)	**76**	(1.8)	89	(1.1)	92	(1.0)	**97**	(0.5)
	Liechtenstein	**99**	(1.5)	99	(1.3)	96	(2.1)	**100**	(0.0)	**50**	(5.4)	72	(4.7)	80	(3.6)	**91**	(2.6)
	Macao-China	**74**	(3.2)	89	(2.4)	89	(2.0)	**96**	(1.1)	**33**	(3.5)	53	(3.2)	55	(3.7)	**78**	(2.5)
	Russian Federation	**80**	(1.7)	94	(0.7)	95	(0.6)	**97**	(0.5)	**69**	(1.6)	89	(1.1)	92	(1.0)	**97**	(0.5)
	Serbia	**72**	(2.2)	87	(1.3)	92	(0.9)	**94**	(0.7)	**54**	(1.7)	75	(1.6)	85	(1.1)	**92**	(0.7)
	Thailand	**58**	(2.3)	86	(1.2)	91	(1.0)	**96**	(0.6)	**45**	(1.8)	74	(1.6)	77	(1.3)	**85**	(1.1)
	Tunisia	**24**	(1.8)	48	(1.8)	64	(1.6)	**81**	(1.4)	**24**	(1.7)	44	(1.7)	64	(1.6)	**79**	(1.4)
	Uruguay	**75**	(1.4)	86	(1.4)	92	(1.1)	**96**	(0.5)	**77**	(1.0)	90	(1.0)	94	(0.8)	**96**	(0.6)
	United Kingdom[1]	**91**	(0.9)	99	(0.3)	99	(0.3)	**100**	(0.2)	77	(1.2)	89	(0.9)	96	(0.7)	**98**	(0.4)

Note: Statistically significant differences are marked in bold.

1. Response rate too low to ensure comparability.

Table 2.4
Mean of various ICT resources at school and percentage of various type of computers out of computers in school all together
Results based on school principals' reports

		PISA 2003																PISA 2000			
		Percentage of students whose principals report there is at least one computer at school		For students whose principals report there is at least one computer at school:				Out of the number of computers in school all together, percentage of computers:										For students whose principals report there is at least one computer at school:			
				The number of computers in the school all together		Computers per student		Available to 15-year-old students		Available only to teachers		Available only to adminis-trative staff		Connected to the Internet/ WWW		Connected to a local area network (LAN)		The number of computers in the school all together		Computers per student	
		%	S.E.	Mean	S.E.	Mean	S.E.	%	S.E.	%	S.E.	%	S.E.	%	S.E.	%	S.E.	Mean	S.E.	Mean	S.E.
OECD countries	Australia	100	(0.0)	255	(12.9)	0.28	(0.01)	69	(1.1)	18	(0.8)	7	(0.6)	93	(0.9)	93	(1.1)	**184**	(13.5)	**0.22**	(0.01)
	Austria	100	(0.0)	128	(11.3)	0.22	(0.01)	77	(1.4)	11	(0.8)	6	(0.3)	87	(1.9)	71	(3.1)	**85**	(7.2)	**0.15**	(0.01)
	Belgium	100	(0.0)	89	(3.3)	0.15	(0.01)	65	(1.3)	10	(0.9)	14	(0.6)	74	(1.5)	54	(2.3)	**67**	(3.1)	**0.11**	(0.00)
	Canada	100	(0.0)	198	(5.3)	0.22	(0.01)	75	(0.9)	14	(0.5)	6	(0.2)	94	(0.7)	87	(1.6)	**176**	(3.0)	a	a
	Czech Republic	100	(0.0)	47	(2.4)	0.11	(0.01)	62	(1.2)	22	(0.9)	11	(0.6)	77	(1.6)	68	(2.6)	**34**	(2.5)	**0.08**	(0.01)
	Denmark	100	(0.0)	68	(2.8)	0.19	(0.01)	67	(1.4)	11	(0.9)	9	(0.4)	88	(1.4)	77	(2.2)	**53**	(2.2)	0.19	(0.03)
	Finland	100	(0.0)	57	(1.9)	0.17	(0.01)	73	(1.4)	12	(0.7)	7	(0.3)	92	(0.9)	76	(2.9)	**45**	(1.5)	**0.13**	(0.01)
	France	w	w	w	w	w	w	w	w	w	w	w	w	w	w	w	w	119	(9.1)	0.13	(0.01)
	Germany	100	(0.0)	48	(2.1)	0.08	(0.00)	69	(1.3)	14	(1.5)	10	(0.4)	71	(2.0)	45	(2.9)	**31**	(1.3)	**0.06**	(0.00)
	Greece	100	(0.0)	24	(2.7)	0.08	(0.01)	69	(2.2)	18	(1.4)	10	(1.7)	69	(3.7)	56	(4.4)	**15**	(1.5)	**0.05**	(0.00)
	Hungary	100	(0.0)	90	(3.6)	0.23	(0.01)	66	(1.5)	12	(0.6)	9	(0.4)	79	(2.0)	79	(2.2)	**61**	(3.7)	**0.16**	(0.01)
	Iceland	100	(0.0)	73	(0.2)	0.18	(0.00)	38	(0.1)	25	(0.1)	7	(0.0)	96	(0.1)	89	(0.1)	**39**	(0.1)	**0.12**	(0.00)
	Ireland	100	(0.0)	60	(3.4)	0.11	(0.00)	69	(2.1)	12	(1.3)	8	(0.7)	67	(2.6)	36	(3.5)	**41**	(1.7)	**0.08**	(0.00)
	Italy	100	(0.0)	77	(3.6)	0.13	(0.01)	57	(1.6)	8	(0.6)	13	(0.7)	71	(2.1)	50	(2.7)	74	(7.2)	**0.10**	(0.00)
	Japan	100	(0.0)	128	(7.2)	0.19	(0.02)	61	(1.5)	25	(1.2)	5	(0.3)	74	(2.5)	73	(2.3)	**92**	(4.4)	**0.11**	(0.01)
	Korea	100	(0.0)	289	(7.4)	0.27	(0.01)	52	(1.5)	32	(0.6)	3	(0.1)	92	(1.2)	91	(1.4)	**198**	(7.2)	**0.21**	(0.03)
	Luxembourg	100	(0.0)	254	(0.2)	0.18	(0.00)	59	(0.0)	8	(0.0)	8	(0.0)	96	(0.0)	95	(0.0)	**159**	(0.1)	**0.11**	(0.00)
	Mexico	99	(0.6)	59	(3.6)	0.09	(0.01)	73	(1.7)	22	(2.9)	18	(1.1)	44	(4.2)	51	(4.4)	**32**	(2.3)	**0.06**	(0.01)
	Netherlands	100	(0.0)	129	(5.8)	0.14	(0.01)	68	(1.6)	12	(1.1)	10	(0.7)	85	(2.6)	81	(3.0)	**101**	(6.8)	**0.11**	(0.01)
	New Zealand	100	(0.0)	232	(8.0)	0.23	(0.01)	68	(1.0)	23	(0.8)	7	(0.3)	92	(1.3)	92	(1.6)	**169**	(5.8)	**0.18**	(0.01)
	Norway	100	(0.0)	50	(1.8)	0.18	(0.01)	46	(1.5)	21	(0.9)	11	(0.4)	81	(1.7)	48	(3.2)	**37**	(1.2)	**0.21**	(0.01)
	Poland	100	(0.0)	21	(0.7)	0.07	(0.00)	79	(0.7)	9	(0.6)	10	(0.5)	83	(2.0)	64	(2.8)	**25**	(1.4)	**0.10**	(0.01)
	Portugal	100	(0.0)	69	(2.9)	0.07	(0.00)	51	(1.9)	13	(0.6)	15	(0.7)	60	(2.3)	50	(3.4)	**27**	(1.8)	0.09	(0.03)
	Slovak Republic	100	(0.0)	29	(1.1)	0.07	(0.00)	60	(1.5)	14	(0.9)	18	(1.1)	51	(1.9)	53	(2.2)	a	a	a	a
	Spain	100	(0.0)	52	(2.8)	0.08	(0.00)	56	(1.6)	19	(1.1)	8	(0.5)	79	(1.7)	59	(3.3)	**42**	(2.4)	**0.06**	(0.00)
	Sweden	100	(0.0)	85	(3.8)	0.16	(0.00)	55	(1.5)	18	(0.7)	10	(0.4)	92	(1.1)	80	(2.2)	**64**	(3.6)	0.14	(0.01)
	Switzerland	100	(0.0)	70	(6.3)	0.17	(0.03)	70	(1.7)	15	(0.9)	7	(0.5)	80	(1.8)	70	(2.9)	**47**	(4.2)	0.14	(0.01)
	Turkey	100	(0.0)	25	(3.9)	0.04	(0.00)	47	(4.5)	9	(1.5)	38	(4.2)	28	(3.1)	12	(2.4)	a	a	a	a
	United States	100	(0.0)	377	(15.9)	0.30	(0.01)	69	(1.7)	23	(1.4)	9	(1.4)	91	(1.3)	84	(2.0)	**237**	(21.4)	**0.22**	(0.01)
	OECD average	***100***	***(0.0)***	***115***	***(1.1)***	***0.16***	***(0.00)***	***64***	***(0.3)***	***16***	***(0.2)***	***10***	***(0.2)***	***78***	***(0.4)***	***68***	***(0.5)***	***82***	***(1.2)***	***0.13***	***(0.00)***
Partner countries	Brazil	90	(2.6)	23	(4.5)	0.02	(0.00)	47	(2.8)	18	(2.0)	39	(2.5)	42	(3.3)	32	(3.2)	16	(2.7)	0.13	(0.09)
	Hong Kong-China	100	(0.0)	222	(5.2)	0.22	(0.01)	68	(1.7)	22	(0.9)	5	(0.3)	91	(1.2)	89	(1.5)	**200**	(5.7)	**0.20**	(0.00)
	Indonesia	84	(2.4)	12	(1.2)	0.04	(0.01)	31	(3.1)	4	(0.6)	39	(2.8)	4	(0.8)	4	(1.5)	10	(1.4)	0.03	(0.00)
	Latvia	100	(0.0)	35	(4.4)	0.06	(0.00)	70	(1.7)	26	(2.9)	14	(1.1)	61	(3.4)	71	(2.5)	**22**	(1.0)	**0.16**	(0.03)
	Liechtenstein	100	(0.0)	70	(0.2)	0.33	(0.00)	70	(0.2)	16	(0.2)	5	(0.0)	97	(0.2)	97	(0.2)	**35**	(0.1)	**0.19**	(0.00)
	Macao-China	100	(0.0)	225	(0.4)	0.12	(0.00)	71	(0.1)	13	(0.0)	5	(0.0)	91	(0.1)	84	(0.1)	a	a	a	a
	Russian Federation	99	(0.4)	20	(2.2)	0.03	(0.00)	75	(2.4)	9	(0.7)	13	(2.0)	16	(2.5)	34	(2.9)	**12**	(0.8)	**0.02**	(0.00)
	Serbia	100	(0.0)	26	(1.4)	0.03	(0.00)	70	(2.0)	8	(1.1)	12	(0.8)	16	(2.1)	28	(3.3)	a	a	a	a
	Thailand	100	(0.3)	84	(7.3)	0.05	(0.00)	67	(1.5)	22	(1.0)	6	(0.6)	40	(2.8)	38	(2.6)	70	(8.1)	0.05	(0.01)
	Tunisia	96	(2.0)	12	(1.2)	0.01	(0.00)	49	(5.1)	20	(3.9)	28	(2.7)	68	(4.8)	16	(4.3)	a	a	a	a
	Uruguay	99	(0.0)	21	(1.1)	0.05	(0.00)	57	(2.6)	15	(1.9)	22	(1.9)	27	(2.1)	32	(2.5)	a	a	a	a
	United Kingdom[1]	100	(0.0)	245	(8.2)	0.23	(0.01)	78	(0.9)	16	(1.3)	7	(0.7)	90	(1.3)	88	(1.7)	**140**	(4.8)	**0.14**	(0.00)

Note: Statistically significant differences are marked in bold.
1. Response rate too low to ensure comparability.

Table 2.5

Percentage of students in schools whose principals report that instruction is hindered by a shortage of ICT resources

Results based on school principals' reports

		Instruction is hindered by a shortage of:															
		Computers for instruction								Computer software for instruction							
		Not at all		Very little		To some extent		A lot		Not at all		Very little		To some extent		A lot	
		%	S.E.	%	S.E.	%	S.E.	%	S.E.	%	S.E.	%	S.E.	%	S.E.	%	S.E.
OECD countries	Australia	30	(3.1)	35	(3.1)	28	(2.7)	6	(1.3)	32	(3.3)	37	(2.9)	28	(3.0)	3	(1.0)
	Austria	40	(3.4)	24	(3.1)	30	(2.9)	7	(2.1)	31	(3.5)	31	(3.4)	31	(3.7)	8	(2.2)
	Belgium	22	(2.7)	35	(3.0)	35	(3.7)	9	(1.8)	25	(3.0)	37	(3.2)	31	(3.0)	7	(1.6)
	Canada	20	(2.1)	34	(2.3)	35	(2.3)	11	(1.7)	18	(2.1)	35	(2.5)	39	(2.3)	8	(1.2)
	Czech Republic	23	(3.2)	34	(3.3)	33	(2.9)	10	(2.2)	15	(2.5)	38	(3.4)	37	(3.0)	9	(1.9)
	Denmark	17	(2.8)	36	(3.7)	39	(3.9)	8	(2.4)	14	(2.5)	45	(3.7)	33	(3.5)	7	(1.8)
	Finland	14	(2.5)	47	(4.1)	34	(4.1)	5	(1.8)	10	(2.2)	44	(4.0)	42	(4.2)	5	(1.7)
	France	w	w	w	w	w	w	w	w	w	w	w	w	w	w	w	w
	Germany	34	(3.5)	33	(3.4)	27	(3.3)	7	(1.7)	26	(3.4)	31	(3.2)	34	(3.3)	9	(2.0)
	Greece	26	(4.2)	25	(5.1)	22	(4.9)	27	(4.6)	12	(3.3)	28	(5.6)	30	(5.1)	30	(4.3)
	Hungary	43	(3.8)	30	(3.5)	23	(3.5)	4	(1.1)	22	(3.5)	33	(3.8)	32	(4.0)	13	(2.8)
	Iceland	36	(0.2)	30	(0.2)	31	(0.2)	2	(0.1)	25	(0.2)	40	(0.2)	32	(0.2)	2	(0.1)
	Ireland	24	(3.8)	27	(3.9)	41	(4.3)	8	(2.5)	18	(3.6)	25	(3.9)	37	(4.4)	20	(3.6)
	Italy	35	(3.5)	36	(3.2)	23	(3.1)	6	(1.3)	30	(3.3)	40	(3.6)	22	(3.5)	9	(2.4)
	Japan	27	(3.9)	34	(4.0)	32	(4.1)	7	(2.1)	20	(3.8)	34	(4.1)	38	(4.3)	9	(2.4)
	Korea	57	(3.9)	33	(3.9)	9	(2.1)	2	(1.1)	41	(4.1)	48	(4.1)	9	(2.2)	2	(1.1)
	Luxembourg	26	(0.1)	50	(0.1)	11	(0.0)	12	(0.0)	38	(0.1)	46	(0.1)	12	(0.0)	3	(0.0)
	Mexico	21	(2.7)	19	(2.6)	38	(3.4)	22	(2.7)	21	(2.7)	21	(2.5)	33	(3.6)	25	(3.1)
	Netherlands	30	(3.9)	32	(4.6)	31	(3.9)	7	(1.8)	26	(3.8)	30	(4.1)	33	(4.2)	11	(2.5)
	New Zealand	24	(2.7)	33	(3.3)	38	(3.3)	4	(1.3)	23	(2.4)	40	(3.3)	33	(3.2)	5	(1.2)
	Norway	6	(1.9)	21	(2.8)	55	(3.7)	18	(3.1)	8	(2.2)	31	(3.6)	48	(3.8)	14	(2.6)
	Poland	19	(3.0)	26	(3.0)	40	(3.6)	15	(2.8)	7	(2.1)	21	(3.5)	53	(4.2)	19	(3.1)
	Portugal	18	(3.6)	27	(4.2)	45	(4.0)	10	(2.6)	14	(2.7)	27	(4.2)	51	(4.2)	8	(2.4)
	Slovak Republic	10	(1.8)	23	(2.5)	49	(3.8)	18	(2.5)	4	(1.3)	21	(3.2)	50	(3.7)	25	(2.7)
	Spain	19	(2.9)	23	(3.2)	44	(3.3)	14	(2.4)	15	(2.9)	25	(3.2)	45	(3.9)	16	(2.6)
	Sweden	17	(2.7)	33	(3.8)	42	(3.9)	8	(2.2)	16	(2.8)	37	(3.8)	41	(3.7)	7	(2.0)
	Switzerland	44	(3.7)	35	(3.3)	17	(2.6)	4	(1.3)	27	(3.4)	48	(4.2)	18	(2.9)	7	(1.9)
	Turkey	6	(2.1)	13	(2.9)	37	(4.2)	45	(4.8)	6	(2.0)	16	(3.7)	33	(4.3)	45	(4.4)
	United States	38	(3.7)	35	(2.8)	20	(2.8)	7	(1.7)	36	(3.6)	37	(2.9)	23	(2.8)	4	(1.3)
	OECD average	***26***	***(0.6)***	***31***	***(0.6)***	***33***	***(0.6)***	***11***	***(0.4)***	***21***	***(0.5)***	***34***	***(0.7)***	***34***	***(0.7)***	***12***	***(0.4)***
Partner countries	Brazil	22	(3.1)	11	(2.3)	20	(2.7)	47	(3.5)	16	(2.8)	14	(2.9)	17	(2.5)	52	(3.4)
	Hong Kong-China	30	(4.2)	43	(4.6)	24	(3.7)	4	(1.6)	15	(2.8)	44	(4.3)	33	(3.5)	8	(2.4)
	Indonesia	32	(3.1)	21	(3.3)	17	(3.2)	31	(3.0)	33	(3.0)	20	(2.9)	15	(2.8)	32	(3.3)
	Latvia	22	(4.1)	26	(3.7)	40	(3.7)	12	(3.1)	14	(3.6)	33	(4.1)	40	(4.3)	13	(3.2)
	Liechtenstein	46	(0.5)	42	(0.4)	12	(0.4)	0	(0.0)	35	(0.4)	46	(0.4)	19	(0.5)	0	(0.0)
	Macao-China	21	(0.1)	30	(0.3)	43	(0.2)	7	(0.1)	15	(0.1)	16	(0.3)	57	(0.2)	13	(0.2)
	Russian Federation	13	(2.7)	10	(2.8)	32	(3.7)	46	(3.9)	9	(2.0)	11	(3.0)	35	(3.7)	46	(3.9)
	Serbia	9	(2.2)	13	(2.6)	48	(4.1)	30	(4.2)	7	(1.9)	5	(1.4)	40	(4.3)	48	(4.2)
	Thailand	17	(3.5)	20	(3.1)	36	(3.7)	28	(3.1)	18	(3.3)	20	(3.1)	31	(3.4)	31	(3.4)
	Tunisia	21	(3.4)	11	(2.5)	34	(4.2)	34	(3.9)	21	(3.4)	16	(2.9)	26	(3.4)	37	(3.4)
	Uruguay	16	(2.9)	13	(2.3)	29	(3.6)	41	(4.2)	15	(3.0)	12	(2.0)	28	(3.5)	45	(4.6)
	United Kingdom[1]	19	(2.5)	34	(3.3)	36	(3.3)	11	(2.2)	17	(2.4)	35	(3.6)	40	(3.2)	7	(1.7)

1. Response rate too low to ensure comparability.

Table 2.5 *(continued)*

Percentage of students in schools whose principals report that instruction is hindered by a shortage of ICT resources

Results based on school principals' reports

		A shortage of computers hinders instruction to some extent or a lot				Number of computers per student in schools whose principals report that a shortage of computers hinders instruction							
		PISA 2000		PISA 2003		Not at all		Very little		To some extent		A lot	
		%	S.E.	%	S.E.	Mean	S.E.	Mean	S.E.	Mean	S.E.	Mean	S.E.
OECD countries	Australia	30	(3.9)	34	(2.8)	0.36	(0.02)	0.26	(0.01)	0.24	(0.01)	0.18	(0.02)
	Austria	38	(4.3)	36	(3.4)	0.26	(0.02)	0.22	(0.02)	0.17	(0.02)	0.19	(0.04)
	Belgium	**18**	(2.4)	**43**	(3.3)	0.18	(0.01)	0.15	(0.01)	0.13	(0.01)	0.13	(0.06)
	Canada	**30**	(1.7)	**45**	(2.6)	0.27	(0.03)	0.22	(0.01)	0.19	(0.01)	0.21	(0.02)
	Czech Republic	22	(3.5)	21	(2.9)	0.14	(0.02)	0.13	(0.01)	0.09	(0.01)	0.07	(0.01)
	Denmark	**27**	(3.5)	**46**	(4.4)	0.27	(0.06)	0.21	(0.01)	0.14	(0.01)	0.11	(0.02)
	Finland	43	(3.9)	39	(4.2)	0.22	(0.02)	0.18	(0.01)	0.14	(0.01)	0.12	(0.02)
	France	28	(3.3)	w	w	w	w	w	w	w	w	w	w
	Germany	**50**	(3.8)	**34**	(3.3)	0.10	(0.01)	0.07	(0.00)	0.08	(0.01)	0.05	(0.01)
	Greece	**70**	(4.4)	**49**	(5.8)	0.12	(0.02)	0.08	(0.01)	0.07	(0.01)	0.07	(0.01)
	Hungary	**12**	(2.7)	**27**	(3.5)	0.28	(0.02)	0.23	(0.03)	0.15	(0.01)	0.14	(0.05)
	Iceland	**45**	(0.1)	**34**	(0.2)	0.20	(0.00)	0.18	(0.00)	0.15	(0.00)	0.14	(0.01)
	Ireland	41	(4.5)	50	(4.1)	0.16	(0.01)	0.11	(0.01)	0.09	(0.01)	0.06	(0.01)
	Italy	32	(3.9)	29	(3.1)	0.15	(0.01)	0.13	(0.01)	0.10	(0.01)	0.10	(0.02)
	Japan	31	(4.3)	39	(4.2)	0.22	(0.03)	0.14	(0.01)	0.22	(0.06)	0.21	(0.04)
	Korea	**22**	(3.7)	**10**	(2.4)	0.26	(0.01)	0.29	(0.02)	0.29	(0.03)	0.12	(0.00)
	Luxembourg	**23**	(0.2)	**23**	(0.1)	0.24	(0.00)	0.16	(0.00)	0.17	(0.00)	0.17	(0.00)
	Mexico	69	(3.7)	60	(3.1)	0.13	(0.02)	0.07	(0.01)	0.07	(0.01)	0.08	(0.01)
	Netherlands	39	(6.0)	38	(4.0)	0.15	(0.01)	0.15	(0.01)	0.13	(0.01)	0.15	(0.02)
	New Zealand	40	(3.4)	42	(3.5)	0.26	(0.02)	0.23	(0.01)	0.20	(0.01)	0.22	(0.03)
	Norway	**61**	(4.1)	**74**	(3.1)	0.30	(0.06)	0.22	(0.02)	0.16	(0.01)	0.13	(0.01)
	Poland	**38**	(4.8)	**55**	(3.6)	0.07	(0.01)	0.08	(0.01)	0.06	(0.01)	0.06	(0.01)
	Portugal	**39**	(3.8)	**55**	(4.1)	0.08	(0.00)	0.08	(0.01)	0.07	(0.00)	0.06	(0.00)
	Slovak Republic	a	a	a	a	0.10	(0.01)	0.09	(0.01)	0.07	(0.00)	0.03	(0.00)
	Spain	**29**	(3.8)	**58**	(3.4)	0.10	(0.01)	0.09	(0.01)	0.08	(0.01)	0.07	(0.01)
	Sweden	51	(4.1)	50	(4.1)	0.21	(0.01)	0.16	(0.01)	0.14	(0.01)	0.12	(0.01)
	Switzerland	37	(4.0)	43	(3.2)	0.21	(0.06)	0.15	(0.01)	0.11	(0.01)	0.20	(0.05)
	Turkey	a	a	a	a	0.12	(0.06)	0.03	(0.01)	0.03	(0.00)	0.03	(0.00)
	United States	26	(4.7)	26	(3.0)	0.32	(0.02)	0.30	(0.02)	0.24	(0.01)	0.21	(0.02)
	OECD average	***37***	***(0.7)***	***41***	***(0.7)***	***0.20***	***(0.01)***	***0.16***	***(0.00)***	***0.14***	***(0.00)***	***0.13***	***(0.00)***
Partner countries	Brazil	63	(3.8)	67	(3.4)	0.06	(0.02)	0.02	(0.01)	0.02	(0.00)	0.01	(0.00)
	Hong Kong-China	**15**	(3.4)	**28**	(3.8)	0.24	(0.01)	0.21	(0.01)	0.21	(0.01)	0.26	(0.06)
	Indonesia	58	(4.7)	48	(3.4)	0.08	(0.06)	0.03	(0.00)	0.03	(0.00)	0.04	(0.01)
	Latvia	**40**	(4.1)	**52**	(4.4)	0.08	(0.01)	0.06	(0.00)	0.06	(0.00)	0.05	(0.00)
	Liechtenstein	**41**	(0.3)	**12**	(0.4)	0.46	(0.00)	0.19	(0.00)	0.10	(0.00)	a	a
	Macao-China	a	a	a	a	0.13	(0.00)	0.15	(0.00)	0.10	(0.00)	0.12	(0.00)
	Russian Federation	**86**	(2.7)	**77**	(3.7)	0.04	(0.01)	0.05	(0.01)	0.03	(0.00)	0.02	(0.00)
	Serbia	a	a	a	a	0.05	(0.01)	0.03	(0.00)	0.04	(0.00)	0.02	(0.00)
	Thailand	62	(4.1)	63	(3.2)	0.08	(0.01)	0.06	(0.00)	0.05	(0.00)	0.03	(0.00)
	Tunisia	a	a	a	a	0.01	(0.00)	0.01	(0.00)	0.01	(0.00)	0.01	(0.00)
	Uruguay	a	a	a	a	0.06	(0.01)	0.06	(0.01)	0.07	(0.01)	0.03	(0.00)
	United Kingdom[1]	56	(3.4)	46	(3.3)	0.30	(0.02)	0.23	(0.01)	0.20	(0.01)	0.20	(0.02)

Note: Statistically significant differences are marked in bold. See Annex A2 for an examination of the cross-cultural comparability of this indicator.
1. Response rate too low to ensure comparability.

Table 2.6

Mean and percentage of various ICT resources at school, by school location

Results based on school principals' reports

		Computers per student by school location:				Percentage of students in schools whose principals report that instruction is hindered by a shortage of:							
						Computers for instruction				Computer software for instruction			
		Rural locations or towns		Cities		Rural locations or towns		Cities		Rural locations or towns		Cities	
		Mean	S.E.	Mean	S.E.	%	S.E.	%	S.E.	%	S.E.	%	S.E.
OECD countries	Australia	0.26	(0.01)	0.29	(0.01)	**42**	(4.5)	**30**	(3.7)	34	(4.9)	29	(4.0)
	Austria	**0.24**	(0.01)	**0.17**	(0.02)	34	(3.8)	42	(7.7)	37	(5.0)	44	(7.5)
	Belgium	0.15	(0.01)	0.14	(0.03)	**39**	(3.7)	**60**	(6.5)	35	(3.5)	48	(7.6)
	Canada	0.22	(0.00)	0.22	(0.02)	41	(3.6)	50	(3.8)	46	(3.3)	49	(3.7)
	Czech Republic	0.11	(0.01)	0.12	(0.02)	46	(3.7)	32	(7.2)	49	(3.5)	38	(7.4)
	Denmark	**0.19**	(0.01)	**0.15**	(0.01)	45	(4.6)	59	(11.0)	39	(4.2)	50	(10.3)
	Finland	0.17	(0.01)	0.16	(0.01)	39	(4.6)	40	(8.7)	44	(4.9)	54	(10.1)
	France	w	w	w	w	w	w	w	w	w	w	w	w
	Germany	0.08	(0.00)	0.08	(0.01)	32	(4.0)	38	(6.2)	41	(3.8)	50	(6.4)
	Greece	0.08	(0.00)	0.09	(0.03)	46	(6.9)	58	(9.6)	56	(7.1)	69	(9.0)
	Hungary	0.24	(0.02)	0.21	(0.02)	26	(5.0)	28	(5.6)	46	(5.9)	45	(6.6)
	Iceland	**0.18**	(0.00)	**0.18**	(0.00)	**35**	(0.2)	**29**	(0.3)	**40**	(0.2)	**13**	(0.2)
	Ireland	**0.12**	(0.01)	**0.10**	(0.01)	49	(5.1)	52	(8.2)	58	(5.3)	54	(8.2)
	Italy	**0.14**	(0.01)	**0.10**	(0.01)	29	(4.0)	28	(4.7)	33	(4.0)	25	(4.7)
	Japan	0.20	(0.02)	0.18	(0.03)	42	(7.4)	37	(5.0)	48	(7.3)	45	(5.5)
	Korea	**0.37**	(0.03)	**0.25**	(0.01)	16	(7.2)	9	(2.5)	20	(7.7)	9	(2.6)
	Luxembourg	0.18	(0.00)	c	c	23	(0.1)	c	c	16	(0.1)	c	c
	Mexico	0.09	(0.01)	0.09	(0.01)	**69**	(3.7)	**49**	(5.6)	**65**	(4.1)	**50**	(5.3)
	Netherlands	0.15	(0.01)	0.14	(0.01)	37	(5.2)	40	(6.9)	42	(5.3)	48	(6.8)
	New Zealand	0.23	(0.01)	0.22	(0.01)	47	(5.2)	36	(3.8)	**44**	(5.1)	**29**	(4.3)
	Norway	**0.18**	(0.01)	**0.14**	(0.01)	73	(3.6)	78	(7.8)	62	(3.9)	63	(8.7)
	Poland	**0.06**	(0.00)	**0.08**	(0.01)	54	(4.5)	60	(6.5)	74	(4.3)	67	(7.9)
	Portugal	0.07	(0.00)	0.07	(0.01)	57	(4.4)	46	(11.2)	61	(4.7)	50	(11.3)
	Slovak Republic	**0.06**	(0.00)	**0.09**	(0.01)	67	(3.4)	70	(7.5)	77	(3.6)	69	(9.8)
	Spain	0.09	(0.00)	0.08	(0.01)	55	(4.2)	62	(6.0)	58	(4.1)	64	(5.7)
	Sweden	0.16	(0.01)	0.15	(0.01)	47	(4.6)	60	(7.4)	46	(4.6)	55	(7.9)
	Switzerland	0.17	(0.03)	0.15	(0.01)	19	(3.3)	30	(8.8)	23	(3.0)	46	(12.2)
	Turkey	0.04	(0.01)	0.04	(0.01)	81	(5.7)	82	(4.6)	78	(6.5)	79	(5.2)
	United States	0.30	(0.01)	0.28	(0.02)	26	(3.5)	28	(5.8)	25	(3.3)	32	(6.3)
	OECD average	***0.16***	***(0.00)***	***0.15***	***(0.00)***	***43***	***(0.8)***	***46***	***(1.3)***	***46***	***(0.9)***	***47***	***(1.4)***
Partner countries	Brazil	**0.01**	(0.00)	**0.03**	(0.01)	**74**	(4.2)	**60**	(4.9)	**76**	(4.1)	**62**	(5.0)
	Hong Kong-China	a	a	a	a	a	a	a	a	a	a	a	a
	Indonesia	0.04	(0.02)	0.03	(0.00)	44	(4.1)	57	(5.9)	46	(4.4)	53	(6.5)
	Latvia	**0.06**	(0.00)	**0.05**	(0.00)	56	(5.8)	44	(6.3)	57	(5.8)	46	(7.4)
	Liechtenstein	0.33	(0.00)	c	c	12	(0.4)	c	c	19	(0.5)	c	c
	Macao-China	a	a	a	a	a	a	a	a	a	a	a	a
	Russian Federation	0.03	(0.00)	0.03	(0.00)	77	(5.2)	78	(4.7)	78	(4.6)	83	(4.7)
	Serbia	**0.04**	(0.00)	**0.03**	(0.00)	78	(4.5)	77	(5.2)	87	(3.3)	90	(3.3)
	Thailand	0.05	(0.00)	0.06	(0.01)	**71**	(3.5)	**39**	(8.5)	**71**	(3.9)	**38**	(8.3)
	Tunisia	0.01	(0.00)	0.01	(0.00)	70	(4.1)	56	(11.2)	66	(4.3)	47	(11.3)
	Uruguay	0.05	(0.00)	0.05	(0.01)	72	(4.6)	69	(4.2)	74	(4.1)	71	(4.2)
	United Kingdom[1]	0.22	(0.01)	0.25	(0.01)	45	(3.8)	50	(5.9)	50	(4.0)	42	(5.7)

Note: Statistically significant differences are marked in bold.

1. Response rate too low to ensure comparability.

Table 3.1

Percentage of students using computers at home, school or other places, by frequency of use

Results based on students' self-reports

		Percentage of students using computers at school						Percentage of students using computers at home						Percentage of students using computers in other places					
		Frequent use		Moderate use		Rare or no use		Frequent use		Moderate use		Rare or no use		Frequent use		Moderate use		Rare or no use	
		%	S.E.	%	S.E.	%	S.E.	%	S.E.	%	S.E.	%	S.E.	%	S.E.	%	S.E.	%	S.E.
OECD countries	Australia	59	(1.0)	27	(0.7)	14	(0.7)	87	(0.5)	7	(0.3)	6	(0.3)	14	(0.6)	27	(0.7)	59	(0.6)
	Austria	53	(2.0)	31	(1.5)	16	(1.3)	81	(0.8)	12	(0.6)	6	(0.4)	16	(0.7)	25	(0.8)	59	(1.0)
	Belgium	27	(0.9)	35	(0.9)	39	(1.2)	84	(0.5)	8	(0.4)	9	(0.4)	15	(0.5)	22	(0.6)	63	(0.7)
	Canada	40	(0.9)	31	(0.7)	29	(0.8)	90	(0.3)	4	(0.2)	6	(0.3)	30	(0.5)	34	(0.5)	37	(0.5)
	Czech Republic	41	(1.6)	44	(1.6)	15	(1.4)	70	(0.9)	11	(0.5)	19	(0.7)	19	(0.6)	29	(0.7)	52	(0.9)
	Denmark	68	(1.6)	25	(1.1)	7	(0.7)	84	(0.7)	10	(0.6)	6	(0.4)	25	(0.8)	25	(0.9)	49	(1.1)
	Finland	36	(1.5)	41	(1.0)	23	(1.3)	78	(0.6)	11	(0.4)	11	(0.5)	21	(0.7)	28	(0.7)	52	(0.8)
	Germany	23	(1.2)	28	(1.4)	48	(1.7)	82	(0.6)	10	(0.5)	7	(0.4)	16	(0.7)	19	(0.7)	65	(0.9)
	Greece	45	(2.4)	27	(1.7)	28	(1.9)	57	(1.2)	6	(0.3)	37	(1.3)	26	(0.8)	20	(0.6)	54	(0.8)
	Hungary	80	(1.2)	10	(0.8)	9	(1.0)	67	(1.0)	6	(0.5)	27	(0.9)	26	(0.6)	28	(0.8)	46	(0.9)
	Iceland	41	(0.8)	40	(0.8)	19	(0.7)	89	(0.6)	7	(0.5)	4	(0.4)	21	(0.7)	30	(0.7)	50	(0.9)
	Ireland	24	(1.4)	27	(1.8)	49	(2.3)	61	(0.9)	19	(0.7)	20	(0.8)	9	(0.5)	18	(0.8)	73	(0.9)
	Italy	51	(2.0)	20	(0.9)	30	(1.9)	76	(0.8)	8	(0.4)	16	(0.7)	19	(0.7)	18	(0.5)	64	(0.8)
	Japan	26	(2.3)	33	(2.7)	41	(3.1)	37	(1.2)	22	(0.8)	41	(1.1)	2	(0.3)	5	(0.4)	93	(0.5)
	Korea	28	(1.9)	29	(1.8)	43	(2.6)	86	(0.6)	11	(0.6)	3	(0.3)	21	(0.9)	33	(1.0)	47	(1.2)
	Mexico	54	(1.9)	16	(0.9)	30	(1.7)	48	(1.8)	44	(0.3)	28	(0.3)	28	(0.4)	74	(0.2)	9	(0.1)
	New Zealand	43	(1.2)	26	(0.8)	31	(1.2)	79	(0.7)	8	(0.5)	12	(0.6)	17	(0.7)	26	(0.6)	57	(0.8)
	Poland	44	(1.8)	34	(1.4)	22	(2.4)	59	(1.1)	4	(0.3)	38	(1.1)	25	(0.7)	22	(0.7)	53	(0.9)
	Portugal	34	(1.5)	25	(0.9)	41	(1.6)	78	(0.9)	5	(0.4)	18	(0.8)	23	(0.8)	22	(0.8)	55	(1.1)
	Slovak Republic	42	(1.5)	30	(1.5)	27	(2.0)	65	(1.0)	9	(0.5)	26	(0.9)	21	(0.8)	31	(0.9)	48	(1.2)
	Sweden	48	(1.5)	30	(0.8)	22	(1.2)	89	(0.5)	7	(0.4)	4	(0.3)	20	(0.7)	28	(0.6)	52	(0.8)
	Switzerland	30	(1.4)	36	(1.1)	34	(1.7)	81	(0.6)	12	(0.5)	7	(0.5)	13	(0.7)	17	(0.6)	70	(0.8)
	Turkey	46	(3.5)	8	(0.9)	46	(3.7)	48	(2.1)	3	(0.5)	49	(2.2)	43	(1.2)	21	(0.9)	36	(1.3)
	United States	43	(1.4)	28	(0.9)	29	(1.2)	83	(0.7)	6	(0.4)	11	(0.5)	23	(0.7)	26	(0.8)	51	(1.0)
	OECD average	*44*	*(0.3)*	*28*	*(0.3)*	*28*	*(0.4)*	*74*	*(0.2)*	*9*	*(0.1)*	*18*	*(0.2)*	*21*	*(0.2)*	*24*	*(0.1)*	*55*	*(0.2)*
Partner countries	Latvia	35	(1.9)	26	(1.4)	39	(2.3)	49	(1.7)	5	(0.7)	46	(1.6)	30	(1.0)	25	(0.8)	44	(1.4)
	Liechtenstein	56	(2.4)	29	(2.5)	14	(2.1)	89	(1.7)	7	(1.4)	4	(1.2)	18	(2.1)	23	(2.8)	59	(2.8)
	Russian Federation	43	(2.1)	38	(1.3)	19	(1.7)	43	(2.0)	2	(0.2)	55	(2.0)	36	(1.2)	23	(0.9)	41	(1.1)
	Serbia	57	(1.8)	37	(1.6)	6	(1.1)	50	(1.3)	3	(0.4)	47	(1.3)	40	(1.2)	17	(0.7)	44	(1.1)
	Thailand	55	(1.8)	24	(1.1)	21	(1.7)	30	(1.6)	3	(0.3)	66	(1.6)	18	(1.1)	16	(0.8)	66	(1.3)
	Tunisia	23	(2.2)	12	(1.0)	65	(2.7)	52	(1.8)	5	(0.6)	43	(1.8)	35	(1.1)	23	(1.0)	42	(1.2)
	Uruguay	27	(1.8)	11	(0.8)	62	(2.3)	57	(1.4)	3	(0.3)	40	(1.3)	38	(1.0)	21	(0.8)	42	(1.0)
	United Kingdom[1]	71	(1.4)	15	(0.8)	14	(1.0)	81	(1.0)	9	(0.6)	11	(0.7)	18	(1.0)	27	(0.9)	55	(1.3)

1. Response rate too low to ensure comparability.

Table 3.2
Index of ICT use for the Internet and entertainment, by national quarters of the index
Results based on students' self-reports

		Index of ICT use for the Internet and entertainment											
		All students		Females		Males		Gender difference (M-F)		Bottom quarter		Second quarter	
		Mean index	S.E.	Mean index	S.E.	Mean index	S.E.	Dif.	S.E.	Mean index	S.E.	Mean index	S.E.
OECD countries	Australia	0.27	(0.02)	0.07	(0.01)	0.47	(0.02)	**0.40**	(0.03)	-0.71	(0.01)	-0.07	(0.00)
	Austria	0.03	(0.02)	-0.21	(0.02)	0.27	(0.03)	**0.48**	(0.03)	-0.96	(0.02)	-0.27	(0.00)
	Belgium	0.14	(0.02)	-0.13	(0.02)	0.40	(0.02)	**0.53**	(0.03)	-1.09	(0.02)	-0.18	(0.00)
	Canada	0.63	(0.01)	0.41	(0.02)	0.87	(0.02)	**0.47**	(0.02)	-0.48	(0.01)	0.22	(0.00)
	Czech Republic	-0.08	(0.02)	-0.32	(0.02)	0.16	(0.02)	**0.49**	(0.03)	-1.03	(0.02)	-0.39	(0.00)
	Denmark	0.11	(0.02)	-0.29	(0.02)	0.51	(0.03)	**0.80**	(0.03)	-0.85	(0.01)	-0.28	(0.00)
	Finland	-0.13	(0.01)	-0.45	(0.01)	0.20	(0.02)	**0.65**	(0.02)	-0.96	(0.01)	-0.46	(0.00)
	Germany	-0.06	(0.01)	-0.40	(0.02)	0.30	(0.02)	**0.70**	(0.03)	-1.16	(0.02)	-0.41	(0.00)
	Greece	-0.11	(0.02)	-0.33	(0.02)	0.13	(0.03)	**0.46**	(0.03)	-1.22	(0.02)	-0.39	(0.00)
	Hungary	-0.24	(0.02)	-0.39	(0.02)	-0.11	(0.03)	**0.28**	(0.03)	-1.12	(0.01)	-0.49	(0.00)
	Iceland	0.26	(0.02)	-0.11	(0.02)	0.62	(0.02)	**0.74**	(0.03)	-0.69	(0.01)	-0.10	(0.00)
	Ireland	-0.43	(0.02)	-0.53	(0.03)	-0.32	(0.03)	**0.22**	(0.04)	-1.46	(0.02)	-0.66	(0.01)
	Italy	-0.16	(0.02)	-0.41	(0.02)	0.10	(0.02)	**0.51**	(0.03)	-1.35	(0.02)	-0.45	(0.00)
	Japan	-0.91	(0.02)	-0.96	(0.02)	-0.85	(0.03)	**0.11**	(0.03)	-1.87	(0.02)	-1.12	(0.00)
	Korea	0.34	(0.02)	0.18	(0.02)	0.45	(0.02)	**0.27**	(0.02)	-0.39	(0.01)	0.08	(0.00)
	Mexico	-0.21	(0.04)	-0.34	(0.04)	-0.08	(0.05)	**0.26**	(0.04)	-1.59	(0.02)	-0.50	(0.01)
	New Zealand	0.26	(0.02)	0.09	(0.02)	0.43	(0.03)	**0.34**	(0.03)	-0.76	(0.01)	-0.09	(0.00)
	Poland	-0.06	(0.02)	-0.33	(0.03)	0.20	(0.03)	**0.53**	(0.03)	-1.24	(0.02)	-0.43	(0.00)
	Portugal	0.07	(0.02)	-0.20	(0.03)	0.37	(0.03)	**0.57**	(0.03)	-1.08	(0.01)	-0.26	(0.01)
	Slovak Republic	-0.43	(0.02)	-0.61	(0.02)	-0.25	(0.03)	**0.36**	(0.03)	-1.39	(0.01)	-0.69	(0.00)
	Sweden	0.28	(0.02)	-0.10	(0.02)	0.65	(0.03)	**0.75**	(0.03)	-0.70	(0.01)	-0.11	(0.00)
	Switzerland	-0.06	(0.02)	-0.38	(0.02)	0.24	(0.03)	**0.62**	(0.03)	-1.14	(0.02)	-0.38	(0.00)
	Turkey	-0.23	(0.03)	-0.58	(0.03)	-0.02	(0.03)	**0.55**	(0.04)	-1.57	(0.04)	-0.49	(0.01)
	United States	0.46	(0.02)	0.35	(0.02)	0.58	(0.03)	**0.23**	(0.03)	-0.63	(0.01)	0.06	(0.00)
	OECD average	***0.00***	***(0.00)***	***-0.24***	***(0.00)***	***0.23***	***(0.01)***	***0.47***	***(0.01)***	***-1.05***	***(0.00)***	***-0.32***	***(0.00)***
Partner countries	Latvia	-0.35	(0.03)	-0.60	(0.03)	-0.09	(0.03)	**0.51**	(0.03)	-1.44	(0.02)	-0.65	(0.01)
	Liechtenstein	0.29	(0.06)	-0.01	(0.07)	0.58	(0.09)	**0.58**	(0.11)	-0.76	(0.05)	-0.07	(0.02)
	Russian Federation	-0.81	(0.04)	-1.05	(0.03)	-0.58	(0.05)	**0.47**	(0.04)	-1.96	(0.02)	-1.20	(0.00)
	Serbia	-0.48	(0.03)	-0.74	(0.03)	-0.22	(0.04)	**0.52**	(0.04)	-1.76	(0.02)	-0.99	(0.01)
	Thailand	-0.64	(0.03)	-0.72	(0.04)	-0.54	(0.04)	**0.18**	(0.04)	-1.87	(0.03)	-0.92	(0.01)
	Tunisia	-0.47	(0.04)	-0.59	(0.04)	-0.36	(0.04)	**0.22**	(0.04)	-1.80	(0.03)	-0.67	(0.01)
	Uruguay	-0.31	(0.02)	-0.47	(0.03)	-0.14	(0.03)	**0.33**	(0.03)	-1.68	(0.02)	-0.60	(0.01)
	United Kingdom[3]	0.30	(0.03)	0.06	(0.03)	0.55	(0.04)	**0.48**	(0.04)	-0.79	(0.02)	-0.06	(0.01)

		Index of ICT use for the Internet and entertainment				Difference in index when students have a computer available to use at home[1]				Difference in index when students have a computer available to use at school[2]			
		Third quarter		Top quarter		Observed difference		Accounting for ESCS		Observed difference		Accounting for ESCS	
		Mean index	S.E.	Mean index	S.E.	Dif.	S.E.	Dif.	S.E.	Dif.	S.E.	Dif.	S.E.
OECD countries	Australia	0.37	(0.00)	1.48	(0.02)	**0.73**	(0.11)	**0.63**	(0.11)	**0.37**	(0.18)	0.33	(0.18)
	Austria	0.15	(0.00)	1.21	(0.03)	**0.74**	(0.10)	**0.59**	(0.10)	**0.23**	(0.11)	0.18	(0.09)
	Belgium	0.34	(0.00)	1.50	(0.02)	**1.07**	(0.06)	**0.97**	(0.07)	**0.22**	(0.06)	**0.19**	(0.06)
	Canada	0.75	(0.00)	2.05	(0.02)	**0.97**	(0.04)	**0.85**	(0.04)	**0.53**	(0.12)	**0.45**	(0.12)
	Czech Republic	0.03	(0.00)	1.09	(0.03)	**0.63**	(0.03)	**0.46**	(0.03)	**0.34**	(0.07)	**0.24**	(0.07)
	Denmark	0.19	(0.01)	1.37	(0.03)	**0.55**	(0.09)	**0.49**	(0.09)	c	c	c	c
	Finland	-0.06	(0.00)	0.95	(0.02)	**0.59**	(0.03)	**0.52**	(0.03)	**0.34**	(0.06)	**0.35**	(0.05)
	Germany	0.11	(0.01)	1.23	(0.03)	**0.97**	(0.07)	**0.84**	(0.07)	0.05	(0.07)	0.01	(0.07)
	Greece	0.09	(0.00)	1.09	(0.02)	**0.67**	(0.03)	**0.58**	(0.03)	**0.27**	(0.06)	**0.30**	(0.06)
	Hungary	-0.09	(0.00)	0.74	(0.02)	**0.44**	(0.03)	**0.34**	(0.03)	0.14	(0.16)	0.13	(0.16)
	Iceland	0.34	(0.00)	1.50	(0.03)	**0.96**	(0.10)	**0.82**	(0.10)	**0.31**	(0.12)	**0.30**	(0.12)
	Ireland	-0.20	(0.00)	0.63	(0.02)	**0.67**	(0.05)	**0.52**	(0.04)	0.08	(0.06)	0.08	(0.06)
	Italy	0.08	(0.00)	1.07	(0.02)	**0.80**	(0.05)	**0.61**	(0.05)	0.09	(0.05)	**0.16**	(0.05)
	Japan	-0.70	(0.00)	0.06	(0.02)	**0.71**	(0.04)	**0.60**	(0.04)	0.02	(0.05)	0.02	(0.04)
	Korea	0.41	(0.00)	1.27	(0.02)	**0.44**	(0.07)	**0.43**	(0.08)	**0.13**	(0.03)	**0.13**	(0.03)
	Mexico	0.09	(0.00)	1.15	(0.03)	**0.94**	(0.04)	**0.58**	(0.05)	**0.16**	(0.06)	**0.15**	(0.05)
	New Zealand	0.37	(0.00)	1.51	(0.03)	**0.64**	(0.05)	**0.58**	(0.05)	**0.26**	(0.11)	**0.25**	(0.12)
	Poland	0.08	(0.01)	1.34	(0.03)	**0.87**	(0.04)	**0.61**	(0.04)	-0.01	(0.08)	0.03	(0.07)
	Portugal	0.28	(0.01)	1.36	(0.03)	**0.73**	(0.04)	**0.44**	(0.05)	0.10	(0.16)	0.08	(0.15)
	Slovak Republic	-0.23	(0.00)	0.61	(0.03)	**0.48**	(0.04)	**0.29**	(0.04)	**0.26**	(0.05)	**0.17**	(0.05)
	Sweden	0.36	(0.00)	1.56	(0.03)	**0.69**	(0.06)	**0.59**	(0.07)	0.02	(0.10)	0.00	(0.10)
	Switzerland	0.11	(0.00)	1.19	(0.02)	**0.93**	(0.07)	**0.79**	(0.07)	**0.20**	(0.08)	**0.21**	(0.09)
	Turkey	0.05	(0.01)	1.07	(0.04)	**0.73**	(0.05)	**0.49**	(0.05)	**0.16**	(0.06)	**0.18**	(0.06)
	United States	0.57	(0.01)	1.86	(0.03)	**0.84**	(0.05)	**0.66**	(0.05)	**0.29**	(0.11)	0.14	(0.12)
	OECD average	***0.16***	***(0.00)***	***1.22***	***(0.01)***	*0.74*	***(0.01)***	*0.60*	***(0.01)***	*0.20*	***(0.02)***	*0.18*	***(0.02)***
Partner countries	Latvia	-0.15	(0.01)	0.82	(0.02)	**0.67**	(0.03)	**0.55**	(0.04)	0.02	(0.06)	0.03	(0.06)
	Liechtenstein	0.40	(0.02)	1.61	(0.09)	c	c	c	c	c	c	c	c
	Russian Federation	-0.62	(0.01)	0.52	(0.03)	**1.01**	(0.04)	**0.91**	(0.04)	0.00	(0.05)	-0.05	(0.05)
	Serbia	-0.24	(0.01)	1.06	(0.03)	**1.14**	(0.05)	**1.00**	(0.05)	-0.18	(0.11)	-0.07	(0.10)
	Thailand	-0.30	(0.01)	0.56	(0.02)	**0.97**	(0.04)	**0.54**	(0.03)	**0.79**	(0.09)	**0.47**	(0.15)
	Tunisia	-0.15	(0.01)	0.75	(0.03)	**0.74**	(0.06)	**0.57**	(0.05)	**0.16**	(0.06)	**0.21**	(0.06)
	Uruguay	0.00	(0.01)	1.05	(0.02)	**1.07**	(0.04)	**0.83**	(0.04)	**0.27**	(0.05)	**0.19**	(0.04)
	United Kingdom[3]	0.43	(0.01)	1.63	(0.03)	**0.74**	(0.08)	**0.69**	(0.08)	c	c	c	c

Note: Statistically significant differences are marked in bold.
1. Results based on less than 3% of students in Denmark, Iceland, Korea and Sweden (see Table 2.2a).
2. Results based on less than 3% of students in Australia, Canada, Hungary, Iceland, New Zealand and Sweden (see Table 2.2a).
3. Response rate too low to ensure comparability.

Table 3.3

Percentage of males and females frequently using ICT for the Internet and entertainment

Results based on students' self-reports

		Games on a computer				The Internet to download software (including games)				The Internet to download music				The Internet to look up information about people, things or ideas				The Internet to collaborate with a group or team				A computer for electronic communication (*e.g.* e-mail or chat rooms)			
		Males		Females		Males		Females		Males		Females		Males		Females		Males		Females		Males		Females	
		%	S.E.	%	S.E.	%	S.E.	%	S.E.	%	S.E.	%	S.E.	%	S.E.	%	S.E.	%	S.E.	%	S.E.	%	S.E.	%	S.E.
OECD countries	Australia	**67**	(0.7)	**33**	(1.0)	**58**	(1.0)	**35**	(0.8)	**62**	(1.1)	**53**	(0.8)	**76**	(0.8)	**72**	(0.9)	**46**	(1.3)	**40**	(0.8)	68	(1.1)	69	(0.9)
	Austria	**66**	(1.3)	**20**	(1.0)	**52**	(1.4)	**25**	(1.2)	**59**	(1.3)	**41**	(1.2)	63	(1.3)	62	(1.3)	**30**	(1.2)	**22**	(1.1)	**56**	(1.3)	**60**	(1.1)
	Belgium	**68**	(0.8)	**30**	(0.7)	**56**	(0.9)	**31**	(0.8)	**65**	(0.9)	**51**	(0.9)	**65**	(0.8)	**55**	(1.1)	**39**	(0.9)	**27**	(0.8)	**72**	(1.0)	**69**	(0.9)
	Canada	**75**	(0.7)	**44**	(0.7)	**70**	(0.6)	**46**	(0.9)	**80**	(0.7)	**75**	(0.6)	**77**	(0.6)	**73**	(0.7)	**55**	(0.9)	**44**	(0.8)	**81**	(0.7)	**85**	(0.6)
	Czech Republic	**75**	(1.1)	**30**	(1.2)	**41**	(1.1)	**13**	(0.8)	**43**	(1.0)	**24**	(1.0)	**58**	(1.4)	**50**	(1.5)	**33**	(1.1)	**27**	(1.3)	50	(1.3)	47	(1.5)
	Denmark	**84**	(0.8)	**33**	(1.1)	**60**	(1.2)	**18**	(0.9)	**59**	(1.2)	**28**	(1.2)	**76**	(1.0)	**59**	(1.2)	**43**	(1.3)	**26**	(1.3)	64	(1.4)	61	(1.5)
	Finland	**75**	(0.9)	**30**	(1.1)	**51**	(1.0)	**9**	(0.6)	**56**	(1.2)	**21**	(0.9)	**49**	(1.0)	**31**	(0.9)	**20**	(0.9)	**7**	(0.5)	**55**	(1.2)	**63**	(1.2)
	Germany	**77**	(0.9)	**27**	(1.1)	**53**	(1.2)	**22**	(1.0)	**60**	(1.2)	**36**	(1.1)	**62**	(0.9)	**44**	(1.0)	**28**	(0.9)	**15**	(0.8)	**59**	(1.1)	**49**	(1.2)
	Greece	**73**	(1.1)	**50**	(1.3)	**56**	(1.3)	**37**	(1.4)	**58**	(1.5)	**43**	(1.4)	**54**	(1.3)	**37**	(1.5)	**32**	(1.2)	**19**	(0.9)	**43**	(1.2)	**29**	(1.0)
	Hungary	**77**	(1.0)	**44**	(1.3)	**34**	(1.3)	**13**	(0.7)	**41**	(1.1)	**24**	(1.1)	41	(1.3)	43	(1.6)	34	(1.1)	32	(1.2)	**44**	(1.4)	**51**	(1.5)
	Iceland	**77**	(1.0)	**28**	(1.1)	**60**	(1.2)	**24**	(1.1)	**73**	(1.1)	**43**	(1.1)	**79**	(1.0)	**66**	(1.2)	**33**	(1.1)	**18**	(1.0)	72	(1.1)	69	(1.1)
	Ireland	**59**	(1.1)	**35**	(1.2)	**30**	(1.3)	**18**	(1.2)	**40**	(1.2)	**27**	(1.5)	**42**	(1.2)	**35**	(1.8)	**18**	(1.0)	**15**	(1.1)	34	(1.2)	34	(1.5)
	Italy	**73**	(0.8)	**42**	(1.2)	**56**	(1.1)	**31**	(1.1)	**57**	(1.1)	**38**	(1.0)	**61**	(1.2)	**48**	(1.3)	**28**	(1.1)	**22**	(1.1)	**44**	(1.3)	**38**	(1.2)
	Japan	**25**	(1.1)	**15**	(1.0)	**14**	(1.1)	**5**	(0.6)	**15**	(1.1)	**9**	(0.7)	**27**	(1.2)	**24**	(1.0)	7	(0.7)	6	(0.7)	21	(1.2)	24	(1.0)
	Korea	**74**	(1.4)	**33**	(1.2)	**60**	(1.5)	**29**	(1.3)	80	(0.9)	78	(1.0)	**58**	(1.2)	**61**	(1.2)	48	(0.9)	51	(1.5)	**71**	(1.0)	**77**	(0.8)
	Mexico	**54**	(1.5)	**37**	(1.1)	**43**	(1.7)	**29**	(1.1)	**51**	(1.6)	**42**	(1.2)	**53**	(1.5)	**46**	(1.3)	**42**	(1.4)	**38**	(1.4)	**50**	(1.7)	**45**	(1.5)
	New Zealand	**69**	(1.3)	**42**	(1.4)	**58**	(1.4)	**36**	(1.1)	**62**	(1.1)	**54**	(1.1)	**67**	(1.1)	**63**	(1.2)	**43**	(1.2)	**35**	(1.2)	68	(1.2)	70	(1.1)
	Poland	**75**	(1.1)	**37**	(1.0)	**44**	(1.4)	**20**	(1.1)	**48**	(1.4)	**33**	(1.1)	**51**	(1.4)	**37**	(1.5)	**41**	(1.4)	**35**	(1.3)	**47**	(1.4)	**42**	(1.2)
	Portugal	**79**	(0.9)	**42**	(1.3)	**58**	(1.4)	**26**	(1.2)	**60**	(1.4)	**42**	(1.5)	**64**	(1.2)	**53**	(1.6)	**49**	(1.3)	**38**	(1.4)	**58**	(1.3)	**49**	(1.8)
	Slovak Republic	**72**	(1.1)	**41**	(1.4)	**27**	(0.9)	**10**	(0.8)	**29**	(1.1)	**15**	(0.9)	**40**	(1.4)	**32**	(1.6)	27	(1.2)	25	(1.2)	**32**	(1.2)	**27**	(1.3)
	Sweden	**81**	(0.8)	**32**	(1.4)	**62**	(1.2)	**27**	(0.9)	**71**	(1.3)	**52**	(1.2)	**71**	(1.3)	**54**	(1.2)	**38**	(1.3)	**19**	(1.1)	75	(1.4)	75	(1.1)
	Switzerland	**65**	(1.1)	**20**	(0.9)	**52**	(1.2)	**20**	(0.9)	**58**	(1.1)	**34**	(1.0)	**63**	(1.9)	**51**	(1.2)	**32**	(1.2)	**19**	(1.0)	**60**	(1.3)	**57**	(1.2)
	Turkey	**66**	(1.5)	**40**	(2.0)	**48**	(1.1)	**27**	(1.4)	**52**	(1.3)	**39**	(1.7)	**45**	(1.5)	**27**	(1.6)	**34**	(1.4)	**21**	(1.3)	**50**	(1.8)	**32**	(1.6)
	United States	**70**	(1.0)	**54**	(1.2)	**61**	(1.0)	**43**	(1.1)	**68**	(0.9)	**61**	(1.1)	74	(0.9)	74	(1.1)	**44**	(1.0)	**40**	(1.1)	**69**	(1.1)	**73**	(1.2)
	OECD average	*70*	*(0.2)*	*35*	*(0.2)*	*51*	*(0.2)*	*25*	*(0.2)*	*56*	*(0.2)*	*40*	*(0.2)*	*59*	*(0.2)*	*50*	*(0.3)*	*36*	*(0.2)*	*27*	*(0.2)*	*56*	*(0.3)*	*55*	*(0.3)*
Partner countries	Latvia	**71**	(1.4)	**31**	(1.5)	**40**	(1.6)	**16**	(1.2)	**46**	(1.5)	**26**	(1.5)	**46**	(1.7)	**29**	(1.4)	**28**	(1.3)	**16**	(1.0)	**43**	(1.5)	**38**	(1.8)
	Liechtenstein	**67**	(3.7)	**27**	(3.5)	**65**	(4.0)	**39**	(4.2)	**71**	(3.8)	**52**	(3.8)	72	(3.5)	61	(4.3)	**40**	(3.6)	**24**	(3.3)	72	(3.4)	80	(3.8)
	Russian Federation	**67**	(1.3)	**44**	(1.5)	**29**	(1.6)	**15**	(0.8)	**28**	(1.6)	**15**	(1.0)	**25**	(1.6)	**12**	(1.0)	**16**	(1.3)	**9**	(0.9)	**23**	(1.5)	**13**	(1.0)
	Serbia	**76**	(1.2)	**54**	(1.3)	**34**	(1.3)	**20**	(0.9)	**40**	(1.2)	**32**	(1.2)	**33**	(1.3)	**23**	(1.1)	**26**	(1.2)	**18**	(1.0)	**33**	(1.2)	**24**	(1.2)
	Thailand	**54**	(1.8)	**40**	(1.4)	**29**	(1.4)	**22**	(1.2)	**31**	(1.6)	**24**	(1.1)	31	(1.7)	30	(1.7)	23	(1.4)	25	(1.3)	25	(1.4)	23	(1.5)
	Tunisia	**56**	(1.9)	**43**	(1.7)	**34**	(1.6)	**24**	(1.4)	**36**	(1.4)	**31**	(1.6)	**43**	(1.7)	**33**	(1.7)	**28**	(1.4)	**20**	(1.4)	**33**	(1.7)	**25**	(1.4)
	Uruguay	**63**	(1.2)	**47**	(1.2)	**41**	(1.2)	**25**	(1.3)	**45**	(1.4)	**32**	(1.3)	**48**	(1.2)	**42**	(1.3)	31	(1.3)	28	(1.4)	45	(1.5)	42	(1.5)
	United Kingdom[1]	**76**	(1.3)	**40**	(1.6)	**61**	(1.5)	**37**	(1.7)	**66**	(1.7)	**50**	(1.8)	**69**	(1.4)	**61**	(1.8)	**46**	(1.7)	**36**	(1.6)	69	(1.7)	69	(1.8)

Note: Statistically significant differences are marked in bold.

1. Response rate too low to ensure comparability.

Table 3.4
Index of ICT use for programs and software, by national quarters of the index

Results based on students' self-reports

		Index of ICT use for programs and software											
		All students		Females		Males		Gender difference (M-F)		Bottom quarter		Second quarter	
		Mean index	S.E.	Mean index	S.E.	Mean index	S.E.	Dif.	S.E.	Mean index	S.E.	Mean index	S.E.
OECD countries	Australia	0.23	(0.01)	0.14	(0.02)	0.33	(0.01)	**0.19**	(0.02)	-0.74	(0.01)	0.01	(0.00)
	Austria	0.13	(0.02)	0.06	(0.02)	0.20	(0.03)	**0.15**	(0.04)	-0.90	(0.02)	-0.09	(0.00)
	Belgium	-0.19	(0.01)	-0.31	(0.02)	-0.07	(0.02)	**0.24**	(0.03)	-1.38	(0.02)	-0.41	(0.00)
	Canada	0.15	(0.01)	0.05	(0.02)	0.25	(0.02)	**0.19**	(0.02)	-0.99	(0.01)	-0.10	(0.00)
	Czech Republic	0.08	(0.02)	-0.02	(0.02)	0.18	(0.03)	**0.20**	(0.03)	-1.01	(0.02)	-0.12	(0.00)
	Denmark	0.17	(0.02)	-0.07	(0.02)	0.41	(0.03)	**0.48**	(0.03)	-0.78	(0.02)	-0.11	(0.00)
	Finland	-0.28	(0.01)	-0.42	(0.02)	-0.13	(0.02)	**0.29**	(0.02)	-1.19	(0.01)	-0.49	(0.00)
	Germany	-0.03	(0.02)	-0.19	(0.02)	0.12	(0.02)	**0.31**	(0.03)	-1.19	(0.02)	-0.25	(0.00)
	Greece	0.11	(0.02)	-0.03	(0.03)	0.26	(0.03)	**0.29**	(0.04)	-1.18	(0.02)	-0.16	(0.01)
	Hungary	0.03	(0.02)	-0.04	(0.02)	0.09	(0.02)	**0.12**	(0.03)	-1.00	(0.03)	-0.16	(0.00)
	Iceland	0.10	(0.02)	-0.07	(0.02)	0.27	(0.03)	**0.34**	(0.03)	-0.93	(0.02)	-0.14	(0.00)
	Ireland	-0.35	(0.02)	-0.26	(0.02)	-0.43	(0.03)	**-0.17**	(0.03)	-1.61	(0.02)	-0.57	(0.01)
	Italy	0.23	(0.02)	0.08	(0.02)	0.39	(0.03)	**0.31**	(0.04)	-0.97	(0.02)	-0.05	(0.00)
	Japan	-1.03	(0.03)	-0.97	(0.03)	-1.10	(0.04)	**-0.13**	(0.04)	-2.27	(0.02)	-1.19	(0.01)
	Korea	-0.33	(0.02)	-0.30	(0.02)	-0.36	(0.02)	**-0.06**	(0.03)	-1.39	(0.02)	-0.50	(0.00)
	Mexico	0.18	(0.03)	0.09	(0.03)	0.29	(0.03)	**0.20**	(0.03)	-1.29	(0.02)	-0.07	(0.01)
	New Zealand	0.16	(0.02)	0.13	(0.02)	0.18	(0.02)	0.05	(0.03)	-0.94	(0.02)	-0.10	(0.00)
	Poland	0.22	(0.02)	0.02	(0.03)	0.43	(0.03)	**0.41**	(0.04)	-1.22	(0.03)	-0.07	(0.01)
	Portugal	0.23	(0.02)	0.11	(0.02)	0.36	(0.03)	**0.26**	(0.03)	-0.94	(0.02)	0.03	(0.00)
	Slovak Republic	0.02	(0.02)	-0.12	(0.02)	0.15	(0.03)	**0.26**	(0.04)	-1.28	(0.02)	-0.22	(0.00)
	Sweden	-0.17	(0.01)	-0.36	(0.02)	0.02	(0.02)	**0.38**	(0.02)	-1.16	(0.01)	-0.40	(0.00)
	Switzerland	-0.15	(0.02)	-0.34	(0.02)	0.03	(0.03)	**0.37**	(0.03)	-1.31	(0.02)	-0.38	(0.00)
	Turkey	0.10	(0.04)	-0.09	(0.06)	0.22	(0.05)	**0.31**	(0.06)	-1.62	(0.04)	-0.16	(0.01)
	United States	0.33	(0.02)	0.31	(0.02)	0.35	(0.02)	0.04	(0.03)	-0.82	(0.02)	0.06	(0.01)
	OECD average	*0.00*	*(0.00)*	*-0.09*	*(0.00)*	*0.11*	*(0.01)*	*0.20*	*(0.01)*	*-1.15*	*(0.00)*	*-0.22*	*(0.00)*
Partner countries	Latvia	-0.23	(0.03)	-0.42	(0.03)	-0.02	(0.04)	**0.41**	(0.04)	-1.53	(0.03)	-0.47	(0.01)
	Liechtenstein	0.13	(0.05)	-0.13	(0.06)	0.38	(0.07)	**0.51**	(0.10)	-0.89	(0.06)	-0.12	(0.01)
	Russian Federation	-0.30	(0.04)	-0.41	(0.04)	-0.19	(0.05)	**0.23**	(0.05)	-1.82	(0.02)	-0.56	(0.01)
	Serbia	0.07	(0.03)	0.00	(0.03)	0.14	(0.03)	**0.14**	(0.04)	-1.30	(0.02)	-0.25	(0.01)
	Thailand	-0.05	(0.03)	-0.03	(0.04)	-0.07	(0.04)	-0.04	(0.03)	-1.30	(0.04)	-0.25	(0.01)
	Tunisia	0.00	(0.04)	-0.13	(0.05)	0.12	(0.06)	**0.26**	(0.06)	-1.84	(0.03)	-0.22	(0.01)
	Uruguay	0.24	(0.03)	0.16	(0.04)	0.33	(0.03)	**0.18**	(0.05)	-1.48	(0.03)	0.00	(0.01)
	United Kingdom[3]	0.32	(0.03)	0.31	(0.03)	0.33	(0.03)	0.02	(0.04)	-0.75	(0.02)	0.11	(0.01)

		Index of ICT use for programs and software				Difference in index when students have a computer available to use at home[1]				Difference in index when students have a computer available to use at school[2]			
		Third quarter		Top quarter		Observed difference		Accounting for ESCS		Observed difference		Accounting for ESCS	
		Mean index	S.E.	Mean index	S.E.	Dif.	S.E.	Dif.	S.E.	Dif.	S.E.	Dif.	S.E.
OECD countries	Australia	0.44	(0.00)	1.22	(0.01)	**0.46**	(0.08)	**0.39**	(0.08)	**0.64**	(0.23)	**0.62**	(0.22)
	Austria	0.36	(0.00)	1.15	(0.02)	**0.61**	(0.10)	**0.58**	(0.10)	**0.50**	(0.13)	**0.51**	(0.12)
	Belgium	0.11	(0.00)	0.93	(0.02)	**0.90**	(0.07)	**0.87**	(0.07)	**0.37**	(0.05)	**0.36**	(0.05)
	Canada	0.39	(0.00)	1.29	(0.02)	**0.65**	(0.05)	**0.49**	(0.05)	**0.84**	(0.14)	**0.76**	(0.13)
	Czech Republic	0.34	(0.00)	1.11	(0.02)	**0.83**	(0.04)	**0.75**	(0.04)	**0.49**	(0.09)	**0.41**	(0.08)
	Denmark	0.34	(0.00)	1.22	(0.02)	**0.59**	(0.09)	**0.51**	(0.09)	c	c	c	c
	Finland	-0.08	(0.00)	0.64	(0.02)	**0.50**	(0.03)	**0.42**	(0.04)	**0.37**	(0.06)	**0.38**	(0.06)
	Germany	0.24	(0.01)	1.07	(0.02)	**0.94**	(0.09)	**0.89**	(0.09)	**0.20**	(0.07)	**0.19**	(0.07)
	Greece	0.40	(0.01)	1.38	(0.03)	**0.69**	(0.04)	**0.71**	(0.04)	**0.47**	(0.08)	**0.48**	(0.07)
	Hungary	0.26	(0.00)	1.01	(0.02)	**0.58**	(0.04)	**0.61**	(0.04)	**0.49**	(0.16)	**0.49**	(0.15)
	Iceland	0.30	(0.00)	1.18	(0.03)	**0.89**	(0.12)	**0.77**	(0.12)	**0.52**	(0.15)	**0.51**	(0.14)
	Ireland	-0.01	(0.00)	0.81	(0.02)	**0.40**	(0.06)	**0.33**	(0.06)	**0.35**	(0.05)	**0.35**	(0.05)
	Italy	0.47	(0.00)	1.48	(0.03)	**0.60**	(0.07)	**0.62**	(0.07)	**0.35**	(0.05)	**0.36**	(0.05)
	Japan	-0.68	(0.01)	0.01	(0.02)	**0.26**	(0.05)	**0.17**	(0.05)	**0.47**	(0.06)	**0.47**	(0.05)
	Korea	-0.04	(0.00)	0.60	(0.01)	**0.73**	(0.08)	**0.55**	(0.08)	**0.27**	(0.04)	**0.27**	(0.04)
	Mexico	0.55	(0.00)	1.54	(0.02)	**0.71**	(0.04)	**0.56**	(0.06)	**0.50**	(0.08)	**0.50**	(0.07)
	New Zealand	0.39	(0.01)	1.28	(0.02)	**0.23**	(0.08)	**0.18**	(0.08)	**0.59**	(0.13)	**0.59**	(0.14)
	Poland	0.53	(0.01)	1.66	(0.03)	**1.07**	(0.04)	**0.97**	(0.05)	**0.23**	(0.10)	**0.26**	(0.09)
	Portugal	0.51	(0.00)	1.32	(0.02)	**0.68**	(0.05)	**0.63**	(0.05)	0.09	(0.16)	0.08	(0.17)
	Slovak Republic	0.32	(0.00)	1.27	(0.03)	**0.92**	(0.04)	**0.84**	(0.04)	**0.31**	(0.05)	**0.24**	(0.05)
	Sweden	0.05	(0.00)	0.83	(0.02)	**0.43**	(0.09)	**0.29**	(0.10)	**0.26**	(0.08)	**0.25**	(0.08)
	Switzerland	0.12	(0.00)	0.97	(0.03)	**0.79**	(0.10)	**0.71**	(0.11)	**0.34**	(0.08)	**0.35**	(0.08)
	Turkey	0.53	(0.01)	1.66	(0.04)	**0.80**	(0.08)	**0.80**	(0.06)	**0.59**	(0.07)	**0.59**	(0.07)
	United States	0.55	(0.00)	1.55	(0.03)	**0.46**	(0.07)	**0.32**	(0.07)	0.11	(0.16)	0.03	(0.15)
	OECD average	*0.28*	*(0.00)*	*1.14*	*(0.00)*	*0.64*	*(0.01)*	*0.57*	*(0.01)*	*0.41*	*(0.02)*	*0.39*	*(0.02)*
Partner countries	Latvia	0.13	(0.01)	0.97	(0.02)	**0.82**	(0.04)	**0.76**	(0.04)	**0.31**	(0.06)	**0.33**	(0.06)
	Liechtenstein	0.34	(0.02)	1.22	(0.08)	c	c	c	c	c	c	c	c
	Russian Federation	0.10	(0.01)	1.09	(0.02)	**1.08**	(0.05)	**0.96**	(0.05)	**0.40**	(0.06)	**0.36**	(0.06)
	Serbia	0.33	(0.01)	1.51	(0.04)	**0.93**	(0.05)	**0.96**	(0.05)	**0.31**	(0.14)	**0.37**	(0.14)
	Thailand	0.29	(0.01)	1.07	(0.02)	**0.50**	(0.04)	**0.29**	(0.04)	**0.68**	(0.21)	**0.52**	(0.24)
	Tunisia	0.50	(0.01)	1.56	(0.04)	**1.12**	(0.07)	**0.99**	(0.07)	**0.36**	(0.07)	**0.42**	(0.08)
	Uruguay	0.67	(0.01)	1.79	(0.02)	**1.40**	(0.05)	**1.32**	(0.07)	**0.47**	(0.07)	**0.40**	(0.07)
	United Kingdom[3]	0.55	(0.00)	1.37	(0.03)	**0.35**	(0.09)	**0.33**	(0.09)	c	c	c	c

Note: Statistically significant differences are marked in bold.
1. Results based on less than 3% of students in Denmark, Iceland, Korea and Sweden (see Table 2.2a).
2. Results based on less than 3% of students in Australia, Canada, Hungary, Iceland, New Zealand and Sweden (see Table 2.2a).
3. Response rate too low to ensure comparability.

Table 3.5
Percentage of males and females frequently using ICT for programs and software

Results based on students' self-reports

	Computer for programming				Drawing, painting or graphics programs on a computer				Speadsheets (*e.g.* <Lotus 123®> or Microsoft Excel®>)				Computer to help learn school material				Educational software such as mathematics programs				Word processing (*e.g.* <Word®> or WordPerfect®>)			
	Males		Females		Males		Females		Males		Females		Males		Females		Males		Females		Males		Females	
	%	S.E.	%	S.E.	%	S.E.	%	S.E.	%	S.E.	%	S.E.	%	S.E.	%	S.E.	%	S.E.	%	S.E.	%	S.E.	%	S.E.
OECD countries																								
Australia	**32**	(1.0)	**17**	(0.7)	**38**	(0.7)	**27**	(0.7)	**25**	(0.7)	**20**	(0.8)	**34**	(0.9)	**30**	(0.7)	**13**	(0.5)	**8**	(0.5)	**67**	(0.8)	**73**	(0.9)
Austria	**33**	(1.6)	**14**	(0.9)	**33**	(1.1)	**22**	(1.1)	26	(1.2)	24	(1.4)	31	(1.1)	31	(1.2)	**12**	(0.9)	**6**	(0.5)	**52**	(1.7)	**67**	(1.6)
Belgium	**31**	(0.8)	**15**	(0.8)	**25**	(0.9)	**13**	(0.6)	**20**	(0.7)	**14**	(0.7)	24	(0.9)	23	(1.0)	**9**	(0.6)	**4**	(0.3)	48	(1.0)	51	(1.0)
Canada	**38**	(0.7)	**21**	(0.7)	**39**	(0.7)	**30**	(0.8)	**20**	(0.7)	**14**	(0.6)	**30**	(0.8)	**27**	(0.7)	**11**	(0.5)	**8**	(0.4)	**60**	(0.9)	**64**	(0.7)
Czech Republic	**29**	(1.2)	**9**	(0.8)	**35**	(1.0)	**20**	(1.0)	**27**	(1.0)	**17**	(1.2)	25	(1.3)	27	(1.1)	15	(0.9)	15	(0.7)	47	(1.2)	45	(1.4)
Denmark	**31**	(1.2)	**9**	(0.7)	**32**	(1.3)	**11**	(0.8)	**24**	(1.4)	**12**	(0.9)	**56**	(1.3)	**47**	(1.4)	**23**	(1.1)	**7**	(0.7)	**66**	(1.1)	**63**	(1.3)
Finland	**19**	(0.8)	**3**	(0.3)	**27**	(0.9)	**10**	(0.6)	**9**	(0.8)	**3**	(0.4)	18	(0.8)	18	(0.7)	**4**	(0.4)	**2**	(0.2)	28	(1.0)	26	(1.0)
Germany	**33**	(1.1)	**13**	(0.8)	**30**	(1.1)	**18**	(0.9)	**24**	(1.1)	**14**	(0.7)	28	(1.1)	26	(1.0)	**13**	(0.8)	**10**	(0.9)	**53**	(1.3)	**45**	(1.2)
Greece	**36**	(1.3)	**21**	(0.7)	44	(1.0)	45	(1.2)	**31**	(1.2)	**23**	(1.1)	**27**	(1.3)	**19**	(1.1)	**26**	(1.0)	**18**	(1.1)	46	(1.4)	44	(1.3)
Hungary	**22**	(1.1)	**11**	(0.8)	**32**	(1.0)	**28**	(1.2)	33	(1.3)	31	(1.4)	**33**	(1.1)	**28**	(1.1)	**13**	(0.6)	**7**	(0.6)	52	(1.3)	54	(1.5)
Iceland	**30**	(1.1)	**13**	(0.8)	**32**	(1.2)	**14**	(0.8)	**19**	(1.0)	**9**	(0.6)	**40**	(1.2)	**35**	(1.3)	**14**	(0.9)	**9**	(0.6)	**47**	(1.3)	**41**	(1.3)
Ireland	**15**	(0.8)	**11**	(1.0)	26	(1.2)	27	(1.2)	**13**	(0.9)	**16**	(0.9)	**14**	(0.8)	**17**	(1.1)	8	(0.6)	9	(0.6)	**27**	(1.1)	**41**	(1.5)
Italy	**38**	(1.3)	**24**	(1.0)	**45**	(1.1)	**38**	(1.0)	**36**	(1.1)	**26**	(1.3)	45	(1.2)	42	(1.2)	**24**	(1.1)	**16**	(1.1)	60	(1.1)	59	(1.4)
Japan	**4**	(0.5)	**2**	(0.4)	**7**	(0.7)	**10**	(0.8)	7	(0.9)	9	(1.6)	4	(0.5)	5	(0.6)	**2**	(0.3)	**1**	(0.2)	**15**	(1.3)	**19**	(1.6)
Korea	**9**	(0.6)	**7**	(0.6)	**14**	(0.7)	**17**	(0.9)	8	(0.6)	6	(0.8)	**16**	(0.9)	**22**	(1.2)	6	(0.5)	7	(0.5)	**29**	(1.2)	**35**	(1.6)
Mexico	**37**	(1.3)	**27**	(1.2)	**50**	(1.1)	**46**	(1.3)	**35**	(1.2)	**30**	(1.6)	**48**	(1.2)	**42**	(1.3)	**29**	(1.0)	**22**	(1.1)	**43**	(1.2)	**34**	(1.3)
New Zealand	**29**	(1.3)	**20**	(1.0)	33	(1.2)	32	(1.1)	22	(1.0)	22	(1.1)	31	(1.1)	30	(1.1)	12	(0.7)	12	(0.9)	**51**	(1.3)	**57**	(1.2)
Poland	**39**	(1.3)	**18**	(1.0)	**46**	(1.1)	**33**	(1.2)	**38**	(1.2)	**27**	(1.2)	**29**	(1.1)	**23**	(1.1)	**29**	(1.0)	**22**	(1.0)	**53**	(1.2)	**42**	(1.3)
Portugal	**42**	(1.2)	**26**	(1.1)	**33**	(1.1)	**24**	(1.0)	**33**	(1.2)	**23**	(1.2)	56	(1.6)	58	(1.3)	**17**	(1.1)	**13**	(0.9)	**56**	(1.2)	**51**	(1.4)
Slovak Republic	**28**	(0.9)	**11**	(0.8)	**38**	(1.1)	**27**	(1.0)	**29**	(1.0)	**16**	(0.9)	**34**	(1.2)	**31**	(1.0)	**21**	(1.0)	**15**	(0.8)	**46**	(1.1)	**41**	(1.4)
Sweden	**29**	(1.1)	**7**	(0.5)	**34**	(1.2)	**15**	(0.8)	**11**	(0.7)	**5**	(0.5)	**27**	(1.2)	**19**	(1.0)	**7**	(0.6)	**3**	(0.4)	46	(1.2)	48	(1.5)
Switzerland	**30**	(1.0)	**11**	(0.7)	**29**	(1.1)	**15**	(0.7)	**24**	(1.1)	**15**	(0.9)	**22**	(1.1)	**17**	(0.6)	**11**	(0.8)	**6**	(0.4)	**49**	(1.7)	**40**	(1.4)
Turkey	37	(1.4)	36	(2.2)	46	(1.7)	44	(2.5)	**35**	(1.9)	**26**	(1.8)	**35**	(1.6)	**27**	(1.7)	**30**	(1.7)	**19**	(1.8)	**45**	(1.9)	**39**	(2.1)
United States	**38**	(1.0)	**27**	(1.1)	**43**	(1.1)	**39**	(1.1)	**24**	(1.1)	**20**	(0.9)	35	(1.1)	37	(1.0)	19	(0.9)	16	(1.0)	**56**	(1.1)	**67**	(1.1)
OECD average	***30***	*(0.2)*	***16***	*(0.2)*	***34***	*(0.2)*	***26***	*(0.2)*	***24***	*(0.2)*	***18***	*(0.2)*	***31***	*(0.2)*	***29***	*(0.2)*	***15***	*(0.2)*	***11***	*(0.2)*	***48***	*(0.3)*	***49***	*(0.3)*
Partner countries																								
Latvia	**23**	(1.0)	**9**	(0.7)	**36**	(1.4)	**22**	(1.3)	**25**	(1.5)	**15**	(1.6)	**28**	(1.5)	**22**	(1.2)	**18**	(1.1)	**10**	(0.7)	**38**	(1.8)	**27**	(1.5)
Liechtenstein	**34**	(3.1)	**11**	(2.7)	**40**	(3.6)	**24**	(3.1)	**34**	(3.6)	**14**	(3.0)	24	(3.3)	18	(2.4)	10	(2.1)	10	(2.2)	**69**	(3.7)	**49**	(4.3)
Russian Federation	**25**	(1.3)	**16**	(1.3)	**35**	(1.5)	**24**	(1.4)	**24**	(1.1)	**17**	(1.3)	**25**	(1.2)	**19**	(1.0)	**21**	(1.0)	**15**	(1.0)	**38**	(1.4)	**31**	(1.6)
Serbia	**33**	(1.3)	**24**	(1.1)	**54**	(1.2)	**58**	(1.2)	**25**	(1.1)	**16**	(0.9)	29	(1.3)	26	(1.1)	**24**	(1.2)	**13**	(1.0)	**49**	(1.4)	**55**	(1.7)
Thailand	23	(1.2)	23	(1.4)	40	(1.5)	38	(1.3)	21	(1.2)	18	(1.3)	**33**	(1.7)	**40**	(1.4)	18	(1.0)	17	(1.1)	**34**	(1.6)	**38**	(1.3)
Tunisia	**36**	(1.6)	**28**	(1.4)	**37**	(1.5)	**31**	(1.2)	**30**	(1.7)	**18**	(1.1)	40	(1.7)	39	(1.5)	**38**	(1.8)	**29**	(1.5)	**38**	(1.8)	**29**	(1.7)
Uruguay	**28**	(1.5)	**18**	(1.1)	**37**	(1.1)	**34**	(1.2)	**37**	(1.1)	**31**	(1.5)	54	(1.2)	54	(1.6)	46	(1.3)	46	(1.5)	52	(1.6)	51	(1.8)
United Kingdom[1]	**34**	(1.3)	**19**	(1.4)	**41**	(1.5)	**32**	(1.4)	**28**	(1.8)	**34**	(1.7)	33	(1.5)	36	(1.6)	18	(1.1)	21	(1.5)	**60**	(1.5)	**72**	(1.6)

Note: Statistically significant differences are marked in bold.

1. Response rate too low to ensure comparability.

Table 3.6
Index of attitudes towards computers, by national quarters of the index
Results based on students' self-reports

		Index of attitudes towards computers											
		All students		Females		Males		Gender difference (M-F)		Bottom quarter		Second quarter	
		Mean index	S.E.	Mean index	S.E.	Mean index	S.E.	Dif.	S.E.	Mean index	S.E.	Mean index	S.E.
OECD countries	Australia	-0.10	(0.01)	-0.26	(0.02)	0.07	(0.02)	**0.33**	(0.02)	-1.23	(0.01)	-0.49	(0.00)
	Austria	0.31	(0.02)	0.18	(0.03)	0.45	(0.02)	**0.27**	(0.04)	-1.08	(0.03)	0.12	(0.01)
	Belgium	0.13	(0.01)	-0.07	(0.02)	0.31	(0.02)	**0.38**	(0.03)	-1.18	(0.02)	-0.25	(0.00)
	Canada	0.15	(0.01)	0.03	(0.02)	0.28	(0.01)	**0.24**	(0.02)	-1.09	(0.01)	-0.20	(0.00)
	Czech Republic	0.01	(0.02)	-0.29	(0.02)	0.29	(0.02)	**0.58**	(0.03)	-1.13	(0.02)	-0.36	(0.01)
	Denmark	-0.24	(0.02)	-0.67	(0.03)	0.19	(0.03)	**0.86**	(0.03)	-1.58	(0.02)	-0.67	(0.01)
	Finland	-0.38	(0.02)	-0.63	(0.02)	-0.12	(0.02)	**0.51**	(0.03)	-1.54	(0.02)	-0.74	(0.01)
	Germany	0.25	(0.02)	-0.03	(0.02)	0.54	(0.02)	**0.57**	(0.03)	-1.16	(0.02)	-0.01	(0.01)
	Greece	0.08	(0.01)	-0.09	(0.02)	0.26	(0.02)	**0.35**	(0.03)	-1.10	(0.02)	-0.26	(0.01)
	Hungary	-0.20	(0.02)	-0.49	(0.03)	0.06	(0.02)	**0.54**	(0.04)	-1.49	(0.02)	-0.57	(0.01)
	Iceland	0.15	(0.02)	-0.15	(0.02)	0.43	(0.03)	**0.58**	(0.04)	-1.15	(0.02)	-0.16	(0.01)
	Ireland	-0.32	(0.01)	-0.39	(0.02)	-0.26	(0.02)	**0.13**	(0.03)	-1.51	(0.02)	-0.65	(0.01)
	Italy	-0.07	(0.01)	-0.24	(0.02)	0.11	(0.02)	**0.34**	(0.03)	-1.18	(0.01)	-0.42	(0.01)
	Japan	-0.41	(0.03)	-0.41	(0.03)	-0.42	(0.04)	-0.02	(0.04)	-1.97	(0.03)	-0.78	(0.01)
	Korea	0.25	(0.02)	0.11	(0.02)	0.34	(0.02)	**0.23**	(0.03)	-0.89	(0.01)	-0.15	(0.01)
	Mexico	-0.13	(0.02)	-0.18	(0.02)	-0.08	(0.02)	**0.10**	(0.03)	-1.21	(0.02)	-0.46	(0.01)
	New Zealand	-0.10	(0.02)	-0.23	(0.02)	0.02	(0.02)	**0.26**	(0.03)	-1.26	(0.02)	-0.48	(0.01)
	Poland	0.26	(0.02)	0.05	(0.02)	0.48	(0.02)	**0.43**	(0.03)	-0.91	(0.02)	-0.18	(0.01)
	Portugal	0.27	(0.02)	0.06	(0.03)	0.50	(0.02)	**0.44**	(0.03)	-0.89	(0.02)	-0.09	(0.01)
	Slovak Republic	-0.01	(0.02)	-0.25	(0.02)	0.22	(0.03)	**0.47**	(0.03)	-1.14	(0.02)	-0.32	(0.01)
	Sweden	-0.10	(0.02)	-0.39	(0.02)	0.20	(0.02)	**0.59**	(0.03)	-1.43	(0.02)	-0.45	(0.01)
	Switzerland	-0.02	(0.02)	-0.28	(0.03)	0.23	(0.03)	**0.51**	(0.05)	-1.49	(0.02)	-0.33	(0.01)
	Turkey	0.14	(0.03)	-0.04	(0.04)	0.24	(0.03)	**0.28**	(0.04)	-1.16	(0.03)	-0.21	(0.01)
	United States	0.07	(0.01)	0.02	(0.02)	0.12	(0.02)	**0.10**	(0.03)	-1.08	(0.01)	-0.29	(0.00)
	OECD average	***0.00***	***(0.00)***	***-0.19***	***(0.00)***	***0.19***	***(0.00)***	***0.38***	***(0.01)***	***-1.24***	***(0.00)***	***-0.35***	***(0.00)***
Partner countries	Latvia	-0.17	(0.02)	-0.35	(0.03)	0.03	(0.03)	**0.37**	(0.04)	-1.27	(0.02)	-0.53	(0.01)
	Liechtenstein	0.26	(0.06)	0.05	(0.10)	0.46	(0.07)	**0.41**	(0.13)	-1.10	(0.08)	0.06	(0.03)
	Russian Federation	0.12	(0.02)	-0.01	(0.03)	0.23	(0.03)	**0.24**	(0.04)	-1.12	(0.02)	-0.31	(0.00)
	Serbia	0.50	(0.03)	0.37	(0.04)	0.63	(0.04)	**0.26**	(0.05)	-0.85	(0.03)	0.35	(0.01)
	Thailand	0.02	(0.02)	0.07	(0.02)	-0.03	(0.02)	**-0.09**	(0.03)	-0.85	(0.02)	-0.32	(0.00)
	Tunisia	0.31	(0.02)	0.36	(0.03)	0.27	(0.03)	**-0.10**	(0.04)	-0.93	(0.03)	0.03	(0.01)
	Uruguay	0.06	(0.02)	-0.03	(0.02)	0.15	(0.02)	**0.18**	(0.03)	-1.05	(0.02)	-0.27	(0.01)
	United Kingdom[3]	0.07	(0.02)	-0.09	(0.03)	0.23	(0.03)	**0.31**	(0.04)	-1.12	(0.02)	-0.29	(0.01)

		Index of attitudes towards computers				Difference in index when students have a computer available to use at home[1]				Difference in index when students have a computer available to use at school[2]			
		Third quarter		Top quarter		Observed difference		Accounting for ESCS		Observed difference		Accounting for ESCS	
		Mean index	S.E.	Mean index	S.E.	Dif.	S.E.	Dif.	S.E.	Dif.	S.E.	Dif.	S.E.
OECD countries	Australia	0.18	(0.01)	1.15	(0.01)	**0.42**	(0.05)	**0.38**	(0.06)	0.30	(0.20)	0.28	(0.20)
	Austria	0.85	(0.01)	1.35	(0.00)	**0.69**	(0.11)	**0.72**	(0.11)	**0.14**	(0.07)	**0.15**	(0.07)
	Belgium	0.58	(0.01)	1.34	(0.00)	**0.75**	(0.08)	**0.79**	(0.08)	0.06	(0.06)	0.07	(0.06)
	Canada	0.57	(0.01)	1.34	(0.00)	**0.53**	(0.06)	**0.51**	(0.06)	0.11	(0.10)	0.07	(0.11)
	Czech Republic	0.31	(0.01)	1.21	(0.01)	**0.52**	(0.04)	**0.53**	(0.04)	**0.16**	(0.08)	0.13	(0.08)
	Denmark	0.14	(0.01)	1.13	(0.01)	**0.45**	(0.14)	**0.44**	(0.14)	c	c	c	c
	Finland	-0.15	(0.01)	0.93	(0.01)	**0.40**	(0.05)	**0.41**	(0.05)	0.20	(0.12)	0.20	(0.12)
	Germany	0.80	(0.01)	1.35	(0.00)	**0.83**	(0.10)	**0.86**	(0.11)	**0.15**	(0.07)	**0.15**	(0.07)
	Greece	0.41	(0.01)	1.27	(0.01)	**0.41**	(0.03)	**0.39**	(0.03)	**0.24**	(0.08)	**0.26**	(0.08)
	Hungary	0.13	(0.01)	1.11	(0.01)	**0.58**	(0.05)	**0.68**	(0.05)	**0.34**	(0.12)	**0.34**	(0.12)
	Iceland	0.57	(0.01)	1.34	(0.00)	**0.89**	(0.16)	**0.81**	(0.16)	0.24	(0.13)	0.23	(0.13)
	Ireland	-0.08	(0.01)	0.96	(0.01)	**0.32**	(0.06)	**0.27**	(0.06)	0.06	(0.07)	0.06	(0.07)
	Italy	0.19	(0.01)	1.13	(0.01)	**0.33**	(0.05)	**0.39**	(0.05)	0.09	(0.05)	0.09	(0.05)
	Japan	-0.05	(0.01)	1.15	(0.01)	**0.58**	(0.06)	**0.46**	(0.06)	0.09	(0.08)	0.10	(0.08)
	Korea	0.68	(0.01)	1.35	(0.00)	**0.28**	(0.10)	**0.24**	(0.10)	**0.13**	(0.04)	**0.13**	(0.04)
	Mexico	0.11	(0.01)	1.05	(0.01)	**0.37**	(0.03)	**0.23**	(0.04)	**0.14**	(0.05)	**0.14**	(0.05)
	New Zealand	0.17	(0.01)	1.15	(0.01)	**0.29**	(0.05)	**0.26**	(0.05)	0.22	(0.16)	0.22	(0.16)
	Poland	0.80	(0.01)	1.35	(0.00)	**0.48**	(0.03)	**0.44**	(0.04)	-0.03	(0.06)	-0.02	(0.06)
	Portugal	0.72	(0.01)	1.34	(0.00)	**0.58**	(0.04)	**0.57**	(0.05)	-0.04	(0.14)	-0.04	(0.14)
	Slovak Republic	0.29	(0.01)	1.15	(0.01)	**0.42**	(0.04)	**0.42**	(0.04)	**0.13**	(0.05)	0.10	(0.05)
	Sweden	0.29	(0.01)	1.19	(0.01)	**0.44**	(0.15)	**0.39**	(0.14)	-0.15	(0.15)	-0.15	(0.16)
	Switzerland	0.46	(0.00)	1.30	(0.01)	**0.76**	(0.10)	**0.77**	(0.09)	0.04	(0.11)	0.04	(0.11)
	Turkey	0.57	(0.01)	1.34	(0.00)	**0.48**	(0.05)	**0.45**	(0.06)	**0.21**	(0.05)	**0.22**	(0.05)
	United States	0.39	(0.01)	1.27	(0.01)	**0.37**	(0.05)	**0.28**	(0.05)	-0.08	(0.14)	-0.14	(0.15)
	OECD average	***0.37***	***(0.00)***	***1.22***	***(0.00)***	***0.51***	***(0.02)***	***0.49***	***(0.02)***	***0.12***	***(0.02)***	***0.11***	***(0.02)***
Partner countries	Latvia	0.05	(0.01)	1.09	(0.01)	**0.34**	(0.04)	**0.33**	(0.04)	0.01	(0.06)	0.00	(0.06)
	Liechtenstein	0.75	(0.03)	1.34	(0.00)	c	c	c	c	c	c	c	c
	Russian Federation	0.54	(0.01)	1.34	(0.00)	**0.48**	(0.03)	**0.38**	(0.05)	**0.17**	(0.05)	**0.14**	(0.04)
	Serbia	1.17	(0.01)	1.35	(0.00)	**0.46**	(0.04)	**0.42**	(0.04)	0.18	(0.10)	**0.21**	(0.10)
	Thailand	0.19	(0.01)	1.07	(0.01)	**0.33**	(0.03)	**0.16**	(0.03)	**0.25**	(0.03)	**0.15**	(0.04)
	Tunisia	0.81	(0.01)	1.35	(0.00)	**0.29**	(0.05)	0.10	(0.05)	-0.04	(0.05)	0.01	(0.04)
	Uruguay	0.34	(0.01)	1.22	(0.01)	**0.27**	(0.05)	**0.31**	(0.06)	0.01	(0.04)	0.00	(0.04)
	United Kingdom[3]	0.41	(0.01)	1.27	(0.01)	**0.50**	(0.09)	**0.48**	(0.09)	c	c	c	c

Note: Statistically significant differences are marked in bold.
1. Results based on less than 3% of students in Denmark, Iceland, Korea and Sweden (see Table 2.2a).
2. Results based on less than 3% of students in Australia, Canada, Hungary, Iceland, New Zealand and Sweden (see Table 2.2a).
3. Response rate too low to ensure comparability.

Table 3.7

Factors influencing students' attitudes towards computers

Results based on students' self-reports

	Percentage of variance explained in students' attitudes towards computers by:					Total percentage of variance explained by these factors
	Student is female	Student has a computer at home	Student uses a computer frequently	Student taught him/herself how to use a computer	Combination of all these factors	
OECD countries						
Australia	2.2	0.3	2.1	2.2	1.3	8.2
Austria	1.7	0.4	1.5	2.1	1.0	6.8
Belgium	2.9	1.9	0.6	3.7	1.9	11.0
Canada	0.8	0.8	1.1	3.1	1.2	7.1
Czech Republic	7.2	2.0	0.7	2.0	5.1	17.1
Denmark	12.4	0.1	1.9	2.1	5.2	21.8
Finland	3.3	0.8	2.2	2.9	4.7	13.9
Germany	7.2	1.7	0.8	1.5	2.2	13.4
Greece	2.2	1.6	1.6	2.1	3.7	11.3
Hungary	4.7	3.5	1.3	1.8	4.1	15.4
Iceland	5.7	0.8	0.6	2.7	3.5	13.2
Ireland	0.6	0.9	1.0	2.5	0.6	5.5
Italy	2.7	0.7	1.5	2.6	1.5	8.9
Japan	0.0	2.9	1.6	4.7	0.8	10.0
Korea	1.4	0.1	0.7	1.8	0.0	4.0
Mexico	0.1	2.8	1.3	1.5	1.1	6.9
New Zealand	1.9	0.3	3.8	2.5	1.0	9.5
Poland	3.5	2.1	0.4	1.3	4.0	11.3
Portugal	3.8	4.6	1.0	1.7	2.5	13.6
Slovak Republic	6.7	2.5	1.3	0.9	3.4	14.7
Sweden	5.4	0.4	2.0	2.4	2.9	13.1
Switzerland	3.8	0.8	0.5	3.2	2.5	10.8
Turkey	1.3	3.1	1.7	2.2	3.4	11.7
United States	0.1	1.0	1.6	2.5	0.6	5.9
Partner countries						
Latvia	2.4	1.5	0.5	1.6	2.7	8.7
Liechtenstein	0.6	1.2	4.3	2.6	3.9	12.6
Russian Federation	1.0	3.0	0.7	0.6	2.4	7.7
Serbia	0.9	3.4	0.3	0.8	1.9	7.2
Thailand	0.4	3.2	1.4	1.3	1.3	7.6
Tunisia	0.0	1.5	0.0	2.9	1.5	5.9
Uruguay	0.9	1.2	0.4	0.8	1.2	4.5
United Kingdom[1]	2.3	1.2	2.1	2.5	1.0	9.1

1. Response rate too low to ensure comparability.

Table 3.8
Index of confidence in routine ICT tasks, by national quarters of the index
Results based on students' self-reports

		Index of confidence in routine ICT tasks											
		All students		Females		Males		Gender difference (M-F)		Bottom quarter		Second quarter	
		Mean index	S.E.	Mean index	S.E.	Mean index	S.E.	Dif.	S.E.	Mean index	S.E.	Mean index	S.E.
OECD countries	Australia	0.39	(0.01)	0.32	(0.01)	0.46	(0.01)	**0.13**	(0.02)	-0.70	(0.02)	0.63	(0.01)
	Austria	0.25	(0.02)	0.22	(0.02)	0.27	(0.03)	0.05	(0.04)	-1.02	(0.03)	0.39	(0.01)
	Belgium	0.11	(0.02)	-0.02	(0.02)	0.24	(0.02)	**0.25**	(0.03)	-1.22	(0.02)	0.06	(0.01)
	Canada	0.33	(0.01)	0.23	(0.01)	0.44	(0.01)	**0.21**	(0.01)	-0.78	(0.01)	0.48	(0.01)
	Czech Republic	0.20	(0.02)	-0.02	(0.03)	0.42	(0.02)	**0.43**	(0.03)	-1.08	(0.02)	0.27	(0.01)
	Denmark	0.15	(0.02)	-0.15	(0.02)	0.47	(0.02)	**0.62**	(0.03)	-1.09	(0.02)	0.09	(0.01)
	Finland	0.08	(0.01)	-0.30	(0.02)	0.46	(0.02)	**0.76**	(0.03)	-1.26	(0.02)	-0.05	(0.01)
	Germany	0.15	(0.02)	-0.07	(0.03)	0.38	(0.02)	**0.44**	(0.03)	-1.14	(0.02)	0.11	(0.01)
	Greece	-0.38	(0.03)	-0.55	(0.03)	-0.21	(0.03)	**0.34**	(0.03)	-1.77	(0.01)	-0.81	(0.01)
	Hungary	-0.12	(0.02)	-0.38	(0.03)	0.12	(0.03)	**0.49**	(0.05)	-1.55	(0.02)	-0.39	(0.01)
	Iceland	0.21	(0.02)	-0.09	(0.02)	0.49	(0.02)	**0.58**	(0.03)	-1.13	(0.02)	0.34	(0.02)
	Ireland	-0.03	(0.02)	-0.06	(0.03)	-0.01	(0.02)	0.05	(0.04)	-1.33	(0.02)	-0.28	(0.01)
	Italy	-0.20	(0.02)	-0.33	(0.03)	-0.06	(0.03)	**0.27**	(0.04)	-1.59	(0.02)	-0.49	(0.01)
	Japan	-0.80	(0.03)	-0.87	(0.03)	-0.73	(0.05)	**0.14**	(0.05)	-2.31	(0.04)	-1.20	(0.01)
	Korea	0.08	(0.01)	-0.07	(0.02)	0.19	(0.02)	**0.26**	(0.03)	-1.03	(0.01)	-0.16	(0.01)
	Mexico	-0.68	(0.05)	-0.74	(0.05)	-0.61	(0.05)	**0.12**	(0.04)	-2.23	(0.03)	-1.13	(0.01)
	New Zealand	0.20	(0.01)	0.11	(0.02)	0.29	(0.02)	**0.18**	(0.03)	-1.02	(0.02)	0.20	(0.01)
	Poland	0.04	(0.03)	-0.07	(0.03)	0.16	(0.03)	**0.23**	(0.04)	-1.54	(0.02)	0.08	(0.02)
	Portugal	0.21	(0.02)	0.12	(0.03)	0.30	(0.03)	**0.17**	(0.03)	-1.18	(0.02)	0.38	(0.02)
	Slovak Republic	-0.36	(0.03)	-0.64	(0.03)	-0.10	(0.04)	**0.54**	(0.05)	-1.95	(0.02)	-0.75	(0.01)
	Sweden	0.21	(0.01)	-0.05	(0.02)	0.48	(0.01)	**0.53**	(0.03)	-1.05	(0.02)	0.29	(0.01)
	Switzerland	-0.02	(0.02)	-0.26	(0.03)	0.20	(0.02)	**0.46**	(0.03)	-1.42	(0.02)	-0.27	(0.01)
	Turkey	-0.74	(0.05)	-0.84	(0.05)	-0.68	(0.06)	**0.16**	(0.06)	-2.26	(0.03)	-1.22	(0.01)
	United States	0.26	(0.02)	0.25	(0.02)	0.28	(0.02)	0.04	(0.03)	-0.99	(0.03)	0.42	(0.01)
	OECD average	*0.00*	*(0.00)*	*-0.16*	*(0.01)*	*0.14*	*(0.01)*	*0.31*	*(0.01)*	*-1.34*	*(0.00)*	*-0.11*	*(0.00)*
Partner countries	Latvia	-0.33	(0.03)	-0.60	(0.04)	-0.05	(0.03)	**0.54**	(0.04)	-1.81	(0.02)	-0.74	(0.01)
	Liechtenstein	0.24	(0.05)	0.06	(0.07)	0.42	(0.06)	**0.35**	(0.10)	-0.99	(0.07)	0.36	(0.04)
	Russian Federation	-0.57	(0.05)	-0.75	(0.05)	-0.41	(0.07)	**0.34**	(0.06)	-2.26	(0.04)	-1.04	(0.01)
	Serbia	-0.60	(0.03)	-0.72	(0.04)	-0.48	(0.04)	**0.24**	(0.04)	-2.04	(0.03)	-1.03	(0.01)
	Thailand	-0.91	(0.04)	-0.88	(0.04)	-0.95	(0.05)	-0.07	(0.05)	-2.19	(0.03)	-1.33	(0.01)
	Tunisia	-1.44	(0.06)	-1.57	(0.06)	-1.32	(0.06)	**0.26**	(0.05)	-3.02	(0.04)	-1.91	(0.01)
	Uruguay	-0.23	(0.03)	-0.27	(0.03)	-0.18	(0.04)	0.08	(0.04)	-1.86	(0.03)	-0.50	(0.01)
	United Kingdom[3]	0.25	(0.02)	0.16	(0.03)	0.34	(0.02)	**0.19**	(0.03)	-0.92	(0.03)	0.30	(0.02)

		Index of confidence in routine ICT tasks				Difference in index when students have a computer available to use at home[1]				Difference in index when students have a computer available to use at school[2]			
		Third quarter		Top quarter		Observed difference		Accounting for ESCS		Observed difference		Accounting for ESCS	
		Mean index	S.E.	Mean index	S.E.	Dif.	S.E.	Dif.	S.E.	Dif.	S.E.	Dif.	S.E.
OECD countries	Australia	0.81	(0.00)	0.82	(0.00)	**0.74**	(0.13)	**0.64**	(0.13)	**0.46**	(0.16)	**0.42**	(0.16)
	Austria	0.81	(0.00)	0.82	(0.00)	**1.14**	(0.10)	**0.98**	(0.10)	**0.30**	(0.07)	**0.25**	(0.06)
	Belgium	0.80	(0.00)	0.82	(0.00)	**1.20**	(0.08)	**1.05**	(0.08)	**0.29**	(0.05)	**0.26**	(0.04)
	Canada	0.81	(0.00)	0.82	(0.00)	**0.70**	(0.05)	**0.59**	(0.05)	**0.48**	(0.12)	**0.41**	(0.11)
	Czech Republic	0.80	(0.00)	0.82	(0.00)	**0.99**	(0.05)	**0.85**	(0.05)	**0.32**	(0.10)	**0.20**	(0.08)
	Denmark	0.80	(0.00)	0.82	(0.00)	**0.80**	(0.11)	**0.67**	(0.11)	c	c	c	c
	Finland	0.80	(0.00)	0.82	(0.00)	**0.83**	(0.05)	**0.76**	(0.05)	**0.49**	(0.09)	**0.50**	(0.08)
	Germany	0.80	(0.00)	0.82	(0.00)	**1.00**	(0.10)	**0.85**	(0.10)	0.13	(0.07)	0.09	(0.07)
	Greece	0.24	(0.02)	0.81	(0.00)	**1.01**	(0.04)	**0.86**	(0.04)	0.10	(0.08)	**0.15**	(0.06)
	Hungary	0.66	(0.01)	0.82	(0.00)	**1.05**	(0.04)	**0.86**	(0.05)	**0.35**	(0.16)	**0.31**	(0.13)
	Iceland	0.81	(0.00)	0.82	(0.00)	**0.85**	(0.19)	**0.76**	(0.19)	**0.33**	(0.14)	**0.31**	(0.14)
	Ireland	0.67	(0.01)	0.82	(0.00)	**0.79**	(0.06)	**0.60**	(0.06)	**0.15**	(0.06)	**0.16**	(0.06)
	Italy	0.46	(0.01)	0.81	(0.00)	**0.88**	(0.06)	**0.72**	(0.06)	**0.18**	(0.06)	**0.25**	(0.05)
	Japan	-0.41	(0.01)	0.71	(0.01)	**1.03**	(0.06)	**0.85**	(0.05)	0.11	(0.08)	0.13	(0.07)
	Korea	0.70	(0.01)	0.82	(0.00)	**0.76**	(0.10)	**0.54**	(0.11)	**0.09**	(0.04)	**0.10**	(0.04)
	Mexico	-0.17	(0.01)	0.81	(0.00)	**1.23**	(0.05)	**0.80**	(0.04)	**0.39**	(0.09)	**0.39**	(0.07)
	New Zealand	0.80	(0.00)	0.82	(0.00)	**0.64**	(0.05)	**0.48**	(0.06)	**0.31**	(0.12)	**0.27**	(0.13)
	Poland	0.80	(0.00)	0.82	(0.00)	**1.09**	(0.04)	**0.83**	(0.04)	0.03	(0.07)	0.07	(0.05)
	Portugal	0.81	(0.00)	0.82	(0.00)	**1.08**	(0.05)	**0.94**	(0.05)	-0.02	(0.14)	-0.04	(0.14)
	Slovak Republic	0.47	(0.01)	0.81	(0.00)	**1.23**	(0.05)	**1.02**	(0.05)	**0.40**	(0.07)	**0.26**	(0.07)
	Sweden	0.80	(0.00)	0.82	(0.00)	**0.58**	(0.11)	**0.43**	(0.11)	0.05	(0.09)	0.03	(0.08)
	Switzerland	0.80	(0.00)	0.82	(0.00)	**1.08**	(0.08)	**0.84**	(0.09)	0.16	(0.09)	0.18	(0.10)
	Turkey	-0.28	(0.02)	0.81	(0.00)	**1.08**	(0.05)	**0.70**	(0.07)	**0.35**	(0.08)	**0.39**	(0.06)
	United States	0.81	(0.00)	0.82	(0.00)	**0.72**	(0.05)	**0.51**	(0.06)	**0.58**	(0.13)	**0.48**	(0.12)
	OECD average	*0.61*	*(0.00)*	*0.81*	*(0.00)*	*0.93*	*(0.02)*	*0.75*	*(0.02)*	*0.26*	*(0.02)*	*0.24*	*(0.02)*
Partner countries	Latvia	0.41	(0.02)	0.81	(0.00)	**1.04**	(0.06)	**0.84**	(0.06)	0.08	(0.07)	0.11	(0.07)
	Liechtenstein	0.81	(0.00)	0.82	(0.00)	c	c	c	c	c	c	c	c
	Russian Federation	0.19	(0.02)	0.81	(0.00)	**1.36**	(0.05)	**1.07**	(0.06)	**0.33**	(0.08)	**0.25**	(0.07)
	Serbia	-0.12	(0.02)	0.81	(0.00)	**1.09**	(0.04)	**0.83**	(0.04)	0.01	(0.11)	0.15	(0.13)
	Thailand	-0.66	(0.01)	0.54	(0.02)	**1.06**	(0.05)	**0.70**	(0.05)	**0.79**	(0.15)	**0.47**	(0.22)
	Tunisia	-1.20	(0.01)	0.37	(0.03)	**1.24**	(0.07)	**0.76**	(0.06)	-0.08	(0.12)	0.07	(0.09)
	Uruguay	0.64	(0.01)	0.82	(0.00)	**1.10**	(0.04)	**0.84**	(0.06)	**0.16**	(0.06)	0.08	(0.05)
	United Kingdom[3]	0.81	(0.00)	0.82	(0.00)	**0.72**	(0.08)	**0.56**	(0.08)	c	c	c	c

Note: Statistically significant differences are marked in bold.

1. Results based on less than 3% of students in Denmark, Iceland, Korea and Sweden (see Table 2.2a).
2. Results based on less than 3% of students in Australia, Canada, Hungary, Iceland, New Zealand and Sweden (see Table 2.2a).
3. Response rate too low to ensure comparability.

Table 3.9

Percentage of students who are confident performing routine ICT tasks

Percentage of students reporting they can complete the following tasks either very well by themselves or with help from someone

		Start a computer game				Open a file				Create/edit a document				Scroll a document up and down a screen				Copy a file from a floppy disk			
		Yes		Yes with help		Yes		Yes with help		Yes		Yes with help		Yes		Yes with help		Yes		Yes with help	
		%	S.E.	%	S.E.	%	S.E.	%	S.E.	%	S.E.	%	S.E.	%	S.E.	%	S.E.	%	S.E.	%	S.E.
OECD countries	Australia	91	(0.4)	8	(0.3)	96	(0.2)	3	(0.2)	92	(0.3)	6	(0.2)	96	(0.2)	2	(0.2)	89	(0.5)	8	(0.4)
	Austria	92	(0.5)	6	(0.4)	96	(0.5)	3	(0.4)	91	(0.8)	7	(0.5)	82	(0.8)	9	(0.5)	87	(0.8)	8	(0.4)
	Belgium	87	(0.5)	9	(0.4)	94	(0.4)	4	(0.3)	88	(0.5)	9	(0.4)	87	(0.5)	8	(0.4)	79	(0.6)	15	(0.5)
	Canada	90	(0.3)	7	(0.2)	96	(0.2)	3	(0.2)	90	(0.3)	7	(0.3)	93	(0.3)	5	(0.2)	87	(0.4)	9	(0.3)
	Czech Republic	94	(0.4)	5	(0.4)	96	(0.3)	3	(0.2)	79	(0.8)	14	(0.6)	93	(0.5)	4	(0.4)	79	(0.8)	13	(0.6)
	Denmark	91	(0.5)	7	(0.4)	92	(0.5)	6	(0.4)	87	(0.6)	9	(0.5)	90	(0.5)	6	(0.4)	83	(0.8)	11	(0.6)
	Finland	90	(0.5)	8	(0.4)	93	(0.4)	5	(0.4)	76	(0.6)	17	(0.6)	88	(0.5)	7	(0.4)	73	(0.7)	18	(0.5)
	Germany	94	(0.4)	5	(0.3)	95	(0.4)	3	(0.3)	86	(0.7)	10	(0.6)	95	(0.4)	3	(0.3)	78	(0.8)	13	(0.6)
	Greece	83	(0.7)	13	(0.6)	79	(0.9)	15	(0.7)	79	(0.9)	15	(0.7)	87	(0.7)	9	(0.5)	56	(1.2)	24	(0.7)
	Hungary	86	(0.5)	12	(0.5)	90	(0.4)	7	(0.4)	83	(0.7)	13	(0.6)	85	(0.6)	11	(0.5)	72	(1.0)	17	(0.7)
	Iceland	90	(0.5)	6	(0.4)	90	(0.5)	5	(0.4)	86	(0.7)	9	(0.6)	91	(0.5)	4	(0.4)	77	(0.6)	14	(0.6)
	Ireland	90	(0.5)	8	(0.4)	91	(0.6)	6	(0.4)	82	(0.8)	12	(0.5)	90	(0.6)	6	(0.4)	68	(0.9)	18	(0.6)
	Italy	86	(0.7)	10	(0.5)	88	(0.6)	9	(0.5)	62	(0.8)	22	(0.6)	84	(0.6)	10	(0.4)	75	(0.9)	15	(0.6)
	Japan	67	(0.9)	18	(0.8)	80	(0.8)	13	(0.6)	72	(0.9)	20	(0.7)	62	(1.0)	17	(0.7)	45	(1.2)	30	(0.8)
	Korea	89	(0.6)	9	(0.5)	94	(0.4)	5	(0.3)	74	(0.7)	20	(0.6)	91	(0.5)	6	(0.4)	79	(0.7)	15	(0.5)
	Mexico	56	(1.4)	31	(1.0)	71	(1.3)	20	(1.1)	62	(1.6)	24	(1.1)	74	(1.2)	17	(0.8)	61	(1.4)	25	(0.9)
	New Zealand	89	(0.5)	8	(0.5)	93	(0.4)	5	(0.3)	89	(0.5)	7	(0.5)	93	(0.4)	4	(0.3)	75	(0.8)	15	(0.6)
	Poland	88	(0.6)	10	(0.5)	89	(0.6)	8	(0.6)	81	(0.8)	13	(0.6)	87	(0.7)	9	(0.5)	77	(1.1)	15	(0.7)
	Portugal	87	(0.7)	10	(0.6)	90	(0.6)	7	(0.4)	85	(0.8)	10	(0.7)	91	(0.6)	6	(0.4)	85	(0.9)	11	(0.7)
	Slovak Republic	82	(0.9)	13	(0.6)	84	(0.7)	11	(0.6)	63	(1.1)	20	(0.7)	85	(0.7)	9	(0.5)	63	(1.2)	18	(0.7)
	Sweden	91	(0.4)	7	(0.4)	91	(0.5)	7	(0.4)	87	(0.6)	9	(0.5)	88	(0.5)	6	(0.4)	81	(0.7)	13	(0.5)
	Switzerland	86	(0.5)	10	(0.4)	93	(0.5)	5	(0.4)	84	(0.8)	11	(0.5)	78	(0.8)	11	(0.6)	76	(0.9)	15	(0.7)
	Turkey	78	(1.3)	17	(1.0)	74	(1.4)	18	(1.1)	47	(1.7)	35	(1.2)	68	(1.6)	19	(1.0)	60	(1.8)	25	(1.4)
	United States	89	(0.5)	7	(0.4)	93	(0.4)	5	(0.3)	88	(0.6)	8	(0.5)	94	(0.4)	4	(0.3)	85	(0.6)	10	(0.5)
	OECD average	***86***	***(0.1)***	***10***	***(0.1)***	***90***	***(0.1)***	***7***	***(0.1)***	***80***	***(0.2)***	***13***	***(0.1)***	***87***	***(0.1)***	***8***	***(0.1)***	***75***	***(0.2)***	***16***	***(0.1)***
Partner countries	Latvia	79	(0.9)	15	(0.9)	82	(1.0)	12	(0.7)	71	(1.5)	21	(1.1)	75	(1.0)	15	(0.7)	62	(1.4)	22	(1.2)
	Liechtenstein	92	(1.5)	6	(1.2)	97	(1.1)	2	(0.7)	91	(1.4)	6	(1.2)	81	(2.2)	11	(1.8)	88	(1.5)	9	(1.4)
	Russian Federation	73	(1.2)	18	(0.7)	76	(1.5)	13	(0.7)	57	(1.7)	22	(0.8)	71	(1.5)	15	(0.9)	54	(1.5)	21	(0.8)
	Serbia	87	(0.7)	9	(0.5)	77	(1.0)	14	(0.7)	58	(1.2)	24	(0.9)	84	(0.8)	9	(0.6)	52	(1.5)	26	(1.0)
	Thailand	65	(1.3)	26	(1.1)	68	(1.3)	24	(0.9)	46	(1.4)	37	(1.0)	64	(1.2)	25	(0.9)	45	(1.6)	35	(1.1)
	Tunisia	52	(1.4)	29	(1.2)	43	(1.8)	26	(1.2)	41	(1.7)	29	(1.2)	50	(1.7)	24	(1.1)	40	(1.9)	27	(1.1)
	Uruguay	72	(1.0)	18	(0.8)	84	(0.8)	11	(0.7)	72	(0.8)	18	(0.6)	79	(0.9)	12	(0.8)	76	(1.2)	14	(0.9)
	United Kingdom[1]	90	(0.6)	8	(0.5)	95	(0.4)	3	(0.4)	91	(0.6)	7	(0.5)	95	(0.4)	3	(0.3)	76	(1.0)	16	(0.8)

		Save a computer document or file				Print a computer document or file				Delete a computer document or file				Move files from one place to another on a computer				Play computer games				Draw pictures using a mouse			
		Yes		Yes with help		Yes		Yes with help		Yes		Yes with help		Yes		Yes with help		Yes		Yes with help		Yes		Yes with help	
		%	S.E.	%	S.E.	%	S.E.	%	S.E.	%	S.E.	%	S.E.	%	S.E.	%	S.E.	%	S.E.	%	S.E.	%	S.E.	%	S.E.
OECD countries	Australia	97	(0.2)	2	(0.2)	97	(0.2)	2	(0.2)	96	(0.2)	3	(0.2)	89	(0.4)	8	(0.3)	93	(0.3)	6	(0.2)	89	(0.4)	8	(0.3)
	Austria	95	(0.7)	3	(0.4)	95	(0.5)	3	(0.3)	95	(0.6)	3	(0.4)	86	(0.8)	9	(0.6)	93	(0.5)	5	(0.4)	88	(0.6)	8	(0.5)
	Belgium	91	(0.5)	6	(0.4)	93	(0.5)	4	(0.3)	92	(0.5)	5	(0.4)	82	(0.6)	13	(0.4)	90	(0.5)	6	(0.4)	84	(0.5)	11	(0.4)
	Canada	97	(0.2)	3	(0.2)	98	(0.1)	2	(0.1)	97	(0.2)	2	(0.2)	88	(0.4)	9	(0.3)	95	(0.3)	4	(0.2)	89	(0.3)	7	(0.3)
	Czech Republic	92	(0.6)	6	(0.4)	88	(0.7)	9	(0.6)	93	(0.4)	5	(0.3)	82	(0.9)	13	(0.7)	96	(0.4)	3	(0.3)	94	(0.4)	4	(0.3)
	Denmark	96	(0.4)	3	(0.3)	96	(0.3)	3	(0.3)	93	(0.5)	5	(0.4)	76	(0.8)	17	(0.7)	94	(0.5)	4	(0.4)	86	(0.6)	9	(0.5)
	Finland	91	(0.5)	6	(0.3)	93	(0.4)	5	(0.3)	90	(0.4)	7	(0.3)	70	(0.6)	22	(0.5)	94	(0.3)	5	(0.3)	94	(0.4)	4	(0.3)
	Germany	86	(0.7)	9	(0.5)	91	(0.5)	6	(0.4)	92	(0.6)	5	(0.4)	79	(0.9)	14	(0.7)	94	(0.4)	4	(0.3)	87	(0.7)	9	(0.5)
	Greece	74	(1.2)	16	(0.8)	70	(1.0)	20	(0.7)	79	(0.9)	14	(0.7)	62	(1.2)	27	(0.9)	88	(0.7)	8	(0.6)	77	(0.8)	16	(0.7)
	Hungary	87	(0.6)	10	(0.5)	70	(0.9)	20	(0.7)	81	(0.7)	13	(0.6)	66	(1.0)	23	(0.9)	90	(0.5)	8	(0.5)	86	(0.5)	9	(0.4)
	Iceland	94	(0.4)	4	(0.4)	95	(0.4)	3	(0.3)	94	(0.5)	4	(0.3)	85	(0.7)	11	(0.5)	95	(0.4)	3	(0.3)	93	(0.5)	4	(0.4)
	Ireland	91	(0.5)	6	(0.4)	91	(0.6)	5	(0.4)	89	(0.6)	7	(0.5)	66	(0.9)	23	(0.8)	95	(0.4)	4	(0.3)	91	(0.4)	7	(0.5)
	Italy	85	(0.8)	10	(0.6)	85	(0.7)	9	(0.6)	84	(0.7)	10	(0.5)	74	(0.8)	17	(0.7)	90	(0.5)	7	(0.4)	81	(0.7)	13	(0.5)
	Japan	75	(1.1)	16	(0.8)	69	(1.2)	21	(0.9)	67	(1.1)	20	(0.7)	38	(1.3)	35	(0.8)	70	(1.1)	18	(0.8)	77	(0.8)	14	(0.5)
	Korea	96	(0.3)	3	(0.2)	96	(0.4)	3	(0.3)	97	(0.3)	2	(0.2)	88	(0.5)	9	(0.5)	93	(0.5)	5	(0.4)	80	(0.6)	16	(0.5)
	Mexico	73	(1.4)	18	(0.9)	70	(1.5)	20	(1.1)	70	(1.4)	19	(1.1)	57	(1.7)	29	(1.1)	21	(0.9)	7	(0.5)	64	(1.3)	24	(0.9)
	New Zealand	95	(0.4)	4	(0.3)	95	(0.4)	3	(0.3)	93	(0.5)	5	(0.4)	84	(0.5)	12	(0.5)	5	(0.3)	1	(0.2)	88	(0.6)	9	(0.5)
	Poland	82	(0.8)	12	(0.6)	77	(1.0)	14	(0.6)	82	(0.8)	12	(0.5)	80	(0.8)	13	(0.6)	8	(0.4)	2	(0.2)	87	(0.6)	9	(0.5)
	Portugal	90	(0.6)	7	(0.5)	91	(0.7)	6	(0.5)	89	(0.7)	8	(0.6)	81	(1.0)	14	(0.7)	6	(0.5)	2	(0.3)	88	(0.7)	9	(0.5)
	Slovak Republic	76	(0.9)	14	(0.6)	67	(1.1)	18	(0.8)	78	(0.9)	13	(0.6)	66	(1.1)	19	(0.6)	8	(0.4)	2	(0.3)	85	(0.6)	10	(0.4)
	Sweden	95	(0.4)	4	(0.3)	95	(0.4)	3	(0.3)	94	(0.4)	4	(0.4)	82	(0.6)	13	(0.6)	4	(0.3)	1	(0.2)	92	(0.4)	5	(0.3)
	Switzerland	88	(0.5)	8	(0.5)	92	(0.4)	5	(0.3)	92	(0.5)	5	(0.4)	77	(0.9)	15	(0.6)	89	(0.5)	8	(0.4)	83	(0.7)	10	(0.5)
	Turkey	60	(1.8)	24	(1.2)	53	(1.8)	30	(1.4)	64	(1.7)	22	(1.2)	61	(1.6)	25	(1.1)	13	(1.1)	4	(0.4)	76	(1.4)	15	(1.1)
	United States	94	(0.4)	4	(0.3)	94	(0.4)	4	(0.3)	93	(0.4)	5	(0.3)	83	(0.6)	12	(0.5)	4	(0.3)	1	(0.1)	87	(0.5)	8	(0.4)
	OECD average	***88***	***(0.1)***	***8***	***(0.1)***	***86***	***(0.2)***	***9***	***(0.1)***	***88***	***(0.1)***	***8***	***(0.1)***	***76***	***(0.2)***	***17***	***(0.1)***	***65***	***(0.1)***	***5***	***(0.1)***	***85***	***(0.1)***	***10***	***(0.1)***
Partner countries	Latvia	75	(1.1)	15	(0.8)	74	(1.4)	17	(1.2)	80	(1.1)	12	(0.8)	61	(1.3)	24	(1.1)	8	(0.6)	3	(0.5)	91	(0.8)	6	(0.5)
	Liechtenstein	93	(1.5)	4	(1.1)	94	(1.2)	4	(0.9)	94	(1.4)	4	(1.2)	85	(2.0)	11	(1.6)	96	(1.1)	2	(0.8)	89	(2.0)	9	(1.9)
	Russian Federation	73	(1.5)	15	(0.8)	68	(1.5)	17	(0.8)	73	(1.4)	15	(0.8)	62	(1.6)	20	(0.8)	8	(0.5)	5	(0.5)	82	(1.2)	9	(0.6)
	Serbia	70	(1.3)	17	(0.9)	58	(1.1)	25	(0.8)	71	(1.2)	16	(0.8)	57	(1.2)	26	(0.8)	7	(0.6)	3	(0.4)	88	(0.9)	6	(0.5)
	Thailand	60	(1.5)	27	(1.0)	63	(1.1)	26	(1.0)	59	(1.2)	29	(0.9)	36	(1.3)	43	(1.0)	22	(0.8)	4	(0.3)	73	(1.0)	19	(0.7)
	Tunisia	41	(1.9)	29	(1.0)	45	(1.7)	26	(1.1)	42	(1.8)	27	(1.2)	37	(1.9)	25	(1.1)	21	(1.0)	9	(0.7)	55	(1.5)	21	(1.2)
	Uruguay	84	(0.8)	10	(0.6)	80	(0.8)	12	(0.7)	81	(0.9)	12	(0.7)	71	(1.0)	18	(0.8)	9	(0.5)	2	(0.3)	85	(0.9)	9	(0.6)
	United Kingdom[1]	96	(0.4)	3	(0.3)	96	(0.4)	3	(0.4)	94	(0.5)	4	(0.5)	84	(1.0)	12	(0.9)	94	(0.5)	5	(0.4)	91	(0.7)	7	(0.6)

1. Response rate too low to ensure comparability.

Table 3.10
Index of confidence in ICT Internet tasks, by national quarters of the index
Results based on students' self-reports

		Index of confidence in ICT Internet tasks											
		All students		Females		Males		Gender difference (M-F)		Bottom quarter		Second quarter	
		Mean index	S.E.	Mean index	S.E.	Mean index	S.E.	Dif.	S.E.	Mean index	S.E.	Mean index	S.E.
OECD countries	Australia	0.41	(0.01)	0.32	(0.02)	0.49	(0.01)	**0.17**	(0.02)	-0.69	(0.01)	0.56	(0.01)
	Austria	0.24	(0.02)	0.20	(0.02)	0.29	(0.03)	**0.09**	(0.03)	-0.93	(0.03)	0.16	(0.01)
	Belgium	0.23	(0.02)	0.13	(0.02)	0.33	(0.02)	**0.20**	(0.03)	-1.09	(0.02)	0.27	(0.01)
	Canada	0.57	(0.01)	0.52	(0.01)	0.62	(0.01)	**0.09**	(0.01)	-0.33	(0.01)	0.85	(0.00)
	Czech Republic	0.06	(0.02)	-0.18	(0.02)	0.30	(0.02)	**0.48**	(0.03)	-1.18	(0.02)	-0.17	(0.01)
	Denmark	0.11	(0.02)	-0.24	(0.02)	0.47	(0.02)	**0.71**	(0.02)	-1.07	(0.01)	-0.17	(0.01)
	Finland	0.06	(0.01)	-0.33	(0.02)	0.45	(0.01)	**0.79**	(0.02)	-1.08	(0.01)	-0.25	(0.01)
	Germany	0.13	(0.02)	-0.07	(0.02)	0.35	(0.02)	**0.42**	(0.02)	-1.15	(0.02)	-0.08	(0.01)
	Greece	-0.45	(0.03)	-0.65	(0.03)	-0.23	(0.03)	**0.42**	(0.03)	-1.73	(0.02)	-0.83	(0.01)
	Hungary	-0.44	(0.02)	-0.65	(0.03)	-0.25	(0.03)	**0.40**	(0.04)	-1.73	(0.02)	-0.78	(0.01)
	Iceland	0.41	(0.01)	0.21	(0.02)	0.60	(0.02)	**0.39**	(0.02)	-0.66	(0.02)	0.54	(0.01)
	Ireland	-0.37	(0.02)	-0.47	(0.03)	-0.27	(0.03)	**0.20**	(0.04)	-1.62	(0.02)	-0.72	(0.01)
	Italy	-0.39	(0.02)	-0.58	(0.03)	-0.18	(0.03)	**0.40**	(0.04)	-1.82	(0.02)	-0.76	(0.01)
	Japan	-0.71	(0.03)	-0.75	(0.03)	-0.67	(0.04)	0.08	(0.05)	-2.21	(0.03)	-1.06	(0.01)
	Korea	0.77	(0.01)	0.76	(0.01)	0.78	(0.01)	0.02	(0.01)	0.44	(0.02)	0.87	(0.00)
	Mexico	-0.54	(0.04)	-0.61	(0.05)	-0.47	(0.05)	**0.14**	(0.04)	-2.05	(0.04)	-0.92	(0.01)
	New Zealand	0.31	(0.01)	0.22	(0.02)	0.41	(0.02)	**0.18**	(0.03)	-0.86	(0.02)	0.37	(0.01)
	Poland	-0.17	(0.03)	-0.38	(0.03)	0.03	(0.03)	**0.40**	(0.04)	-1.57	(0.02)	-0.56	(0.01)
	Portugal	-0.22	(0.03)	-0.46	(0.04)	0.05	(0.03)	**0.50**	(0.04)	-1.62	(0.02)	-0.61	(0.01)
	Slovak Republic	-0.81	(0.03)	-1.06	(0.03)	-0.59	(0.04)	**0.48**	(0.04)	-2.29	(0.03)	-1.19	(0.01)
	Sweden	0.39	(0.01)	0.20	(0.02)	0.57	(0.01)	**0.37**	(0.02)	-0.68	(0.02)	0.48	(0.01)
	Switzerland	0.09	(0.02)	-0.09	(0.02)	0.26	(0.03)	**0.35**	(0.03)	-1.18	(0.03)	-0.10	(0.01)
	Turkey	-0.55	(0.04)	-0.76	(0.05)	-0.42	(0.05)	**0.34**	(0.05)	-2.06	(0.04)	-0.94	(0.01)
	United States	0.39	(0.01)	0.37	(0.02)	0.42	(0.02)	0.05	(0.03)	-0.72	(0.02)	0.54	(0.01)
	OECD average	*0.00*	*(0.00)*	*-0.17*	*(0.01)*	*0.15*	*(0.01)*	*0.32*	*(0.01)*	*-1.23*	*(0.00)*	*-0.17*	*(0.00)*
Partner countries	Latvia	-0.53	(0.03)	-0.80	(0.04)	-0.25	(0.04)	**0.56**	(0.04)	-1.87	(0.02)	-0.91	(0.01)
	Liechtenstein	0.48	(0.04)	0.37	(0.06)	0.58	(0.05)	**0.21**	(0.08)	-0.50	(0.06)	0.65	(0.04)
	Russian Federation	-1.27	(0.05)	-1.55	(0.05)	-1.00	(0.07)	**0.55**	(0.06)	-2.90	(0.04)	-1.78	(0.01)
	Serbia	-0.93	(0.03)	-1.12	(0.04)	-0.72	(0.04)	**0.40**	(0.05)	-2.47	(0.03)	-1.41	(0.01)
	Thailand	-1.36	(0.04)	-1.39	(0.05)	-1.33	(0.05)	0.06	(0.07)	-2.96	(0.03)	-1.60	(0.01)
	Tunisia	-1.38	(0.04)	-1.53	(0.05)	-1.25	(0.05)	**0.28**	(0.05)	-2.93	(0.04)	-1.71	(0.01)
	Uruguay	-0.46	(0.03)	-0.59	(0.03)	-0.33	(0.04)	**0.26**	(0.05)	-2.08	(0.03)	-0.86	(0.01)
	United Kingdom[3]	0.28	(0.02)	0.15	(0.03)	0.40	(0.02)	**0.25**	(0.03)	-0.88	(0.02)	0.23	(0.02)

		Index of confidence in ICT Internet tasks				Difference in index when students have a computer available to use at home[1]				Difference in index when students have a computer available to use at school[2]			
		Third quarter		Top quarter		Observed difference		Accounting for ESCS		Observed difference		Accounting for ESCS	
		Mean index	S.E.	Mean index	S.E.	Dif.	S.E.	Dif.	S.E.	Dif.	S.E.	Dif.	S.E.
OECD countries	Australia	0.87	(0.00)	0.88	(0.00)	**0.79**	(0.11)	**0.66**	(0.11)	0.30	(0.20)	0.25	(0.20)
	Austria	0.87	(0.00)	0.88	(0.00)	**0.72**	(0.11)	**0.52**	(0.11)	**0.20**	(0.08)	0.13	(0.07)
	Belgium	0.87	(0.00)	0.88	(0.00)	**1.04**	(0.09)	**0.87**	(0.09)	**0.29**	(0.05)	**0.26**	(0.04)
	Canada	0.87	(0.00)	0.88	(0.00)	**0.65**	(0.04)	**0.57**	(0.04)	**0.42**	(0.10)	**0.36**	(0.10)
	Czech Republic	0.73	(0.01)	0.88	(0.00)	**0.63**	(0.04)	**0.41**	(0.04)	**0.46**	(0.09)	**0.34**	(0.08)
	Denmark	0.80	(0.01)	0.88	(0.00)	**0.61**	(0.10)	**0.53**	(0.09)	c	c	c	c
	Finland	0.69	(0.01)	0.88	(0.00)	**0.61**	(0.05)	**0.55**	(0.05)	**0.39**	(0.09)	**0.39**	(0.08)
	Germany	0.87	(0.00)	0.88	(0.00)	**0.90**	(0.08)	**0.71**	(0.09)	0.09	(0.08)	0.04	(0.07)
	Greece	-0.10	(0.01)	0.87	(0.00)	**0.77**	(0.04)	**0.59**	(0.04)	**0.14**	(0.06)	**0.18**	(0.05)
	Hungary	-0.10	(0.01)	0.87	(0.00)	**0.75**	(0.04)	**0.46**	(0.04)	**0.36**	(0.15)	**0.32**	(0.13)
	Iceland	0.87	(0.00)	0.88	(0.00)	**0.75**	(0.14)	**0.65**	(0.14)	0.16	(0.12)	0.15	(0.12)
	Ireland	-0.02	(0.01)	0.88	(0.00)	**0.75**	(0.05)	**0.52**	(0.06)	0.06	(0.08)	0.07	(0.08)
	Italy	0.17	(0.01)	0.88	(0.00)	**0.98**	(0.05)	**0.69**	(0.05)	0.02	(0.06)	**0.12**	(0.05)
	Japan	-0.32	(0.01)	0.76	(0.01)	**1.01**	(0.05)	**0.82**	(0.05)	0.03	(0.08)	0.05	(0.07)
	Korea	0.88	(0.00)	0.89	(0.00)	**0.33**	(0.07)	**0.28**	(0.07)	0.03	(0.02)	**0.03**	(0.02)
	Mexico	-0.07	(0.01)	0.87	(0.00)	**1.02**	(0.05)	**0.53**	(0.04)	0.14	(0.09)	0.12	(0.07)
	New Zealand	0.87	(0.00)	0.88	(0.00)	**0.75**	(0.05)	**0.61**	(0.05)	0.11	(0.11)	0.03	(0.11)
	Poland	0.56	(0.01)	0.88	(0.00)	**0.83**	(0.04)	**0.50**	(0.05)	0.05	(0.08)	0.10	(0.07)
	Portugal	0.50	(0.02)	0.88	(0.00)	**0.90**	(0.05)	**0.53**	(0.05)	0.12	(0.19)	0.09	(0.17)
	Slovak Republic	-0.46	(0.01)	0.68	(0.01)	**0.69**	(0.05)	**0.33**	(0.05)	**0.40**	(0.07)	**0.26**	(0.07)
	Sweden	0.87	(0.00)	0.88	(0.00)	**0.46**	(0.10)	**0.39**	(0.10)	0.04	(0.07)	0.01	(0.06)
	Switzerland	0.78	(0.01)	0.88	(0.00)	**0.95**	(0.08)	**0.74**	(0.08)	0.11	(0.07)	0.12	(0.08)
	Turkey	-0.09	(0.02)	0.88	(0.00)	**0.84**	(0.06)	**0.39**	(0.07)	-0.01	(0.09)	0.02	(0.06)
	United States	0.87	(0.00)	0.88	(0.00)	**0.72**	(0.04)	**0.54**	(0.05)	**0.33**	(0.11)	**0.23**	(0.10)
	OECD average	*0.51*	*(0.00)*	*0.87*	*(0.00)*	*0.76*	*(0.01)*	*0.56*	*(0.01)*	*0.18*	*(0.02)*	*0.16*	*(0.02)*
Partner countries	Latvia	-0.18	(0.01)	0.83	(0.01)	**0.74**	(0.04)	**0.54**	(0.05)	-0.04	(0.08)	-0.04	(0.07)
	Liechtenstein	0.87	(0.00)	0.88	(0.00)	c	c	c	c	c	c	c	c
	Russian Federation	-0.93	(0.01)	0.52	(0.02)	**1.30**	(0.05)	**1.01**	(0.05)	-0.05	(0.07)	**-0.12**	(0.06)
	Serbia	-0.56	(0.01)	0.73	(0.01)	**1.23**	(0.05)	**0.96**	(0.04)	**-0.29**	(0.12)	-0.15	(0.11)
	Thailand	-0.96	(0.01)	0.09	(0.02)	**1.26**	(0.06)	**0.68**	(0.05)	**1.05**	(0.11)	**0.62**	(0.19)
	Tunisia	-1.04	(0.01)	0.15	(0.03)	**0.90**	(0.07)	**0.51**	(0.07)	0.01	(0.09)	0.12	(0.06)
	Uruguay	0.21	(0.01)	0.88	(0.00)	**1.19**	(0.05)	**0.79**	(0.05)	**0.12**	(0.06)	0.00	(0.05)
	United Kingdom[3]	0.87	(0.00)	0.88	(0.00)	**0.65**	(0.09)	**0.54**	(0.10)	c	c	c	c

Note: Statistically significant differences are marked in bold.
1. Results based on less than 3% of students in Denmark, Iceland, Korea and Sweden (see Table 2.2a).
2. Results based on less than 3% of students in Australia, Canada, Hungary, Iceland, New Zealand and Sweden (see Table 2.2a).
3. Response rate too low to ensure comparability.

Table 3.11

Percentage of students who are confident performing Internet tasks

Percentage of students reporting they can complete the following tasks either very well by themselves or with help from someone

		Get onto the Internet				Copy or download files from the Internet				Attach a file to an e-mail message				Download music from the Internet				Write and send e-mails			
		Yes		Yes with help		Yes		Yes with help		Yes		Yes with help		Yes		Yes with help		Yes		Yes with help	
		%	S.E.	%	S.E.	%	S.E.	%	S.E.	%	S.E.	%	S.E.	%	S.E.	%	S.E.	%	S.E.	%	S.E.
OECD countries	Australia	97	(0.2)	2	(0.2)	86	(0.5)	10	(0.4)	76	(0.7)	17	(0.5)	79	(0.5)	15	(0.4)	92	(0.3)	5	(0.2)
	Austria	96	(0.5)	3	(0.3)	87	(0.7)	9	(0.5)	67	(1.2)	21	(0.9)	71	(0.8)	19	(0.8)	88	(0.7)	7	(0.4)
	Belgium	92	(0.5)	5	(0.3)	79	(0.6)	14	(0.4)	69	(0.7)	19	(0.5)	75	(0.6)	15	(0.4)	87	(0.5)	8	(0.4)
	Canada	98	(0.1)	1	(0.1)	91	(0.3)	6	(0.2)	81	(0.5)	13	(0.4)	91	(0.3)	6	(0.3)	96	(0.2)	2	(0.1)
	Switzerland	90	(0.6)	6	(0.4)	74	(1.0)	19	(0.8)	61	(1.0)	26	(0.8)	62	(1.1)	24	(0.7)	85	(0.7)	10	(0.6)
	Czech Republic	99	(0.1)	0	(0.1)	69	(0.9)	19	(0.7)	64	(1.0)	22	(0.8)	64	(0.8)	19	(0.6)	92	(0.5)	5	(0.4)
	Germany	98	(0.2)	1	(0.2)	67	(0.7)	21	(0.6)	58	(0.8)	28	(0.7)	60	(0.8)	22	(0.6)	94	(0.4)	4	(0.3)
	Denmark	93	(0.5)	4	(0.3)	78	(0.7)	15	(0.6)	62	(0.9)	23	(0.7)	68	(0.8)	20	(0.7)	86	(0.7)	8	(0.5)
	Finland	77	(1.2)	16	(1.0)	52	(1.1)	32	(0.8)	36	(1.2)	34	(0.7)	62	(1.0)	24	(0.8)	55	(1.1)	27	(0.8)
	Greece	81	(0.9)	12	(0.5)	51	(1.0)	31	(0.8)	35	(1.1)	36	(0.9)	50	(0.9)	32	(0.7)	67	(1.0)	19	(0.7)
	Hungary	97	(0.3)	2	(0.2)	85	(0.6)	11	(0.5)	78	(0.6)	14	(0.6)	79	(0.7)	16	(0.6)	94	(0.4)	4	(0.4)
	Ireland	87	(0.8)	8	(0.6)	57	(1.0)	25	(0.8)	36	(1.0)	30	(0.9)	55	(1.0)	25	(0.7)	70	(1.0)	17	(0.8)
	Iceland	79	(0.9)	11	(0.5)	61	(0.9)	22	(0.6)	41	(0.9)	27	(0.6)	56	(1.0)	23	(0.6)	60	(1.0)	21	(0.6)
	Italy	73	(1.0)	15	(0.6)	44	(1.1)	29	(0.7)	38	(1.2)	27	(0.8)	35	(1.0)	32	(0.7)	57	(1.0)	21	(0.7)
	Japan	99	(0.1)	1	(0.1)	97	(0.3)	3	(0.2)	96	(0.3)	3	(0.3)	97	(0.3)	2	(0.2)	97	(0.2)	2	(0.2)
	Korea	64	(1.6)	22	(0.9)	52	(1.8)	30	(1.1)	39	(1.5)	36	(0.8)	49	(1.3)	33	(1.1)	54	(1.7)	26	(1.0)
	Mexico	95	(0.4)	3	(0.3)	82	(0.6)	13	(0.5)	71	(0.9)	19	(0.6)	76	(0.7)	16	(0.6)	90	(0.6)	6	(0.4)
	New Zealand	84	(0.9)	10	(0.6)	66	(1.3)	22	(0.8)	51	(1.2)	29	(0.8)	57	(0.9)	26	(0.7)	68	(1.1)	20	(0.7)
	Poland	88	(0.7)	8	(0.5)	54	(1.2)	29	(0.8)	52	(1.2)	29	(0.9)	56	(1.2)	26	(0.8)	67	(1.0)	20	(0.8)
	Portugal	64	(1.2)	15	(0.7)	46	(1.3)	27	(0.7)	27	(1.0)	29	(0.7)	39	(0.9)	28	(0.7)	54	(1.3)	21	(0.7)
	Slovak Republic	99	(0.2)	1	(0.2)	84	(0.7)	12	(0.6)	74	(0.8)	18	(0.6)	78	(0.9)	15	(0.8)	96	(0.4)	3	(0.3)
	Sweden	94	(0.5)	4	(0.3)	79	(1.0)	14	(0.8)	62	(1.1)	22	(0.6)	64	(0.7)	21	(0.5)	85	(0.9)	9	(0.6)
	Turkey	69	(2.0)	19	(1.2)	48	(1.7)	32	(1.1)	39	(1.4)	35	(1.1)	60	(1.2)	25	(0.9)	50	(2.0)	29	(1.4)
	United States	95	(0.4)	3	(0.3)	86	(0.6)	10	(0.4)	74	(0.8)	18	(0.7)	82	(0.6)	12	(0.4)	91	(0.5)	5	(0.3)
	OECD average	***88***	***(0.2)***	***7***	***(0.1)***	***70***	***(0.2)***	***19***	***(0.1)***	***58***	***(0.2)***	***24***	***(0.1)***	***66***	***(0.2)***	***21***	***(0.1)***	***79***	***(0.2)***	***12***	***(0.1)***
Partner countries	Latvia	71	(1.8)	16	(0.9)	46	(1.3)	30	(0.8)	34	(1.5)	34	(1.0)	51	(1.4)	27	(0.9)	66	(1.6)	19	(0.8)
	Liechtenstein	98	(0.7)	2	(0.8)	91	(1.7)	7	(1.3)	83	(2.0)	11	(1.7)	77	(2.3)	16	(1.9)	96	(1.1)	2	(0.8)
	Russian Federation	40	(1.8)	23	(1.0)	32	(1.7)	25	(1.0)	20	(1.2)	27	(1.0)	34	(1.5)	24	(0.9)	32	(1.4)	25	(0.7)
	Serbia	42	(1.2)	25	(0.8)	35	(1.2)	29	(0.9)	28	(1.1)	32	(0.8)	45	(1.1)	26	(0.7)	47	(1.2)	25	(0.8)
	Thailand	46	(1.7)	32	(1.1)	21	(1.2)	40	(1.2)	14	(1.0)	39	(1.0)	25	(1.1)	38	(1.0)	28	(1.4)	34	(1.0)
	Tunisia	31	(1.6)	27	(1.0)	24	(1.2)	30	(1.0)	20	(1.0)	30	(1.1)	36	(1.4)	29	(1.1)	37	(1.3)	27	(1.0)
	Uruguay	68	(1.1)	18	(0.8)	56	(1.2)	25	(1.0)	44	(1.2)	29	(0.7)	51	(1.1)	27	(0.8)	60	(1.2)	20	(0.8)
	United Kingdom[1]	97	(0.3)	2	(0.3)	77	(0.9)	17	(0.9)	70	(1.2)	20	(0.9)	74	(1.1)	16	(0.9)	90	(0.8)	6	(0.6)

1. Response rate too low to ensure comparability.

Table 3.12

Index of confidence in high-level ICT tasks, by national quarters of the index

Results based on students' self-reports

	Index of confidence in high-level ICT tasks											
	All students		Females		Males		Gender difference (M-F)		Bottom quarter		Second quarter	
	Mean index	S.E.	Mean index	S.E.	Mean index	S.E.	Dif.	S.E.	Mean index	S.E.	Mean index	S.E.
OECD countries												
Australia	0.42	(0.01)	0.19	(0.02)	0.65	(0.02)	**0.46**	(0.02)	-0.67	(0.02)	0.06	(0.00)
Austria	0.28	(0.02)	0.08	(0.02)	0.49	(0.03)	**0.41**	(0.04)	-0.82	(0.02)	-0.04	(0.01)
Belgium	0.04	(0.02)	-0.20	(0.01)	0.27	(0.02)	**0.47**	(0.02)	-1.06	(0.02)	-0.27	(0.00)
Canada	0.35	(0.01)	0.10	(0.01)	0.62	(0.01)	**0.52**	(0.02)	-0.78	(0.01)	-0.03	(0.00)
Czech Republic	0.05	(0.03)	-0.30	(0.02)	0.39	(0.03)	**0.70**	(0.03)	-1.09	(0.02)	-0.29	(0.00)
Denmark	0.06	(0.02)	-0.37	(0.02)	0.51	(0.02)	**0.88**	(0.03)	-1.10	(0.02)	-0.31	(0.01)
Finland	-0.04	(0.01)	-0.49	(0.02)	0.41	(0.02)	**0.90**	(0.03)	-1.16	(0.02)	-0.39	(0.01)
Germany	0.08	(0.02)	-0.26	(0.02)	0.43	(0.03)	**0.70**	(0.03)	-1.06	(0.02)	-0.29	(0.01)
Greece	-0.22	(0.02)	-0.45	(0.02)	0.04	(0.03)	**0.49**	(0.03)	-1.35	(0.02)	-0.55	(0.00)
Hungary	-0.33	(0.02)	-0.59	(0.02)	-0.11	(0.02)	**0.48**	(0.03)	-1.44	(0.02)	-0.59	(0.01)
Iceland	0.14	(0.02)	-0.31	(0.02)	0.57	(0.02)	**0.88**	(0.03)	-1.01	(0.02)	-0.24	(0.01)
Ireland	-0.24	(0.02)	-0.30	(0.02)	-0.19	(0.03)	**0.10**	(0.04)	-1.38	(0.02)	-0.56	(0.01)
Italy	-0.15	(0.02)	-0.38	(0.02)	0.09	(0.03)	**0.48**	(0.03)	-1.27	(0.01)	-0.48	(0.00)
Japan	-0.71	(0.02)	-0.76	(0.02)	-0.67	(0.03)	**0.09**	(0.04)	-1.93	(0.03)	-0.91	(0.00)
Korea	-0.09	(0.01)	-0.21	(0.02)	-0.01	(0.02)	**0.20**	(0.03)	-1.03	(0.02)	-0.30	(0.00)
Mexico	-0.13	(0.03)	-0.21	(0.03)	-0.05	(0.04)	**0.16**	(0.04)	-1.34	(0.03)	-0.34	(0.01)
New Zealand	0.22	(0.02)	0.05	(0.02)	0.40	(0.03)	**0.35**	(0.03)	-0.88	(0.02)	-0.13	(0.01)
Poland	0.20	(0.02)	-0.11	(0.03)	0.51	(0.03)	**0.62**	(0.04)	-0.99	(0.02)	-0.18	(0.01)
Portugal	0.12	(0.02)	-0.13	(0.02)	0.39	(0.02)	**0.53**	(0.03)	-1.00	(0.02)	-0.18	(0.00)
Slovak Republic	-0.50	(0.03)	-0.78	(0.03)	-0.25	(0.03)	**0.54**	(0.04)	-1.73	(0.03)	-0.81	(0.00)
Sweden	0.00	(0.02)	-0.36	(0.02)	0.37	(0.03)	**0.72**	(0.03)	-1.13	(0.01)	-0.35	(0.01)
Switzerland	-0.03	(0.02)	-0.39	(0.02)	0.30	(0.02)	**0.69**	(0.03)	-1.20	(0.02)	-0.36	(0.00)
Turkey	-0.16	(0.02)	-0.29	(0.03)	-0.08	(0.03)	**0.20**	(0.04)	-1.45	(0.03)	-0.36	(0.01)
United States	0.43	(0.02)	0.32	(0.02)	0.55	(0.02)	**0.23**	(0.03)	-0.75	(0.01)	0.04	(0.01)
OECD average	*0.00*	*(0.00)*	*-0.24*	*(0.00)*	*0.25*	*(0.01)*	***0.49***	*(0.01)*	*-1.14*	*(0.00)*	*-0.31*	*(0.00)*
Partner countries												
Latvia	-0.35	(0.02)	-0.66	(0.03)	-0.02	(0.03)	**0.63**	(0.03)	-1.43	(0.02)	-0.66	(0.01)
Liechtenstein	0.47	(0.05)	0.07	(0.07)	0.85	(0.07)	**0.78**	(0.11)	-0.72	(0.07)	0.06	(0.02)
Russian Federation	-0.49	(0.04)	-0.72	(0.04)	-0.27	(0.06)	**0.45**	(0.05)	-1.89	(0.03)	-0.83	(0.01)
Serbia	-0.43	(0.02)	-0.61	(0.02)	-0.24	(0.03)	**0.37**	(0.04)	-1.64	(0.03)	-0.74	(0.01)
Thailand	-0.68	(0.03)	-0.67	(0.04)	-0.69	(0.04)	-0.01	(0.04)	-1.98	(0.04)	-0.85	(0.01)
Tunisia	-0.58	(0.04)	-0.78	(0.04)	-0.39	(0.05)	**0.38**	(0.05)	-2.05	(0.04)	-0.82	(0.01)
Uruguay	-0.07	(0.02)	-0.19	(0.02)	0.05	(0.03)	**0.24**	(0.04)	-1.30	(0.03)	-0.35	(0.01)
United Kingdom[3]	0.31	(0.03)	0.09	(0.03)	0.53	(0.03)	**0.45**	(0.04)	-0.84	(0.02)	-0.03	(0.01)

	Index of confidence in high-level ICT tasks				Difference in index when students have a computer available to use at home[1]				Difference in index when students have a computer available to use at school[2]			
	Third quarter		Top quarter		Observed difference		Accounting for ESCS		Observed difference		Accounting for ESCS	
	Mean index	S.E.	Mean index	S.E.	Dif.	S.E.	Dif.	S.E.	Dif.	S.E.	Dif.	S.E.
OECD countries												
Australia	0.62	(0.00)	1.68	(0.01)	**0.64**	(0.10)	**0.52**	(0.11)	0.26	(0.20)	0.22	(0.20)
Austria	0.47	(0.01)	1.52	(0.02)	**0.85**	(0.10)	**0.70**	(0.10)	**0.17**	(0.08)	0.13	(0.07)
Belgium	0.24	(0.00)	1.26	(0.01)	**0.67**	(0.07)	**0.62**	(0.07)	0.02	(0.05)	0.00	(0.05)
Canada	0.55	(0.00)	1.67	(0.01)	**0.61**	(0.05)	**0.46**	(0.05)	**0.42**	(0.12)	**0.34**	(0.11)
Czech Republic	0.26	(0.01)	1.33	(0.02)	**0.73**	(0.04)	**0.57**	(0.04)	**0.36**	(0.10)	**0.25**	(0.09)
Denmark	0.29	(0.01)	1.37	(0.02)	**0.65**	(0.09)	**0.57**	(0.10)	c	c	c	c
Finland	0.16	(0.01)	1.23	(0.02)	**0.56**	(0.04)	**0.50**	(0.05)	**0.46**	(0.06)	**0.46**	(0.06)
Germany	0.28	(0.01)	1.41	(0.02)	**0.66**	(0.09)	**0.56**	(0.09)	**0.22**	(0.07)	**0.19**	(0.07)
Greece	-0.02	(0.01)	1.06	(0.02)	**0.76**	(0.03)	**0.66**	(0.03)	**0.18**	(0.06)	**0.21**	(0.05)
Hungary	-0.09	(0.00)	0.78	(0.02)	**0.68**	(0.04)	**0.57**	(0.04)	**0.44**	(0.13)	**0.41**	(0.12)
Iceland	0.32	(0.01)	1.51	(0.02)	**0.85**	(0.14)	**0.74**	(0.14)	**0.39**	(0.13)	**0.37**	(0.12)
Ireland	-0.03	(0.01)	1.00	(0.02)	**0.54**	(0.05)	**0.36**	(0.05)	**0.22**	(0.07)	**0.23**	(0.08)
Italy	0.05	(0.00)	1.09	(0.02)	**0.63**	(0.04)	**0.53**	(0.04)	**0.18**	(0.06)	**0.22**	(0.06)
Japan	-0.40	(0.00)	0.39	(0.02)	**0.62**	(0.06)	**0.47**	(0.06)	**0.14**	(0.06)	**0.16**	(0.06)
Korea	0.10	(0.00)	0.86	(0.02)	**0.49**	(0.10)	**0.27**	(0.11)	**0.14**	(0.03)	**0.14**	(0.03)
Mexico	0.14	(0.01)	1.02	(0.02)	**0.75**	(0.04)	**0.45**	(0.05)	**0.32**	(0.06)	**0.31**	(0.06)
New Zealand	0.41	(0.01)	1.48	(0.02)	**0.47**	(0.06)	**0.34**	(0.07)	**0.27**	(0.14)	0.25	(0.14)
Poland	0.40	(0.01)	1.57	(0.02)	**0.80**	(0.04)	**0.63**	(0.04)	-0.02	(0.07)	0.02	(0.07)
Portugal	0.33	(0.01)	1.33	(0.02)	**0.74**	(0.05)	**0.60**	(0.05)	-0.02	(0.16)	-0.03	(0.15)
Slovak Republic	-0.24	(0.01)	0.77	(0.02)	**0.79**	(0.04)	**0.58**	(0.05)	**0.23**	(0.06)	**0.13**	(0.06)
Sweden	0.19	(0.00)	1.30	(0.02)	**0.54**	(0.10)	**0.44**	(0.11)	0.11	(0.12)	0.07	(0.11)
Switzerland	0.19	(0.00)	1.24	(0.01)	**0.79**	(0.07)	**0.63**	(0.08)	**0.17**	(0.07)	**0.18**	(0.07)
Turkey	0.12	(0.01)	1.05	(0.03)	**0.59**	(0.05)	**0.39**	(0.06)	**0.25**	(0.05)	**0.27**	(0.05)
United States	0.65	(0.01)	1.79	(0.02)	**0.63**	(0.06)	**0.42**	(0.06)	0.11	(0.12)	0.00	(0.11)
OECD average	*0.22*	*(0.00)*	*1.25*	*(0.00)*	***0.66***	*(0.01)*	***0.52***	*(0.01)*	***0.22***	*(0.02)*	***0.20***	*(0.02)*
Partner countries												
Latvia	-0.15	(0.01)	0.85	(0.02)	**0.69**	(0.03)	**0.59**	(0.04)	0.10	(0.06)	0.11	(0.06)
Liechtenstein	0.70	(0.03)	1.87	(0.04)	c	c	c	c	c	c	c	c
Russian Federation	-0.21	(0.01)	0.96	(0.02)	**1.11**	(0.04)	**0.88**	(0.04)	**0.18**	(0.06)	**0.12**	(0.05)
Serbia	-0.17	(0.01)	0.82	(0.03)	**0.84**	(0.04)	**0.74**	(0.04)	-0.09	(0.09)	-0.01	(0.11)
Thailand	-0.30	(0.00)	0.40	(0.02)	**0.68**	(0.05)	**0.35**	(0.04)	**0.78**	(0.25)	0.56	(0.30)
Tunisia	-0.26	(0.01)	0.82	(0.03)	**0.95**	(0.06)	**0.66**	(0.06)	0.09	(0.08)	**0.18**	(0.06)
Uruguay	0.17	(0.01)	1.19	(0.02)	**0.85**	(0.04)	**0.66**	(0.05)	**0.18**	(0.05)	**0.11**	(0.05)
United Kingdom[3]	0.51	(0.01)	1.58	(0.02)	**0.53**	(0.09)	**0.41**	(0.09)	c	c	c	c

Note: Statistically significant differences are marked in bold.

1. Results based on less than 3% of students in Denmark, Iceland, Korea and Sweden (see Table 2.2a).
2. Results based on less than 3% of students in Australia, Canada, Hungary, Iceland, New Zealand and Sweden (see Table 2.2a).
3. Response rate too low to ensure comparability.

Table 3.13

Percentage of students who are confident performing high-level tasks on computers

Percentage of students reporting they can complete the following tasks either very well by themselves or with help from someone

		Use software to find and get rid of computer viruses		Use a database to produce a list of addresses		Create a computer program (*e.g.* in Logo, Pascal, Basic)		Use a speadsheet to plot a graph		Create a presentation (*e.g.* using <Microsoft® PowerPoint®>)		Create a multimedia presentation (with sound, pictures, video)		Construct a Web page	
		Yes	Yes with help	Yes	Yes with help	Yes	Yes with help	Yes	Yes with help	Yes	Yes with help	Yes	Yes with help	Yes	Yes with help
		% (S.E.)	% (S.E.)	% (S.E.)	% (S.E.)	% (S.E.)	% (S.E.)	% (S.E.)	% (S.E.)	% (S.E.)	% (S.E.)	% (S.E.)	% (S.E.)	% (S.E.)	% (S.E.)
OECD countries	Australia	44 (0.6)	31 (0.5)	68 (0.6)	23 (0.6)	27 (0.5)	34 (0.7)	58 (0.8)	28 (0.6)	77 (0.7)	17 (0.5)	48 (0.6)	35 (0.4)	37 (0.7)	39 (0.5)
	Austria	48 (0.9)	28 (0.7)	58 (1.1)	26 (0.8)	29 (1.0)	34 (0.9)	57 (1.2)	25 (0.8)	66 (1.5)	22 (0.9)	42 (1.1)	35 (0.9)	31 (0.9)	40 (0.8)
	Belgium	43 (0.8)	31 (0.7)	56 (0.9)	29 (0.7)	19 (0.7)	40 (0.6)	33 (0.7)	33 (0.6)	47 (1.0)	30 (0.6)	38 (0.9)	37 (0.6)	29 (0.6)	42 (0.6)
	Canada	50 (0.5)	27 (0.5)	64 (0.5)	23 (0.4)	25 (0.5)	33 (0.5)	51 (0.6)	28 (0.4)	64 (0.7)	22 (0.4)	46 (0.6)	35 (0.6)	42 (0.7)	36 (0.7)
	Switzerland	47 (1.5)	25 (0.8)	60 (1.1)	28 (0.8)	19 (0.9)	37 (0.7)	52 (1.4)	28 (0.9)	33 (1.4)	30 (0.8)	32 (1.0)	34 (0.8)	32 (1.0)	38 (1.0)
	Czech Republic	36 (0.8)	25 (0.6)	47 (0.9)	32 (0.7)	15 (0.7)	34 (0.9)	54 (1.0)	32 (0.8)	49 (1.1)	29 (0.7)	38 (0.7)	34 (0.8)	38 (0.8)	35 (0.7)
	Germany	39 (0.8)	28 (0.8)	46 (0.8)	34 (0.7)	14 (0.6)	33 (0.7)	41 (0.9)	36 (0.8)	42 (1.2)	30 (0.8)	28 (0.7)	36 (0.7)	27 (0.6)	42 (0.8)
	Denmark	48 (1.0)	24 (0.8)	57 (0.9)	28 (0.8)	26 (0.8)	33 (0.8)	49 (0.9)	29 (0.8)	35 (1.2)	30 (0.8)	36 (0.9)	34 (0.7)	30 (0.9)	39 (0.8)
	Finland	22 (0.9)	28 (0.7)	42 (1.0)	38 (0.8)	22 (0.7)	36 (0.9)	29 (0.9)	34 (0.7)	38 (1.3)	29 (0.6)	35 (0.8)	34 (0.7)	21 (0.8)	36 (0.8)
	Greece	38 (1.1)	32 (0.7)	38 (0.9)	40 (0.9)	16 (0.6)	34 (0.8)	31 (0.9)	36 (0.7)	27 (1.2)	31 (0.9)	22 (0.6)	34 (0.7)	14 (0.6)	38 (0.8)
	Hungary	45 (0.8)	24 (0.7)	71 (0.8)	18 (0.7)	20 (0.7)	32 (0.7)	36 (0.8)	30 (0.7)	56 (0.8)	26 (0.7)	31 (0.8)	35 (0.9)	42 (0.8)	40 (0.8)
	Ireland	28 (0.9)	28 (0.7)	49 (1.1)	28 (0.9)	18 (0.7)	30 (0.8)	36 (1.1)	28 (0.8)	41 (1.5)	25 (0.8)	28 (1.0)	32 (0.8)	19 (0.8)	31 (0.9)
	Iceland	32 (1.0)	28 (0.6)	35 (0.9)	31 (0.7)	26 (0.9)	31 (0.6)	46 (0.8)	27 (0.6)	47 (1.0)	28 (0.8)	32 (0.8)	33 (0.8)	19 (0.8)	34 (0.6)
	Italy	11 (0.7)	22 (0.7)	30 (0.8)	35 (0.8)	7 (0.4)	29 (0.7)	23 (1.3)	36 (0.8)	17 (0.9)	30 (1.0)	17 (0.6)	31 (0.7)	13 (0.6)	37 (0.8)
	Japan	43 (1.0)	36 (0.7)	38 (0.7)	45 (0.8)	11 (0.5)	46 (0.7)	13 (0.6)	42 (0.7)	47 (1.0)	41 (0.7)	44 (0.8)	42 (0.7)	19 (0.5)	54 (0.7)
	Korea	22 (0.9)	40 (0.8)	44 (1.3)	36 (0.9)	17 (0.7)	43 (0.8)	37 (1.3)	36 (0.7)	53 (1.3)	29 (0.7)	31 (1.0)	41 (0.7)	20 (1.0)	43 (1.0)
	Mexico	42 (0.9)	29 (0.7)	64 (0.9)	24 (0.7)	25 (1.0)	32 (0.8)	58 (0.9)	27 (0.8)	60 (1.1)	24 (0.8)	39 (1.0)	36 (0.9)	27 (0.8)	37 (0.8)
	New Zealand	43 (1.0)	26 (0.7)	66 (1.0)	23 (0.7)	24 (0.9)	31 (0.7)	64 (1.1)	25 (0.8)	50 (1.4)	29 (0.9)	34 (0.9)	34 (0.8)	36 (1.3)	33 (0.8)
	Poland	42 (1.0)	32 (0.6)	53 (1.0)	33 (0.8)	18 (0.9)	41 (0.8)	52 (1.0)	30 (0.9)	58 (1.1)	25 (0.8)	37 (0.9)	37 (0.9)	20 (0.7)	43 (0.8)
	Portugal	29 (1.1)	24 (0.7)	42 (1.1)	32 (0.7)	14 (0.7)	25 (0.6)	35 (1.1)	26 (0.6)	21 (1.1)	23 (0.7)	18 (0.7)	26 (0.7)	23 (0.8)	27 (0.7)
	Slovak Republic	37 (0.9)	29 (0.7)	44 (0.9)	33 (0.9)	19 (0.7)	35 (0.7)	35 (1.2)	35 (0.9)	50 (1.1)	31 (0.8)	40 (1.1)	34 (0.8)	26 (0.9)	45 (0.9)
	Sweden	39 (0.8)	28 (0.7)	54 (1.1)	28 (0.8)	22 (0.7)	33 (0.9)	46 (0.8)	33 (0.7)	39 (1.4)	29 (0.8)	31 (0.9)	36 (0.8)	25 (0.8)	39 (0.8)
	Turkey	20 (1.1)	42 (1.4)	40 (1.4)	38 (1.1)	27 (1.2)	38 (1.0)	38 (1.3)	36 (1.1)	40 (1.8)	32 (1.4)	34 (1.1)	39 (1.0)	27 (1.1)	43 (1.2)
	United States	47 (0.8)	28 (0.7)	68 (0.8)	21 (0.6)	29 (0.6)	33 (0.7)	53 (1.0)	28 (0.7)	70 (1.1)	19 (0.8)	51 (0.8)	33 (0.8)	45 (0.9)	36 (0.8)
	OECD average	*37 (0.2)*	*29 (0.1)*	*52 (0.2)*	*30 (0.2)*	*21 (0.2)*	*35 (0.2)*	*44 (0.2)*	*31 (0.2)*	*47 (0.2)*	*27 (0.2)*	*35 (0.2)*	*35 (0.2)*	*28 (0.2)*	*39 (0.2)*
Partner countries	Liechtenstein	24 (1.0)	26 (0.9)	40 (1.0)	34 (0.8)	14 (0.8)	31 (0.8)	30 (1.2)	34 (1.1)	28 (1.4)	29 (1.0)	23 (0.9)	33 (0.9)	24 (1.1)	38 (0.8)
	Latvia	48 (2.7)	28 (2.2)	59 (2.5)	26 (2.3)	33 (2.6)	35 (2.6)	61 (2.2)	29 (2.2)	72 (2.5)	16 (2.2)	45 (2.6)	37 (2.3)	41 (2.5)	42 (2.9)
	Russian Federation	26 (1.4)	23 (0.7)	41 (1.2)	30 (0.9)	24 (1.2)	27 (0.8)	34 (1.3)	28 (0.7)	28 (1.5)	22 (0.7)	21 (1.1)	24 (0.8)	21 (0.9)	26 (0.8)
	Serbia	22 (0.9)	31 (0.8)	50 (1.1)	30 (0.9)	18 (0.9)	35 (0.9)	27 (0.9)	29 (0.8)	18 (0.9)	30 (0.9)	24 (0.9)	31 (0.8)	18 (0.9)	33 (0.8)
	Thailand	14 (0.8)	41 (1.0)	24 (1.1)	47 (1.0)	10 (0.7)	37 (1.0)	17 (0.9)	45 (1.0)	28 (1.4)	38 (1.0)	11 (0.6)	40 (1.0)	10 (0.7)	37 (0.9)
	Tunisia	19 (1.2)	31 (1.1)	36 (1.4)	30 (1.1)	16 (0.9)	27 (0.9)	24 (1.1)	28 (1.0)	31 (2.2)	30 (1.3)	34 (1.4)	31 (1.0)	24 (1.1)	29 (0.8)
	Uruguay	30 (1.1)	30 (1.2)	53 (1.1)	28 (0.7)	19 (0.9)	31 (0.8)	48 (1.2)	27 (0.9)	68 (1.0)	19 (0.8)	33 (0.8)	33 (0.8)	20 (1.0)	35 (0.9)
	United Kingdom[1]	38 (1.0)	32 (1.0)	77 (1.0)	16 (0.7)	30 (1.1)	35 (1.0)	60 (1.2)	25 (0.9)	55 (1.6)	27 (1.1)	42 (1.3)	33 (1.0)	36 (1.2)	39 (1.1)

1. Response rate too low to ensure comparability.

Table 3.14

Percentage of males and females who are confident performing high-level tasks on computers

Based on students' self-reports

		Use software to find and get rid of computer viruses				Create a multimedia presentation (with sound, pictures, video)				Create a computer program (*e.g.* in <Logo, Pascal, Basic>)				Construct a Web page				Create a presentation (*e.g.* using <Microsoft® PowerPoint®>)				Use a spreadsheet to plot a graph				Use a database to produce a list of addresses			
		Males		Females		Males		Females		Males		Females		Males		Females		Males		Females		Males		Females		Males		Females	
		%	S.E.	%	S.E.	%	S.E.	%	S.E.	%	S.E.	%	S.E.	%	S.E.	%	S.E.	%	S.E.	%	S.E.	%	S.E.	%	S.E.	%	S.E.	%	S.E.
OECD countries	Australia	**84**	(0.7)	**64**	(0.9)	**88**	(0.5)	**79**	(0.7)	**70**	(0.9)	**52**	(1.0)	**80**	(0.8)	**71**	(0.9)	**95**	(0.4)	**93**	(0.5)	**89**	(0.5)	**84**	(0.7)	**92**	(0.5)	**89**	(0.5)
	Austria	**86**	(0.9)	**66**	(1.1)	**84**	(1.1)	**69**	(1.2)	**69**	(1.1)	**56**	(1.5)	**74**	(1.4)	**67**	(1.4)	88	(1.0)	88	(1.1)	83	(1.2)	83	(1.2)	**86**	(0.9)	**82**	(0.8)
	Belgium	**84**	(0.7)	**65**	(0.8)	**81**	(0.7)	**68**	(0.9)	**65**	(0.9)	**51**	(0.9)	**75**	(0.8)	**66**	(0.8)	**81**	(0.7)	**74**	(0.9)	**73**	(0.8)	**59**	(0.9)	**88**	(0.6)	**82**	(0.7)
	Canada	**87**	(0.5)	**69**	(0.7)	**86**	(0.5)	**76**	(0.6)	**68**	(0.6)	**48**	(0.8)	**82**	(0.6)	**75**	(0.9)	**89**	(0.5)	**84**	(0.7)	**83**	(0.5)	**77**	(0.6)	**89**	(0.5)	**85**	(0.5)
	Czech Republic	**87**	(0.9)	**56**	(1.5)	**78**	(1.0)	**55**	(1.5)	**65**	(1.4)	**47**	(1.2)	**76**	(1.2)	**63**	(1.4)	**72**	(1.3)	**52**	(1.6)	**85**	(1.0)	**74**	(1.2)	**91**	(0.8)	**86**	(0.8)
	Denmark	**84**	(0.9)	**39**	(1.2)	**87**	(0.8)	**58**	(1.1)	**64**	(1.1)	**35**	(1.2)	**84**	(0.8)	**63**	(1.3)	**87**	(0.9)	**68**	(1.2)	**91**	(0.6)	**82**	(1.0)	**89**	(0.7)	**68**	(1.2)
	Finland	**87**	(0.6)	**45**	(1.1)	**82**	(0.8)	**46**	(1.2)	**63**	(1.2)	**32**	(1.1)	**79**	(1.0)	**58**	(1.3)	**85**	(0.9)	**58**	(1.3)	**87**	(0.7)	**67**	(1.1)	**89**	(0.6)	**72**	(1.0)
	Germany	**87**	(0.8)	**57**	(1.0)	**82**	(1.0)	**58**	(1.1)	**68**	(1.1)	**50**	(1.2)	**75**	(0.9)	**63**	(1.3)	**74**	(1.1)	**55**	(1.4)	**84**	(0.8)	**72**	(1.2)	**90**	(0.7)	**81**	(0.9)
	Greece	**66**	(1.2)	**36**	(1.1)	**78**	(1.0)	**62**	(1.0)	**63**	(1.2)	**52**	(1.4)	**63**	(1.3)	**51**	(1.2)	**73**	(1.3)	**60**	(1.4)	**70**	(1.3)	**56**	(1.2)	**82**	(1.0)	**77**	(1.0)
	Hungary	**82**	(0.9)	**55**	(1.3)	**67**	(0.9)	**45**	(1.4)	**56**	(1.1)	**43**	(1.3)	**56**	(1.1)	**47**	(1.3)	**65**	(1.2)	**50**	(1.6)	**72**	(0.8)	**61**	(1.3)	**83**	(0.9)	**71**	(1.1)
	Iceland	**88**	(0.7)	**48**	(1.1)	**80**	(1.0)	**49**	(1.3)	**65**	(1.0)	**39**	(1.2)	**89**	(0.7)	**74**	(1.0)	**89**	(0.8)	**74**	(1.0)	**76**	(1.2)	**56**	(1.1)	**94**	(0.7)	**85**	(1.0)
	Ireland	**62**	(1.1)	**50**	(1.4)	**62**	(1.4)	**57**	(1.6)	**51**	(1.4)	**46**	(1.4)	52	(1.5)	48	(1.6)	64	(1.3)	67	(1.7)	64	(1.1)	64	(1.3)	77	(1.0)	79	(1.0)
	Italy	**76**	(1.0)	**46**	(1.0)	**73**	(1.0)	**58**	(1.3)	**63**	(1.3)	**52**	(1.5)	**60**	(1.2)	**46**	(1.3)	**79**	(0.8)	**73**	(1.0)	**78**	(0.9)	**68**	(1.1)	**72**	(0.9)	**59**	(1.3)
	Japan	**39**	(1.6)	**29**	(1.0)	**50**	(1.2)	**46**	(1.1)	**40**	(1.3)	**33**	(1.3)	51	(1.5)	50	(1.5)	**50**	(1.7)	**45**	(1.5)	59	(1.6)	59	(1.6)	66	(1.3)	65	(1.1)
	Korea	**87**	(0.6)	**67**	(1.1)	86	(0.7)	85	(0.8)	**59**	(0.9)	**54**	(1.2)	73	(0.9)	73	(1.0)	87	(0.9)	88	(1.0)	**58**	(1.0)	**53**	(1.1)	83	(0.7)	81	(1.0)
	Mexico	**67**	(1.6)	**58**	(1.5)	**75**	(1.2)	**70**	(1.5)	**64**	(1.3)	**57**	(1.3)	**64**	(1.5)	**61**	(1.4)	81	(1.1)	81	(1.2)	**76**	(1.3)	**71**	(1.4)	81	(1.2)	80	(1.1)
	New Zealand	**80**	(0.9)	**63**	(1.0)	**79**	(1.0)	**70**	(1.2)	**63**	(1.3)	**52**	(1.3)	**69**	(1.1)	**60**	(1.3)	86	(0.9)	83	(1.0)	**86**	(0.7)	**84**	(0.9)	89	(0.7)	88	(0.8)
	Poland	**83**	(1.0)	**55**	(1.2)	**78**	(1.0)	**58**	(1.4)	**64**	(1.2)	**45**	(1.2)	**77**	(1.4)	**61**	(1.6)	**85**	(1.1)	**73**	(1.5)	**92**	(0.7)	**86**	(1.1)	**91**	(0.8)	**87**	(1.0)
	Portugal	**85**	(0.9)	**62**	(1.1)	**82**	(1.0)	**66**	(1.2)	**67**	(1.2)	**52**	(1.3)	**72**	(1.2)	**54**	(1.4)	**86**	(0.9)	**80**	(1.1)	**85**	(0.8)	**78**	(0.9)	**89**	(0.9)	**84**	(0.9)
	Slovak Republic	**70**	(1.1)	**33**	(1.0)	**55**	(1.3)	**32**	(1.3)	**47**	(1.0)	**30**	(1.3)	**53**	(1.4)	**47**	(1.4)	**54**	(1.2)	**34**	(1.6)	**69**	(1.4)	**53**	(1.3)	**79**	(1.1)	**69**	(1.2)
	Sweden	**85**	(0.8)	**46**	(1.0)	**85**	(0.7)	**63**	(1.2)	**64**	(1.3)	**43**	(1.2)	**79**	(1.0)	**64**	(1.3)	**86**	(0.9)	**76**	(1.0)	**78**	(0.9)	**63**	(1.2)	**85**	(0.7)	**70**	(1.2)
	Switzerland	**82**	(0.8)	**51**	(1.2)	**78**	(1.0)	**54**	(1.2)	**65**	(1.3)	**44**	(1.2)	**72**	(1.0)	**54**	(1.1)	**78**	(0.8)	**59**	(1.4)	**85**	(0.9)	**71**	(0.9)	**87**	(0.6)	**77**	(1.0)
	Turkey	**67**	(1.2)	**55**	(2.1)	**74**	(1.1)	**70**	(1.4)	66	(1.3)	64	(2.1)	**71**	(1.0)	**66**	(1.6)	72	(1.5)	73	(1.9)	73	(1.3)	75	(1.9)	78	(1.2)	78	(1.4)
	United States	**79**	(0.8)	**69**	(1.0)	**85**	(0.7)	**82**	(0.9)	**68**	(1.0)	**57**	(1.3)	80	(1.0)	81	(0.8)	88	(0.7)	89	(0.9)	**83**	(0.8)	**80**	(1.0)	88	(0.7)	88	(0.9)
	OECD average	***79***	*(0.2)*	***54***	*(0.2)*	***77***	*(0.2)*	***62***	*(0.2)*	***63***	*(0.2)*	***48***	*(0.3)*	***71***	*(0.2)*	***61***	*(0.3)*	***79***	*(0.2)*	***70***	*(0.3)*	***79***	*(0.2)*	***70***	*(0.2)*	***85***	*(0.2)*	***79***	*(0.2)*
Partner countries	Latvia	**67**	(1.2)	**34**	(1.5)	**68**	(1.2)	**43**	(1.7)	**56**	(1.4)	**35**	(1.6)	**70**	(1.5)	**56**	(1.5)	**68**	(1.5)	**47**	(1.9)	**74**	(1.4)	**55**	(1.7)	**81**	(1.4)	**69**	(1.2)
	Liechtenstein	**86**	(2.7)	**65**	(3.7)	**89**	(2.5)	**74**	(3.7)	**77**	(3.3)	**60**	(3.6)	**88**	(2.4)	**78**	(3.1)	**96**	(1.6)	**81**	(3.0)	93	(2.1)	87	(2.7)	**90**	(2.3)	**80**	(3.1)
	Russian Federation	**61**	(2.1)	**36**	(1.7)	**53**	(1.8)	**37**	(1.5)	**57**	(1.7)	**45**	(1.7)	**53**	(1.6)	**42**	(1.6)	**55**	(2.0)	**46**	(1.7)	**66**	(1.5)	**57**	(1.6)	**73**	(1.5)	**69**	(1.3)
	Serbia	**62**	(1.3)	**45**	(1.3)	**62**	(1.5)	**50**	(1.2)	**57**	(1.3)	**47**	(1.4)	**55**	(1.4)	**46**	(1.5)	**56**	(1.7)	**41**	(1.4)	**62**	(1.1)	**50**	(1.4)	**82**	(1.1)	**79**	(1.1)
	Thailand	56	(1.7)	54	(1.6)	**53**	(1.4)	**48**	(1.4)	**49**	(1.7)	**45**	(1.5)	47	(1.4)	47	(1.8)	65	(1.7)	68	(1.6)	61	(1.5)	62	(1.6)	**68**	(1.7)	**73**	(1.4)
	Tunisia	**56**	(1.9)	**42**	(1.6)	**67**	(1.8)	**61**	(1.7)	**50**	(1.8)	**35**	(1.6)	**57**	(1.8)	**47**	(1.6)	**66**	(1.9)	**54**	(2.3)	**57**	(1.8)	**46**	(1.5)	68	(1.4)	64	(1.9)
	Uruguay	**68**	(1.4)	**51**	(1.3)	**70**	(1.3)	**62**	(1.2)	**53**	(1.5)	**47**	(1.3)	**57**	(1.2)	**52**	(1.6)	87	(0.9)	87	(1.0)	**78**	(1.2)	**72**	(1.2)	81	(1.2)	80	(1.1)
	United Kingdom[1]	**80**	(1.1)	**62**	(1.5)	**81**	(1.3)	**69**	(1.5)	**72**	(1.6)	**58**	(2.1)	**79**	(1.1)	**70**	(1.5)	**84**	(1.1)	**79**	(1.4)	**87**	(0.9)	**83**	(1.3)	93	(0.6)	93	(0.7)

Note: Statistically significant differences are marked in bold.

1. Response rate too low to ensure comparability.

Table 3.15

Proportion of tertiary qualifications[1] in computing, mathematics and statistics and all fields of education awarded to females (2003)

		Computing	Mathematics and statistics	All fields of education
		%	%	%
OECD countries	Australia	26.7	38.1	56.0
	Austria	9.3	36.7	48.9
	Belgium	10.2	45.2	51.8
	Canada[2]	21.4	41.6	57.6
	Czech Republic	15.5	50.3	53.6
	Denmark	25.7	35.7	61.4
	Finland	42.3	43.2	62.2
	France	22.7	42.2	56.6
	Germany	14.9	48.1	48.2
	Greece	m	m	m
	Hungary	22.6	25.3	62.2
	Iceland	26.8	27.3	65.8
	Ireland	34.0	34.7	60.2
	Italy	20.8	61.0	56.7
	Japan	m	m	38.6
	Korea	39.2	56.3	46.1
	Luxembourg	m	m	m
	Mexico	41.6	47.1	52.5
	Netherlands	15.1	30.2	56.0
	New Zealand	27.0	43.9	60.9
	Norway	19.9	26.0	61.6
	Poland	18.2	72.5	64.9
	Portugal	35.4	69.2	67.4
	Slovak Republic	14.1	47.8	53.8
	Spain	22.0	55.5	58.7
	Sweden	42.0	27.0	61.9
	Switzerland	6.3	25.0	40.5
	Turkey	24.1	45.5	45.6
	United Kingdom	25.7	39.8	55.3
	United States	28.3	44.0	57.2
	OECD average	***24.1***	***42.9***	***56.4***

1. Includes qualifications from theoretically oriented university-level programmes (ISCED 5A) and advanced research programmes such as Ph.D.s (ISCED 6). Excludes vocationally oriented tertiary programmes (ISCED 5B).
2. Data refer to 2001.
Source: OECD Education database.

Table 4.1

Availability of a computer at home or school and student performance on the PISA mathematics scale

Results based on students' self-reports

		Student performance on the PISA mathematics scale							
		Computer available to use at home		Computer not available to use at home[1]		Computer available to use at school		Computer not available to use at school[2]	
		Mean score	S.E.	Mean score	S.E.	Mean score	S.E.	Mean score	S.E.
OECD countries	Australia	530	(2.0)	451	(7.4)	527	(2.1)	489	(18.1)
	Austria	512	(3.0)	444	(7.9)	512	(3.1)	478	(9.5)
	Belgium	547	(2.2)	446	(6.2)	547	(2.6)	497	(6.1)
	Canada	540	(1.6)	483	(4.0)	538	(1.6)	474	(12.4)
	Czech Republic	536	(3.2)	484	(4.2)	528	(3.2)	466	(8.1)
	Denmark	518	(2.7)	458	(11.0)	518	(2.7)	c	c
	Finland	548	(1.8)	510	(4.2)	547	(1.9)	521	(7.3)
	Germany	519	(3.3)	440	(8.1)	520	(3.4)	512	(7.8)
	Greece	465	(4.5)	428	(3.9)	447	(4.0)	466	(8.2)
	Hungary	512	(3.1)	450	(3.4)	494	(2.9)	457	(12.9)
	Iceland	517	(1.4)	478	(13.5)	517	(1.4)	508	(10.0)
	Ireland	513	(2.3)	461	(5.1)	505	(2.6)	505	(6.3)
	Italy	479	(2.9)	422	(5.2)	470	(3.0)	469	(6.0)
	Japan	550	(4.3)	496	(5.2)	537	(4.5)	544	(10.3)
	Korea	545	(3.2)	472	(8.7)	547	(3.7)	551	(5.9)
	Mexico	429	(4.4)	381	(3.4)	402	(4.5)	380	(5.3)
	New Zealand	533	(2.1)	464	(4.8)	528	(2.2)	494	(14.4)
	Poland	507	(2.4)	462	(2.8)	493	(2.6)	475	(6.8)
	Portugal	481	(3.2)	429	(4.2)	472	(3.3)	455	(9.5)
	Slovak Republic	526	(2.6)	475	(5.8)	519	(3.4)	472	(7.0)
	Sweden	513	(2.5)	459	(10.9)	513	(2.5)	492	(9.9)
	Switzerland	532	(3.3)	442	(8.4)	532	(3.5)	506	(7.7)
	Turkey	483	(13.1)	413	(5.0)	430	(10.8)	430	(7.1)
	United States	492	(2.8)	416	(5.8)	488	(2.7)	390	(11.4)
	OECD average	***514***	***(0.8)***	***453***	***(1.4)***	***506***	***(0.7)***	***480***	***(2.0)***
Partner countries	Latvia	504	(4.8)	475	(3.6)	488	(3.9)	477	(7.0)
	Liechtenstein	539	(4.4)	c	c	539	(4.2)	c	c
	Russian Federation	499	(4.9)	462	(4.2)	480	(4.6)	452	(4.9)
	Serbia	461	(4.3)	437	(4.0)	444	(3.7)	428	(12.1)
	Thailand	464	(5.5)	404	(2.9)	419	(3.1)	393	(15.6)
	Tunisia	385	(5.6)	356	(2.5)	359	(7.3)	368	(3.0)
	Uruguay	463	(3.8)	403	(3.6)	436	(4.5)	431	(4.8)
	United Kingdom[3]	530	(2.2)	466	(6.2)	527	(2.2)	c	c

1. Results based on less than 3% of students in Denmark, Iceland, Korea and Sweden (see Table 2.2a).
2. Results based on less than 3% of students in Australia, Canada, Hungary, Iceland, New Zealand and Sweden (see Table 2.2a).
3. Response rate too low to ensure comparability.

Table 4.2

Differences in mathematics performance associated with students' access to a computer at home, school or other places

Results based on students' self-reports

		Students with access to a computer at home versus students without access to a computer at home[1]				Students with access to a computer at school versus students without access to a computer at school[2]				Students with access to a computer in places other than at home or at school versus students without access to a computer in other places[3]			
		Observed performance difference		Performance difference after accounting for differences in socio-economic background (ESCS)		Observed performance difference		Performance difference after accounting for differences in socio-economic background (ESCS)		Observed performance difference		Performance difference after accounting for differences in socio-economic background (ESCS)	
		Score point difference	S.E.	Score point difference	S.E.	Score point difference	S.E.	Score point difference	S.E.	Score point difference	S.E.	Score point difference	S.E.
OECD countries	Australia	**79**	(7.2)	**35**	(7.3)	**38**	(18.0)	24	(17.2)	8	(4.9)	-2	(4.5)
	Austria	**68**	(7.9)	**29**	(7.5)	**34**	(10.4)	**21**	(9.1)	2	(3.9)	-1	(3.5)
	Belgium	**101**	(5.9)	**48**	(5.2)	**50**	(6.3)	**36**	(4.3)	**20**	(5.0)	**13**	(3.5)
	Canada	**56**	(4.0)	**23**	(4.0)	**64**	(12.3)	**47**	(10.1)	**27**	(8.8)	12	(8.1)
	Czech Republic	**53**	(3.8)	**16**	(4.1)	**62**	(8.4)	**42**	(7.6)	8	(4.2)	2	(3.6)
	Denmark	**60**	(11.2)	19	(11.2)	c	c	c	c	-5	(5.1)	**-10**	(4.3)
	Finland	**38**	(4.2)	8	(4.3)	**26**	(7.5)	**25**	(7.9)	**9**	(4.0)	6	(3.9)
	Germany	**79**	(8.6)	**32**	(8.0)	8	(7.9)	-4	(6.8)	-5	(3.9)	-5	(3.6)
	Greece	**38**	(4.8)	**8**	(4.0)	**-19**	(8.2)	**-17**	(8.2)	**33**	(6.0)	**24**	(5.9)
	Hungary	**62**	(4.3)	**17**	(3.8)	**37**	(13.3)	**30**	(9.9)	**24**	(4.6)	**8**	(3.7)
	Iceland	**39**	(13.8)	13	(14.2)	9	(10.3)	6	(9.6)	**-13**	(4.9)	**-16**	(4.6)
	Ireland	**52**	(5.5)	**18**	(5.1)	0	(6.8)	1	(5.6)	3	(4.5)	-4	(4.2)
	Italy	**57**	(4.9)	**25**	(4.8)	1	(6.3)	8	(4.7)	**18**	(3.0)	**8**	(2.7)
	Japan	**54**	(5.6)	**28**	(4.9)	-7	(11.1)	-4	(8.9)	**21**	(3.8)	**14**	(3.2)
	Korea	**73**	(8.5)	**30**	(8.2)	-4	(6.6)	-3	(5.3)	**13**	(5.3)	6	(5.1)
	Mexico	**48**	(4.8)	**14**	(3.8)	**22**	(6.5)	**11**	(4.5)	**52**	(6.2)	**30**	(5.3)
	New Zealand	**69**	(4.7)	**25**	(5.0)	**33**	(14.4)	16	(12.7)	12	(6.8)	-3	(6.3)
	Poland	**45**	(2.6)	**6**	(3.1)	**17**	(7.1)	**17**	(6.1)	**49**	(3.3)	**27**	(3.4)
	Portugal	**52**	(4.2)	**18**	(4.1)	17	(9.4)	12	(9.6)	**27**	(5.6)	**17**	(5.1)
	Slovak Republic	**51**	(5.6)	**16**	(3.6)	**46**	(7.2)	**26**	(4.8)	**37**	(7.8)	**17**	(5.1)
	Sweden	**54**	(11.1)	9	(9.8)	**21**	(10.1)	**17**	(7.9)	2	(6.9)	-3	(5.7)
	Switzerland	**90**	(8.3)	**45**	(8.4)	**27**	(7.4)	**28**	(7.6)	1	(3.5)	-5	(3.4)
	Turkey	**70**	(11.9)	**12**	(6.2)	0	(11.4)	-7	(8.3)	**41**	(6.1)	**16**	(5.4)
	United States	**76**	(5.7)	**31**	(6.2)	**98**	(10.8)	**72**	(9.7)	**60**	(6.3)	**37**	(5.9)
	OECD average	*61*	*(1.4)*	*22*	*(1.3)*	*25*	*(2.1)*	*18*	*(1.8)*	*18*	*(1.1)*	*7*	*(1.0)*
Partner countries	Latvia	**29**	(4.0)	5	(4.2)	11	(7.5)	10	(7.1)	**41**	(8.0)	**26**	(7.7)
	Liechtenstein	c	c	c	c	c	c	c	c	c	c	c	c
	Russian Federation	**38**	(5.0)	10	(5.2)	**29**	(5.7)	**21**	(5.4)	**15**	(4.2)	4	(4.0)
	Serbia	**24**	(4.2)	-2	(3.9)	15	(12.3)	**19**	(8.7)	c	c	c	c
	Thailand	**60**	(5.5)	**34**	(4.8)	26	(15.9)	5	(16.8)	**35**	(4.2)	**22**	(4.3)
	Tunisia	**30**	(5.7)	-3	(3.7)	-8	(8.2)	**-16**	(6.0)	**38**	(4.6)	**15**	(3.2)
	Uruguay	**59**	(4.6)	**21**	(4.3)	5	(6.4)	-6	(4.9)	**34**	(5.0)	**13**	(5.2)
	United Kingdom[4]	**64**	(6.2)	**28**	(6.9)	c	c	c	c	-4	(7.0)	-9	(6.7)

Note: Statistically significant differences are marked in bold.

1. Results based on less than 3% of students in Denmark, Iceland, Korea and Sweden (see Table 2.2a).
2. Results based on less than 3% of students in Australia, Canada, Hungary, Iceland, New Zealand and Sweden (see Table 2.2a).
3. Results based on less than 3% of students in Canada (see Table 2.2a).
4. Response rate too low to ensure comparability.

Table 4.3

Length of time students have been using a computer and student performance on the PISA mathematics scale

Results based on students' self-reports

	Performance on the mathematics scale, by using computers:								Observed difference in mathematics[1]						Difference in mathematics after accounting for the socio-economic background of students[1]					
									Between students who reported using computers less than one year and those using computers:						Between students who reported using computers less than one year and those using computers:					
	Less than one year[1]		One to three years		Three to five years		More than five years		One to three years		Three to five years		More than five years		One to three years		Three to five years		More than five years	
	Mean	S.E.	Mean	S.E.	Mean	S.E.	Mean	S.E.	Diff.	S.E.	Diff.	S.E.	Diff.	S.E.	Diff.	S.E.	Diff.	S.E.	Diff.	S.E.
OECD countries																				
Australia	434	(8.7)	478	(3.7)	511	(3.2)	539	(1.9)	**44**	(8.5)	**77**	(9.9)	**105**	(8.9)	**40**	(7.8)	**63**	(9.3)	**79**	(8.3)
Austria	424	(9.0)	479	(3.7)	523	(3.4)	535	(3.6)	**55**	(8.8)	**99**	(9.3)	**111**	(8.7)	**39**	(8.4)	**72**	(8.8)	**76**	(8.5)
Belgium	442	(5.1)	510	(3.5)	562	(2.9)	568	(2.7)	**68**	(5.1)	**120**	(5.8)	**126**	(5.6)	**50**	(4.7)	**83**	(4.9)	**80**	(5.3)
Canada	467	(7.4)	500	(3.6)	529	(2.2)	548	(1.7)	**33**	(7.9)	**62**	(7.5)	**81**	(7.3)	**29**	(8.0)	**48**	(7.3)	**59**	(7.2)
Czech Republic	465	(6.5)	506	(3.5)	536	(3.1)	559	(4.3)	**41**	(6.2)	**71**	(6.5)	**94**	(6.7)	**27**	(5.5)	**46**	(5.4)	**56**	(5.9)
Denmark	441	(10.3)	490	(4.2)	515	(3.2)	528	(3.1)	**50**	(10.6)	**75**	(10.3)	**87**	(10.4)	**36**	(9.8)	**52**	(9.5)	**54**	(9.4)
Finland	489	(7.9)	516	(2.8)	540	(2.6)	561	(2.3)	**27**	(8.4)	**51**	(8.3)	**72**	(8.0)	**21**	(8.4)	**38**	(8.4)	**52**	(8.1)
Germany	436	(8.3)	492	(3.9)	528	(4.3)	533	(3.5)	**56**	(7.5)	**92**	(7.6)	**97**	(7.9)	**34**	(7.6)	**57**	(7.7)	**55**	(7.8)
Greece	411	(4.0)	441	(4.1)	466	(4.2)	494	(6.9)	**30**	(3.8)	**54**	(4.2)	**83**	(7.1)	**22**	(3.9)	**36**	(4.2)	**49**	(5.3)
Hungary	418	(6.5)	464	(3.6)	501	(3.3)	521	(3.8)	**46**	(7.0)	**83**	(7.1)	**104**	(7.6)	**30**	(6.2)	**54**	(6.3)	**57**	(6.8)
Iceland	435	(10.3)	495	(3.3)	516	(3.1)	528	(2.1)	**60**	(10.9)	**81**	(10.9)	**93**	(10.6)	**50**	(10.3)	**66**	(10.4)	**71**	(10.2)
Ireland	456	(5.2)	480	(3.7)	513	(2.9)	531	(2.9)	**25**	(6.0)	**58**	(5.5)	**76**	(5.8)	**15**	(5.5)	**35**	(4.9)	**44**	(5.3)
Italy	408	(5.3)	458	(3.5)	495	(2.9)	507	(4.0)	**50**	(4.6)	**87**	(5.0)	**99**	(6.0)	**38**	(4.5)	**66**	(4.9)	**71**	(5.5)
Japan	501	(5.5)	535	(4.7)	562	(4.7)	565	(5.7)	**34**	(4.9)	**60**	(5.2)	**64**	(7.1)	**24**	(4.5)	**45**	(4.5)	**42**	(6.5)
Korea	452	(10.9)	500	(4.2)	537	(3.2)	570	(4.3)	**48**	(11.2)	**85**	(10.6)	**118**	(11.7)	**37**	(10.5)	**67**	(9.8)	**87**	(10.1)
Mexico	364	(3.0)	409	(2.8)	439	(4.4)	445	(6.5)	**45**	(3.1)	**75**	(5.0)	**81**	(6.8)	**34**	(3.0)	**53**	(4.7)	**53**	(5.9)
New Zealand	424	(7.1)	479	(4.3)	521	(3.7)	551	(2.2)	**55**	(7.4)	**97**	(7.3)	**127**	(7.0)	**49**	(8.3)	**76**	(8.1)	**94**	(7.7)
Poland	440	(5.4)	482	(2.7)	503	(3.1)	532	(4.2)	**42**	(5.2)	**63**	(5.4)	**92**	(6.4)	**38**	(5.1)	**46**	(4.9)	**57**	(5.6)
Portugal	403	(6.1)	444	(3.8)	472	(3.1)	505	(3.5)	**41**	(5.2)	**69**	(5.8)	**102**	(5.7)	**34**	(5.1)	**49**	(5.8)	**67**	(5.4)
Slovak Republic	471	(3.4)	506	(2.7)	536	(3.7)	555	(4.2)	**36**	(3.6)	**65**	(3.5)	**85**	(4.9)	**22**	(3.3)	**40**	(3.6)	**48**	(4.3)
Sweden	419	(15.3)	465	(5.1)	506	(3.2)	525	(2.8)	**46**	(15.9)	**87**	(15.6)	**106**	(15.3)	26	(14.4)	**57**	(13.7)	**68**	(12.9)
Switzerland	427	(6.4)	501	(3.7)	540	(3.4)	557	(4.2)	**74**	(6.9)	**114**	(6.8)	**130**	(8.1)	**59**	(6.7)	**85**	(6.3)	**94**	(7.4)
Turkey	390	(6.0)	426	(7.3)	468	(10.3)	495	(18.9)	**35**	(6.5)	**77**	(10.1)	**104**	(18.9)	**22**	(6.1)	**45**	(7.8)	**45**	(11.1)
United States	373	(7.6)	430	(4.0)	478	(3.2)	507	(3.0)	**57**	(7.9)	**106**	(8.0)	**134**	(8.0)	**43**	(7.8)	**80**	(8.2)	**94**	(8.0)
OECD average	*433*	*(1.6)*	*479*	*(0.8)*	*513*	*(0.8)*	*532*	*(1.1)*	***46***	*(1.6)*	***79***	*(1.7)*	***98***	*(1.9)*	***34***	*(1.6)*	***56***	*(1.6)*	***64***	*(1.7)*
Partner countries																				
Latvia	449	(5.2)	485	(3.9)	509	(6.0)	514	(6.0)	**37**	(5.7)	**60**	(7.1)	**65**	(6.7)	**29**	(5.5)	**43**	(6.8)	**44**	(6.5)
Liechtenstein	c	c	491	(11.9)	538	(8.2)	560	(8.6)	c	c	c	c	c	c	c	c	c	c	c	c
Russian Federation	451	(5.0)	486	(5.1)	511	(6.0)	520	(7.7)	**35**	(4.2)	**60**	(6.8)	**69**	(8.0)	**26**	(4.2)	**42**	(6.3)	**46**	(7.3)
Serbia	420	(3.6)	448	(4.4)	467	(5.1)	486	(7.4)	**28**	(3.4)	**47**	(4.8)	**66**	(6.8)	**17**	(3.5)	**27**	(4.6)	**37**	(6.3)
Thailand	393	(3.7)	412	(3.1)	443	(4.9)	465	(6.5)	**18**	(3.8)	**50**	(6.1)	**72**	(7.2)	**13**	(3.7)	**34**	(5.6)	**47**	(6.1)
Tunisia	357	(3.1)	400	(6.2)	416	(9.6)	388	(8.6)	**42**	(6.1)	**59**	(9.1)	**30**	(8.0)	**24**	(4.6)	**30**	(6.6)	11	(6.7)
Uruguay	376	(5.3)	399	(4.1)	447	(3.9)	476	(4.4)	**23**	(5.9)	**71**	(5.6)	**100**	(6.0)	**17**	(6.0)	**52**	(5.3)	**69**	(5.5)
United Kingdom[2]	437	(12.7)	490	(4.5)	521	(3.6)	545	(2.6)	**53**	(12.4)	**84**	(12.6)	**108**	(13.0)	**42**	(13.4)	**60**	(13.5)	**73**	(14.2)

Note: Statistically significant differences are marked in bold.

1. Results based on less than 3% of students in Australia, Canada, Denmark, Finland, Korea, Sweden and the United Kingdom (see Table 2.1).

2. Response rate too low to ensure comparability.

Table 4.4

Frequency of use of computers at home and at school and student performance on the PISA mathematics scale

Results based on students' self-reports

		Frequency of use of computers at home						Frequency of use of computers at school					
		Never or less than once a month		Between once a week and once a month		Almost every day or a few times each week		Never or less than once a month		Between once a week and once a month		Almost every day or a few times each week	
		Mean score	S.E.	Mean score	S.E.	Mean score	S.E.	Mean score	S.E.	Mean score	S.E.	Mean score	S.E.
OECD countries	Australia	465	(4.5)	510	(5.3)	533	(2.0)	516	(3.8)	534	(2.6)	528	(2.3)
	Austria	458	(7.7)	496	(4.4)	516	(3.2)	504	(5.9)	512	(4.6)	513	(3.7)
	Belgium	456	(5.8)	526	(4.3)	552	(2.4)	544	(4.1)	559	(2.9)	519	(4.2)
	Canada	491	(3.7)	523	(4.4)	542	(1.6)	534	(2.6)	541	(2.5)	538	(2.1)
	Czech Republic	492	(4.0)	525	(5.0)	541	(3.3)	495	(5.7)	527	(3.2)	542	(5.7)
	Denmark	457	(6.6)	506	(5.1)	522	(3.3)	529	(3.4)	520	(4.6)	490	(6.3)
	Finland	516	(4.3)	547	(3.8)	550	(1.8)	542	(3.1)	551	(2.3)	542	(2.6)
	Germany	472	(7.2)	506	(5.4)	522	(2.7)	508	(7.0)	528	(3.6)	515	(3.1)
	Greece	432	(3.7)	470	(6.3)	467	(4.7)	471	(4.8)	458	(5.5)	431	(4.7)
	Hungary	455	(3.3)	521	(7.1)	512	(3.1)	503	(11.3)	506	(5.8)	491	(3.1)
	Iceland	475	(8.6)	513	(6.0)	518	(1.5)	515	(3.6)	524	(2.3)	511	(2.2)
	Ireland	473	(3.7)	512	(3.9)	518	(2.6)	503	(3.0)	513	(4.4)	506	(4.3)
	Italy	432	(4.7)	486	(5.1)	480	(2.9)	479	(5.4)	494	(4.5)	458	(3.5)
	Japan	512	(4.9)	559	(5.3)	561	(5.1)	553	(6.2)	544	(7.8)	512	(7.2)
	Korea	494	(9.6)	562	(5.8)	544	(3.2)	553	(4.2)	552	(4.5)	535	(6.6)
	Mexico	394	(2.9)	412	(7.3)	429	(4.6)	400	(3.6)	411	(4.9)	405	(5.6)
	New Zealand	471	(4.8)	524	(5.2)	537	(2.1)	536	(3.5)	541	(3.7)	514	(3.2)
	Poland	463	(2.8)	492	(8.9)	510	(2.5)	488	(5.1)	510	(3.2)	483	(3.2)
	Portugal	433	(4.5)	477	(6.6)	482	(3.3)	482	(3.6)	480	(3.6)	454	(4.8)
	Slovak Republic	493	(3.8)	523	(5.1)	528	(2.7)	494	(4.4)	529	(3.5)	525	(4.2)
	Sweden	469	(7.5)	512	(5.0)	515	(2.5)	522	(4.5)	524	(3.4)	500	(2.9)
	Switzerland	467	(5.9)	520	(5.2)	537	(3.5)	526	(3.3)	538	(4.9)	528	(5.5)
	Turkey	430	(6.5)	498	(21.4)	485	(13.5)	466	(9.5)	466	(16.0)	420	(13.6)
	United States	437	(4.3)	461	(6.7)	498	(2.8)	482	(3.8)	502	(3.8)	487	(3.3)
	OECD average	***464***	***(1.1)***	***508***	***(1.4)***	***517***	***(0.8)***	***507***	***(1.0)***	***516***	***(1.0)***	***499***	***(1.0)***
Partner countries	Latvia	480	(3.8)	498	(11.2)	505	(4.7)	489	(3.8)	496	(4.7)	481	(6.2)
	Liechtenstein	c	c	c	c	541	(4.5)	533	(14.6)	555	(9.7)	531	(6.7)
	Russian Federation[1]	473	(5.3)	485	(13.9)	502	(5.1)	466	(5.0)	489	(5.2)	480	(5.1)
	Serbia	438	(3.9)	456	(10.8)	463	(4.3)	436	(10.2)	455	(4.8)	439	(3.6)
	Thailand	408	(3.2)	446	(13.6)	470	(5.3)	427	(5.6)	436	(4.9)	412	(3.7)
	Tunisia	380	(4.2)	358	(10.5)	395	(7.0)	391	(4.5)	368	(11.4)	361	(15.5)
	Uruguay	412	(4.0)	468	(8.7)	463	(3.9)	446	(3.2)	459	(6.7)	408	(9.0)
	United Kingdom[2]	473	(5.5)	519	(5.6)	534	(2.2)	525	(5.4)	534	(4.7)	524	(2.7)

1. Results based on less than 3% of students (see Table 3.1).
2. Response rate too low to ensure comparability.

Table 4.5

Index of ICT use for the Internet and entertainment and performance on the mathematics scale, by national quarters of the index

Results based on students' self-reports

		Performance on the PISA mathematics scale, by national quarters of the index of ICT use for the Internet and entertainment								Change in the mathematics score per unit of the index of ICT use for the Internet and entertainment		Increased likelihood of students in the bottom quarter of this index distribution scoring in the bottom quarter of the national mathematics performance distribution		Explained variance in student performance (r-squared x 100)	
		Bottom quarter		Second quarter		Third quarter		Top quarter							
		Mean score	S.E.	Mean score	S.E.	Mean score	S.E.	Mean score	S.E.	Change	S.E.	Ratio	S.E.	%	S.E.
OECD countries	Australia	525	(2.5)	530	(3.5)	527	(2.7)	524	(2.7)	-0.6	(1.40)	**1.0**	(0.04)	0.0	(0.02)
	Austria	500	(4.1)	517	(4.3)	508	(4.4)	508	(4.5)	2.7	(2.12)	**1.2**	(0.10)	0.1	(0.12)
	Belgium	**512**	(3.6)	546	(3.6)	549	(3.6)	**547**	(3.3)	**11.1**	(1.56)	**1.5**	(0.08)	1.3	(0.37)
	Canada	**532**	(2.4)	538	(2.3)	538	(2.4)	**540**	(2.3)	**2.8**	(0.99)	**1.1**	(0.05)	0.1	(0.08)
	Czech Republic	**512**	(3.7)	531	(4.8)	534	(3.6)	**530**	(3.9)	**5.3**	(1.69)	**1.3**	(0.07)	0.3	(0.18)
	Denmark	518	(3.6)	519	(4.1)	516	(3.6)	513	(3.9)	-1.3	(1.62)	**0.9**	(0.06)	0.0	(0.05)
	Finland	**543**	(3.1)	541	(2.6)	547	(2.7)	**551**	(3.5)	**4.6**	(1.41)	**1.0**	(0.06)	0.2	(0.13)
	Germany	505	(4.5)	521	(4.7)	514	(4.8)	515	(4.6)	**4.5**	(1.81)	**1.1**	(0.08)	0.2	(0.17)
	Greece	444	(4.4)	444	(4.7)	454	(5.0)	449	(5.0)	**3.9**	(1.85)	**1.1**	(0.08)	0.2	(0.16)
	Hungary	**479**	(4.1)	501	(4.2)	497	(4.4)	**495**	(4.4)	**5.6**	(2.77)	**1.3**	(0.11)	0.2	(0.23)
	Iceland	515	(3.5)	523	(3.1)	519	(3.6)	508	(3.0)	**-5.4**	(2.03)	**1.0**	(0.08)	0.3	(0.24)
	Ireland	496	(3.1)	511	(4.1)	511	(3.7)	502	(3.8)	2.5	(1.78)	**1.2**	(0.07)	0.1	(0.10)
	Italy	**459**	(4.1)	479	(3.8)	473	(4.4)	**469**	(4.0)	3.2	(1.72)	**1.2**	(0.08)	0.1	(0.14)
	Japan	**514**	(5.7)	538	(4.7)	550	(5.1)	**550**	(5.5)	**18.8**	(2.96)	**1.5**	(0.10)	2.3	(0.68)
	Korea	**546**	(4.7)	549	(4.0)	549	(3.7)	**530**	(3.9)	**-9.2**	(2.42)	**1.0**	(0.07)	0.5	(0.27)
	Mexico	**386**	(4.1)	402	(4.4)	405	(4.0)	**410**	(4.9)	**8.8**	(1.55)	**1.4**	(0.07)	1.4	(0.49)
	New Zealand	**535**	(3.6)	530	(3.6)	525	(3.3)	**518**	(3.4)	**-5.9**	(1.79)	**0.8**	(0.05)	0.3	(0.21)
	Poland	**483**	(3.7)	494	(2.9)	499	(3.7)	**497**	(3.5)	**5.0**	(1.53)	**1.2**	(0.07)	0.4	(0.22)
	Portugal	**457**	(3.6)	470	(3.7)	467	(5.2)	**479**	(5.2)	**8.3**	(1.85)	**1.2**	(0.09)	0.9	(0.41)
	Slovak Republic	**490**	(3.7)	517	(3.3)	522	(3.8)	**513**	(4.2)	**10.3**	(1.91)	**1.4**	(0.08)	0.9	(0.34)
	Sweden	**515**	(3.6)	514	(4.6)	512	(3.5)	**503**	(3.2)	**-4.8**	(1.52)	**0.9**	(0.06)	0.2	(0.15)
	Switzerland	**511**	(3.9)	535	(4.0)	534	(4.9)	**531**	(5.4)	**9.3**	(1.54)	**1.3**	(0.06)	0.9	(0.27)
	Turkey	430	(7.4)	442	(7.6)	438	(10.3)	431	(11.1)	-0.8	(3.12)	**0.9**	(0.08)	0.0	(0.11)
	United States	**480**	(4.0)	492	(4.1)	485	(3.7)	**491**	(3.8)	3.0	(1.60)	**1.2**	(0.07)	0.1	(0.12)
	OECD average	*497*	*(0.8)*	*509*	*(0.8)*	*508*	*(0.9)*	*505*	*(0.9)*	*3.2*	*(0.38)*	*1.2*	*(0.01)*	*0.4*	*(0.05)*
Partner countries	Latvia	**475**	(4.4)	496	(5.3)	487	(4.8)	**485**	(5.1)	**4.7**	(1.92)	**1.3**	(0.10)	0.3	(0.23)
	Liechtenstein	521	(11.5)	539	(11.9)	546	(10.8)	537	(10.0)	3.4	(5.44)	**1.3**	(0.25)	0.2	(0.47)
	Russian Federation	469	(5.4)	476	(5.3)	475	(6.2)	479	(5.3)	3.8	(1.97)	**1.1**	(0.10)	0.2	(0.19)
	Serbia	440	(5.1)	445	(4.4)	447	(4.8)	442	(5.2)	0.4	(1.55)	**1.0**	(0.08)	0.0	(0.05)
	Thailand	**404**	(4.1)	411	(3.5)	427	(4.2)	**439**	(5.3)	**13.9**	(2.34)	**1.2**	(0.10)	2.8	(0.89)
	Tunisia	381	(4.6)	383	(5.8)	369	(5.0)	370	(6.3)	-2.2	(2.31)	**0.8**	(0.07)	0.1	(0.17)
	Uruguay	**413**	(4.3)	430	(3.8)	439	(4.7)	**441**	(5.7)	**7.7**	(1.67)	**1.2**	(0.07)	0.8	(0.32)
	United Kingdom[1]	528	(4.5)	528	(3.6)	522	(3.9)	520	(3.9)	-2.6	(1.94)	**1.0**	(0.07)	0.1	(0.16)

Note: Statistically significant differences are marked in bold.

1. Response rate too low to ensure comparability.

Table 4.6

Index of ICT use for programs and software and performance on the PISA mathematics scale, by national quarters of the index

Results based on students' self-reports

		Performance on the PISA mathematics scale, by national quarters of the index of ICT use for programs and software								Change in the mathematics score per unit of the index of ICT use for programs and software		Increased likelihood of students in the bottom quarter of this index distribution scoring in the bottom quarter of the national mathematics performance distribution		Explained variance in student performance (r-squared x 100)	
		Bottom quarter		Second quarter		Third quarter		Second quarter							
		Mean score	S.E.	Mean score	S.E.	Mean score	S.E.	Mean score	S.E.	Change	S.E.	Ratio	S.E.	%	S.E.
OECD countries	Australia	**527**	(2.8)	541	(3.2)	529	(2.8)	**509**	(2.9)	**-8.0**	(1.52)	**1.0**	(0.05)	0.5	(0.18)
	Austria	**511**	(4.2)	516	(4.8)	513	(4.1)	**494**	(4.6)	**-6.9**	(2.32)	**1.0**	(0.08)	0.4	(0.28)
	Belgium	523	(3.5)	549	(3.5)	558	(3.1)	527	(3.7)	**4.4**	(1.84)	**1.3**	(0.06)	0.2	(0.15)
	Canada	534	(2.7)	543	(2.4)	543	(1.9)	528	(2.7)	**-2.8**	(1.27)	**1.0**	(0.05)	0.1	(0.09)
	Czech Republic	**509**	(4.2)	538	(4.0)	537	(4.4)	**525**	(3.6)	**7.1**	(1.70)	**1.3**	(0.08)	0.5	(0.23)
	Denmark	508	(3.5)	529	(4.2)	525	(4.0)	505	(3.9)	-2.1	(1.94)	**1.1**	(0.07)	0.0	(0.08)
	Finland	539	(2.8)	548	(2.8)	551	(2.9)	545	(3.2)	3.4	(1.78)	**1.1**	(0.06)	0.1	(0.11)
	Germany	**514**	(4.9)	526	(4.2)	522	(4.1)	**494**	(4.6)	**-6.1**	(2.36)	**1.0**	(0.07)	0.4	(0.29)
	Greece	**458**	(4.9)	454	(4.8)	448	(5.0)	**431**	(4.3)	**-6.4**	(1.76)	**0.8**	(0.06)	0.5	(0.29)
	Hungary	483	(4.4)	502	(4.2)	498	(3.5)	489	(4.4)	3.9	(2.57)	**1.3**	(0.09)	0.1	(0.18)
	Iceland	511	(3.9)	532	(2.9)	520	(3.7)	503	(2.9)	**-4.6**	(1.91)	**1.1**	(0.09)	0.2	(0.18)
	Ireland	**504**	(3.5)	515	(3.5)	514	(3.3)	**488**	(3.5)	**-4.8**	(1.70)	**1.1**	(0.07)	0.3	(0.22)
	Italy	**474**	(3.9)	482	(3.5)	471	(4.4)	**453**	(4.0)	**-7.3**	(1.61)	**0.9**	(0.06)	0.6	(0.27)
	Japan	**517**	(5.7)	540	(4.8)	551	(5.2)	**544**	(6.5)	**12.0**	(3.05)	**1.5**	(0.12)	1.2	(0.59)
	Korea	**531**	(4.4)	548	(3.7)	554	(3.9)	**543**	(4.4)	**9.4**	(1.87)	**1.3**	(0.07)	0.7	(0.27)
	Mexico	**402**	(4.0)	408	(4.4)	406	(4.3)	**391**	(5.1)	-1.9	(1.72)	**0.9**	(0.07)	0.1	(0.15)
	New Zealand	**538**	(3.5)	547	(3.3)	527	(3.1)	**496**	(3.4)	**-17.4**	(1.80)	**0.7**	(0.05)	2.8	(0.59)
	Poland	487	(3.6)	503	(3.8)	502	(3.4)	483	(3.1)	0.1	(1.26)	**1.1**	(0.08)	0.0	(0.02)
	Portugal	**462**	(3.8)	481	(4.1)	481	(3.9)	**450**	(5.9)	-2.4	(1.70)	**1.2**	(0.08)	0.1	(0.10)
	Slovak Republic	**496**	(4.0)	519	(4.0)	520	(3.8)	**509**	(3.8)	**5.3**	(1.81)	**1.4**	(0.09)	0.4	(0.26)
	Sweden	507	(3.5)	519	(3.8)	520	(3.6)	500	(3.8)	-2.6	(1.89)	**1.0**	(0.06)	0.1	(0.08)
	Switzerland	517	(3.9)	541	(4.7)	542	(4.4)	512	(3.7)	0.9	(1.71)	**1.2**	(0.06)	0.0	(0.04)
	Turkey	**449**	(9.1)	460	(9.7)	438	(10.4)	**398**	(7.8)	**-12.6**	(2.23)	**0.8**	(0.08)	2.4	(0.80)
	United States	**493**	(3.6)	503	(3.5)	489	(3.7)	**463**	(3.7)	**-10.6**	(1.50)	**0.9**	(0.05)	1.3	(0.37)
	OECD average	*501*	*(0.9)*	*515*	*(0.9)*	*511*	*(0.9)*	*491*	*(0.9)*	-2.4	*(0.38)*	*1.1*	*(0.01)*	*0.6*	*(0.06)*
Partner countries	Latvia	474	(3.6)	490	(4.5)	497	(6.4)	482	(5.1)	**3.8**	(1.77)	**1.3**	(0.08)	0.2	(0.19)
	Liechtenstein	539	(11.1)	540	(11.8)	551	(13.5)	512	(10.9)	-10.2	(6.06)	**0.8**	(0.20)	0.9	(1.02)
	Russian Federation	**455**	(5.5)	473	(5.8)	495	(5.0)	**481**	(4.9)	**9.4**	(1.46)	**1.4**	(0.09)	1.5	(0.43)
	Serbia	**444**	(4.1)	453	(5.1)	455	(4.0)	**428**	(4.9)	**-4.9**	(1.46)	**1.1**	(0.08)	0.5	(0.28)
	Thailand	416	(4.1)	427	(4.0)	426	(4.0)	412	(4.6)	-0.4	(2.18)	**1.0**	(0.08)	0.0	(0.07)
	Tunisia	**382**	(4.7)	379	(5.7)	373	(6.7)	**369**	(5.1)	**-3.4**	(1.62)	**0.8**	(0.09)	0.3	(0.28)
	Uruguay	**415**	(4.2)	441	(4.2)	448	(5.4)	**427**	(5.1)	**3.6**	(1.20)	**1.2**	(0.07)	0.2	(0.16)
	United Kingdom[1]	**530**	(4.0)	538	(3.9)	527	(3.6)	**503**	(4.0)	**-9.5**	(2.16)	**0.9**	(0.07)	1.0	(0.47)

Note: Statistically significant differences are marked in bold.

1. Response rate too low to ensure comparability.

Table 4.7
Students' use of ICT and performance on the PISA reading scale
Results based on students' self-reports

		Performance on the PISA reading scale, by national quarters of the index of ICT use for the Internet and entertainment								Performance on the PISA reading scale, by national quarters of the index of ICT use for programs and software							
		Bottom quarter		Second quarter		Third quarter		Top quarter		Bottom quarter		Second quarter		Third quarter		Top quarter	
		Mean score	S.E.	Mean score	S.E.	Mean score	S.E.	Mean score	S.E.	Mean score	S.E.	Mean score	S.E.	Mean score	S.E.	Mean score	S.E.
OECD countries	Australia	**532**	(2.6)	536	(3.1)	527	(2.5)	**518**	(2.6)	**536**	(2.4)	545	(3.2)	528	(2.9)	**505**	(2.8)
	Austria	491	(4.9)	507	(4.3)	496	(4.8)	484	(4.8)	**498**	(5.0)	511	(4.9)	498	(4.3)	**472**	(4.9)
	Belgium	**497**	(3.7)	527	(4.2)	526	(3.7)	**517**	(3.1)	504	(4.3)	531	(3.5)	536	(3.1)	499	(3.9)
	Canada	532	(2.6)	536	(2.2)	532	(2.7)	530	(2.4)	**531**	(2.7)	541	(2.3)	539	(2.2)	**519**	(2.6)
	Czech Republic	493	(3.7)	508	(4.2)	505	(3.4)	494	(3.4)	490	(3.9)	513	(3.7)	507	(3.9)	492	(3.1)
	Denmark	**505**	(3.6)	502	(3.6)	492	(4.0)	**481**	(4.1)	**495**	(3.6)	512	(3.2)	498	(3.8)	**475**	(3.9)
	Finland	**549**	(2.8)	550	(2.5)	545	(2.6)	**535**	(2.9)	541	(3.0)	551	(2.6)	550	(2.4)	536	(3.1)
	Germany	**504**	(4.3)	518	(4.2)	505	(4.5)	**492**	(4.7)	**513**	(4.4)	521	(4.6)	511	(4.5)	**475**	(4.9)
	Greece	478	(5.7)	476	(4.8)	474	(5.8)	469	(5.4)	**483**	(5.1)	486	(5.4)	475	(5.3)	**454**	(5.3)
	Hungary	474	(4.3)	494	(3.1)	489	(3.9)	481	(3.8)	479	(4.1)	496	(3.8)	490	(3.3)	474	(3.8)
	Iceland	**504**	(3.3)	510	(3.1)	491	(3.4)	**471**	(3.2)	**496**	(4.1)	515	(3.1)	495	(3.7)	**471**	(3.8)
	Ireland	511	(3.6)	527	(4.4)	524	(3.5)	508	(4.0)	**515**	(3.6)	531	(3.6)	529	(3.2)	**498**	(3.8)
	Italy	475	(4.4)	498	(3.4)	483	(4.6)	467	(4.0)	**493**	(3.2)	497	(3.8)	483	(3.7)	**450**	(4.6)
	Japan	**477**	(6.0)	504	(5.1)	516	(5.1)	**520**	(5.2)	**479**	(6.1)	508	(5.1)	519	(4.6)	**511**	(5.8)
	Korea	**542**	(4.2)	540	(4.1)	537	(3.5)	**524**	(3.4)	**520**	(4.0)	541	(3.0)	546	(3.7)	**537**	(4.2)
	Mexico	**401**	(4.3)	422	(5.4)	423	(4.4)	**426**	(5.2)	**420**	(3.9)	430	(4.6)	422	(5.3)	**405**	(5.1)
	New Zealand	**538**	(3.6)	529	(4.0)	519	(3.5)	**516**	(3.6)	**535**	(4.1)	547	(3.7)	527	(3.8)	**494**	(4.0)
	Poland	497	(4.0)	505	(3.8)	504	(4.2)	493	(3.8)	**502**	(4.4)	514	(4.2)	507	(3.5)	**478**	(3.5)
	Portugal	475	(4.3)	486	(4.4)	476	(6.0)	482	(5.6)	**477**	(3.8)	497	(4.6)	490	(4.2)	**456**	(5.9)
	Slovak Republic	**463**	(4.1)	490	(3.2)	495	(3.4)	**476**	(4.4)	467	(4.3)	495	(4.1)	491	(3.5)	472	(3.8)
	Sweden	**529**	(4.0)	525	(3.9)	517	(3.3)	**498**	(3.4)	**519**	(3.5)	529	(3.3)	525	(3.3)	**497**	(3.8)
	Switzerland	494	(4.5)	512	(3.8)	504	(4.7)	491	(5.4)	**499**	(4.3)	518	(4.4)	512	(3.3)	**475**	(4.2)
	Turkey	448	(6.3)	456	(7.8)	449	(8.5)	439	(9.7)	**461**	(7.8)	472	(8.4)	451	(8.9)	**414**	(6.7)
	United States	497	(4.5)	507	(4.1)	497	(4.4)	498	(4.1)	**508**	(4.4)	517	(3.8)	503	(4.0)	**471**	(4.3)
	OECD average	*497*	*(0.9)*	*508*	*(0.8)*	*502*	*(0.9)*	*493*	*(0.9)*	*500*	*(0.9)*	*514*	*(0.8)*	*506*	*(0.8)*	*481*	*(0.9)*
Partner countries	Latvia	491	(4.0)	506	(5.0)	493	(5.4)	481	(5.3)	489	(4.5)	502	(4.3)	501	(4.5)	479	(5.4)
	Liechtenstein	524	(9.0)	529	(10.9)	535	(10.8)	513	(8.3)	**538**	(10.6)	534	(12.6)	529	(11.3)	**500**	(10.3)
	Russian Federation	447	(5.3)	450	(4.9)	449	(5.3)	448	(5.3)	**432**	(5.5)	451	(5.7)	466	(4.3)	**450**	(5.0)
	Serbia	421	(4.2)	416	(4.7)	422	(4.3)	414	(4.7)	**419**	(4.3)	428	(4.9)	429	(4.1)	**404**	(4.4)
	Thailand	**411**	(4.0)	415	(3.3)	427	(4.1)	**438**	(4.8)	416	(3.8)	430	(3.2)	428	(4.2)	417	(4.0)
	Tunisia	**394**	(5.1)	399	(6.7)	383	(6.0)	**380**	(6.8)	**398**	(5.3)	400	(5.9)	382	(6.9)	**377**	(5.9)
	Uruguay	**426**	(5.5)	448	(4.9)	452	(5.5)	**452**	(5.8)	**428**	(5.6)	455	(4.9)	460	(5.2)	**443**	(5.6)
	United Kingdom[1]	**524**	(4.8)	521	(4.2)	513	(4.3)	**507**	(3.7)	**528**	(4.2)	532	(4.2)	520	(3.7)	**487**	(4.1)

Note: Statistically significant differences are marked in bold.
1. Response rate too low to ensure comparability.

Table 4.8

Index of confidence in routine ICT tasks and performance on the PISA mathematics scale, by national quarters of the index

Results based on students' self-reports

		Performance on the PISA mathematics scale, by national quarters of the index of confidence in routine ICT tasks								Change in the mathematics score per unit of the index of confidence in routine ICT tasks		Increased likelihood of students in the bottom quarter of this index distribution scoring in the bottom quarter of the national mathematics performance distribution		Explained variance in student performance (r-squared x 100)	
		Bottom quarter		Second quarter		Third quarter		Top quarter							
		Mean score	S.E.	Mean score	S.E.	Mean score	S.E.	Mean score	S.E.	Change	S.E.	Ratio	S.E.	%	S.E.
OECD countries	Australia	**493**	(2.4)	534	(2.9)	540	(3.2)	**540**	(2.9)	**33.4**	(1.46)	**1.9**	(0.07)	6.8	(0.48)
	Austria	**461**	(4.8)	512	(3.8)	530	(3.8)	**530**	(4.0)	**36.1**	(2.34)	**2.4**	(0.13)	11.3	(1.43)
	Belgium	**487**	(4.4)	544	(3.0)	563	(4.7)	**564**	(3.9)	**38.6**	(2.15)	**2.3**	(0.11)	12.0	(1.17)
	Canada	**508**	(2.7)	540	(2.9)	550	(2.3)	**550**	(2.5)	**27.2**	(1.39)	**1.7**	(0.06)	5.4	(0.54)
	Czech Republic	**480**	(4.1)	530	(3.9)	550	(4.1)	**549**	(4.9)	**35.6**	(2.03)	**2.2**	(0.15)	11.2	(1.11)
	Denmark	**487**	(3.8)	514	(3.7)	533	(3.7)	**532**	(4.3)	**25.4**	(1.89)	**1.7**	(0.10)	5.6	(0.75)
	Finland	**514**	(2.9)	546	(2.9)	560	(2.9)	**559**	(2.9)	**21.8**	(1.48)	**1.7**	(0.09)	5.7	(0.79)
	Germany	**471**	(4.1)	512	(4.2)	536	(4.2)	**538**	(4.5)	**34.4**	(1.84)	**2.1**	(0.12)	9.9	(0.98)
	Greece	**406**	(4.2)	436	(4.6)	467	(5.3)	**482**	(4.9)	**28.6**	(1.71)	**2.3**	(0.14)	10.6	(1.13)
	Hungary	**438**	(3.5)	488	(3.7)	520	(4.0)	**524**	(4.1)	**36.3**	(1.62)	**2.8**	(0.16)	15.8	(1.26)
	Iceland	**491**	(3.5)	523	(4.2)	526	(3.5)	**525**	(4.2)	**20.5**	(1.81)	**1.5**	(0.09)	4.2	(0.75)
	Ireland	**474**	(3.9)	503	(3.3)	520	(4.2)	**522**	(3.9)	**22.8**	(1.71)	**1.8**	(0.10)	6.2	(0.88)
	Italy	**421**	(5.0)	465	(3.4)	494	(3.0)	**501**	(3.3)	**32.1**	(1.87)	**2.3**	(0.12)	11.6	(1.12)
	Japan	**494**	(5.1)	531	(4.5)	555	(4.5)	**575**	(6.7)	**26.9**	(2.17)	**2.0**	(0.12)	10.9	(1.48)
	Korea	**501**	(4.2)	543	(3.5)	564	(4.5)	**567**	(5.6)	**37.0**	(2.00)	**2.1**	(0.11)	10.5	(0.95)
	Mexico	**351**	(3.4)	383	(3.6)	422	(3.4)	**447**	(4.7)	**30.3**	(1.57)	**2.5**	(0.16)	19.5	(1.59)
	New Zealand	**492**	(4.0)	532	(3.8)	541	(3.4)	**544**	(3.1)	**29.2**	(1.94)	**1.9**	(0.12)	6.4	(0.82)
	Poland	**445**	(4.0)	492	(4.0)	517	(3.6)	**519**	(3.1)	**30.3**	(1.55)	**2.4**	(0.13)	12.6	(1.08)
	Portugal	**413**	(4.6)	476	(3.8)	492	(4.6)	**491**	(3.9)	**37.2**	(1.95)	**2.9**	(0.18)	15.4	(1.32)
	Slovak Republic	**460**	(3.7)	501	(3.4)	535	(3.6)	**547**	(4.1)	**30.6**	(1.57)	**2.5**	(0.15)	16.0	(1.24)
	Sweden	**481**	(3.7)	514	(3.7)	526	(3.6)	**526**	(4.7)	**25.3**	(2.05)	**1.7**	(0.09)	5.3	(0.82)
	Switzerland	**475**	(4.5)	523	(3.5)	558	(5.2)	**557**	(4.7)	**37.2**	(1.81)	**2.4**	(0.14)	13.8	(1.14)
	Turkey	**395**	(6.6)	407	(6.5)	441	(8.8)	**496**	(13.6)	**30.5**	(3.87)	**1.6**	(0.14)	11.3	(1.85)
	United States	**447**	(3.8)	495	(4.4)	503	(3.6)	**503**	(3.8)	**33.3**	(1.57)	**2.1**	(0.10)	9.1	(0.85)
	OECD average	*463*	*(0.8)*	*503*	*(0.8)*	*523*	*(0.8)*	*529*	*(1.0)*	*30.7*	*(0.39)*	*2.1*	*(0.02)*	*10.2*	*(0.22)*
Partner countries	Latvia	**444**	(3.9)	477	(4.7)	505	(5.2)	**519**	(5.3)	**27.9**	(1.58)	**2.1**	(0.16)	12.0	(1.33)
	Liechtenstein	**495**	(10.9)	534	(15.0)	559	(11.1)	**554**	(12.9)	**32.3**	(8.54)	**1.8**	(0.38)	7.4	(3.51)
	Russian Federation	**431**	(5.1)	462	(5.4)	498	(4.9)	**513**	(4.8)	**25.3**	(1.43)	**2.2**	(0.14)	12.4	(1.28)
	Serbia	**409**	(3.5)	428	(4.6)	454	(4.1)	**480**	(5.1)	**23.5**	(1.55)	**1.9**	(0.13)	10.4	(1.22)
	Thailand	**389**	(4.2)	405	(3.4)	422	(3.5)	**465**	(5.5)	**27.2**	(2.28)	**1.6**	(0.11)	12.5	(1.83)
	Tunisia	**352**	(3.4)	350	(4.5)	373	(5.2)	**428**	(8.3)	**22.7**	(2.61)	**1.3**	(0.12)	12.6	(2.64)
	Uruguay	**379**	(4.8)	417	(4.3)	456	(6.0)	**469**	(5.4)	**30.4**	(1.83)	**2.2**	(0.11)	12.8	(1.36)
	United Kingdom[1]	**491**	(4.5)	527	(3.7)	540	(4.2)	**540**	(4.7)	**28.1**	(2.46)	**2.0**	(0.14)	7.3	(1.12)

Note: Statistically significant differences are marked in bold.

1. Response rate too low to ensure comparability.

Table 4.9
Index of confidence in Internet ICT tasks and performance on the PISA mathematics scale, by national quarters of the index

Results based on students' self-reports

		Performance on the PISA mathematics scale, by national quarters of the index of confidence in Internet ICT tasks								Change in the mathematics score per unit of the index of confidence in Internet ICT tasks		Increased likelihood of students in the bottom quarter of this index distribution scoring in the bottom quarter of the national mathematics performance distribution		Explained variance in student performance (r-squared x 100)	
		Bottom quarter		Second quarter		Third quarter		Top quarter							
		Mean score	S.E.	Mean score	S.E.	Mean score	S.E.	Mean score	S.E.	Change	S.E.	Ratio	S.E.	%	S.E.
OECD countries	Australia	**504**	(3.5)	532	(2.6)	535	(3.2)	**537**	(2.9)	**22.5**	(2.13)	**1.5**	(0.08)	3.1	(0.54)
	Austria	**478**	(4.4)	508	(3.6)	523	(3.8)	**523**	(4.7)	**25.2**	(2.39)	**1.7**	(0.10)	5.1	(0.96)
	Belgium	**495**	(4.3)	544	(3.5)	560	(4.7)	**560**	(4.1)	**32.7**	(2.36)	**2.0**	(0.10)	8.2	(1.12)
	Canada	**519**	(2.4)	541	(2.6)	545	(2.3)	**544**	(2.3)	**22.9**	(1.75)	**1.4**	(0.05)	2.4	(0.35)
	Czech Republic	**502**	(3.7)	521	(4.1)	540	(4.1)	**546**	(4.2)	**22.0**	(2.08)	**1.5**	(0.09)	4.6	(0.82)
	Denmark	**503**	(3.8)	516	(4.1)	524	(3.7)	**523**	(4.4)	**11.0**	(2.00)	**1.2**	(0.08)	1.0	(0.37)
	Finland	**532**	(2.9)	542	(3.0)	551	(2.9)	**555**	(2.9)	**11.7**	(1.66)	**1.2**	(0.08)	1.4	(0.40)
	Germany	**484**	(4.2)	516	(3.9)	529	(4.2)	**529**	(4.6)	**22.1**	(1.84)	**1.7**	(0.08)	4.2	(0.68)
	Greece	**427**	(4.2)	433	(4.9)	449	(5.3)	**484**	(5.2)	**21.9**	(2.03)	**1.5**	(0.11)	5.7	(0.99)
	Hungary	**454**	(3.4)	483	(3.3)	502	(4.0)	**532**	(4.6)	**29.7**	(1.73)	**2.0**	(0.13)	10.7	(1.14)
	Iceland	507	(3.7)	519	(3.6)	520	(3.5)	520	(4.2)	**12.6**	(2.30)	**1.2**	(0.08)	1.0	(0.38)
	Ireland	**489**	(3.0)	501	(4.3)	510	(4.2)	**522**	(3.9)	**13.6**	(1.61)	**1.3**	(0.08)	2.4	(0.55)
	Italy	**439**	(5.0)	461	(3.7)	481	(3.0)	**499**	(4.0)	**22.1**	(1.77)	**1.6**	(0.10)	6.4	(0.97)
	Japan	**504**	(5.1)	530	(4.9)	557	(4.5)	**565**	(6.0)	**22.9**	(1.93)	**1.8**	(0.09)	7.4	(1.11)
	Korea	**528**	(5.5)	549	(4.4)	549	(4.5)	**549**	(4.2)	**49.4**	(3.76)	**1.4**	(0.13)	4.0	(0.68)
	Mexico	**371**	(3.9)	388	(3.9)	415	(3.4)	**440**	(4.5)	**23.8**	(1.69)	**1.8**	(0.13)	11.3	(1.40)
	New Zealand	**500**	(4.0)	533	(3.5)	540	(3.4)	**537**	(3.8)	**23.3**	(2.21)	**1.6**	(0.09)	3.6	(0.69)
	Poland	**462**	(4.0)	486	(3.3)	510	(3.6)	**516**	(3.7)	**21.2**	(1.62)	**1.7**	(0.10)	6.1	(0.86)
	Portugal	**436**	(4.7)	454	(4.3)	487	(4.6)	**497**	(4.9)	**24.6**	(1.70)	**1.7**	(0.11)	8.7	(1.12)
	Slovak Republic	**477**	(2.9)	506	(3.9)	519	(3.6)	**542**	(3.9)	**21.7**	(1.38)	**1.7**	(0.11)	8.0	(0.92)
	Sweden	**501**	(3.7)	512	(4.4)	516	(3.6)	**518**	(4.2)	**12.4**	(2.40)	**1.2**	(0.07)	0.9	(0.34)
	Switzerland	**489**	(4.0)	528	(3.7)	548	(5.2)	**550**	(5.6)	**30.0**	(2.17)	**2.1**	(0.13)	7.7	(0.93)
	Turkey	**403**	(5.6)	415	(8.4)	447	(8.8)	**488**	(12.9)	**26.9**	(3.92)	**1.6**	(0.17)	8.5	(1.64)
	United States	**456**	(4.0)	495	(4.4)	498	(3.6)	**500**	(5.3)	**28.6**	(1.97)	**1.9**	(0.10)	5.2	(0.71)
	OECD average	*479*	*(0.8)*	*502*	*(0.8)*	*515*	*(0.8)*	*524*	*(1.0)*	*22.7*	*(0.44)*	*1.6*	*(0.02)*	*5.2*	*(0.17)*
Partner countries	Latvia	**466**	(4.0)	484	(5.0)	491	(5.2)	**506**	(5.2)	**15.7**	(1.84)	**1.5**	(0.12)	3.5	(0.85)
	Liechtenstein	507	(14.0)	541	(14.9)	552	(11.1)	542	(15.0)	**29.5**	(9.59)	**1.5**	(0.38)	3.8	(2.42)
	Russian Federation	**456**	(5.1)	472	(4.8)	475	(4.9)	**505**	(5.3)	**13.8**	(1.45)	**1.4**	(0.10)	4.1	(0.88)
	Serbia	**434**	(4.3)	434	(4.0)	446	(4.1)	**468**	(5.2)	**11.7**	(1.53)	**1.2**	(0.08)	3.2	(0.81)
	Thailand	**399**	(4.2)	407	(3.6)	416	(3.5)	**460**	(5.6)	**18.9**	(2.01)	**1.3**	(0.10)	7.8	(1.51)
	Tunisia	**361**	(4.2)	371	(4.3)	368	(5.2)	**405**	(7.9)	**13.8**	(2.50)	**1.2**	(0.10)	3.8	(1.25)
	Uruguay	**394**	(5.1)	414	(4.3)	447	(6.0)	**475**	(5.0)	**26.5**	(1.88)	**1.8**	(0.11)	10.8	(1.46)
	United Kingdom[1]	**511**	(4.0)	527	(4.0)	531	(4.2)	**530**	(4.0)	**11.9**	(2.18)	**1.5**	(0.10)	1.3	(0.48)

Note: Statistically significant differences are marked in bold.

1. Response rate too low to ensure comparability.

Table 4.10
Index of confidence in high-level ICT tasks and performance on the PISA mathematics scale, by national quarters of the index
Results based on students' self-reports

	Performance on the PISA mathematics scale, by national quarters of the index of confidence in high-level ICT tasks								Change in the mathematics score per unit of the index of confidence in high-level ICT tasks		Increased likelihood of students in the bottom quarter of this index distribution scoring in the bottom quarter of the national mathematics performance distribution		Explained variance in student performance (r-squared x 100)	
	Bottom quarter		Second quarter		Third quarter		Top quarter							
	Mean score	S.E.	Mean score	S.E.	Mean score	S.E.	Mean score	S.E.	Change	S.E.	Ratio	S.E.	%	S.E.
Australia	**513**	(2.9)	529	(2.8)	538	(2.9)	**528**	(3.0)	**6.2**	(1.33)	**1.2**	(0.06)	0.4	(0.16)
Austria	**488**	(4.8)	502	(4.0)	517	(3.8)	**525**	(4.6)	**14.4**	(2.21)	**1.4**	(0.09)	2.2	(0.67)
Belgium	**530**	(4.1)	544	(3.1)	541	(3.4)	**543**	(3.4)	**5.9**	(2.05)	**1.2**	(0.07)	0.3	(0.21)
Canada	**524**	(2.5)	538	(2.4)	544	(2.1)	**543**	(2.6)	**7.1**	(1.22)	**1.3**	(0.05)	0.6	(0.21)
Czech Republic	**512**	(3.9)	519	(3.8)	533	(3.7)	**546**	(4.6)	**14.0**	(1.74)	**1.2**	(0.07)	2.2	(0.55)
Denmark	**506**	(3.7)	520	(4.0)	520	(4.1)	**520**	(4.1)	**4.8**	(1.70)	**1.1**	(0.07)	0.3	(0.19)
Finland	**539**	(2.7)	540	(2.8)	544	(3.0)	**558**	(3.3)	**7.8**	(1.46)	**1.0**	(0.06)	0.8	(0.30)
Germany	**500**	(4.3)	515	(4.0)	522	(4.6)	**521**	(5.1)	**7.7**	(2.08)	**1.3**	(0.08)	0.6	(0.35)
Greece	**438**	(4.4)	446	(4.4)	441	(4.3)	**467**	(5.5)	**11.5**	(2.02)	**1.1**	(0.08)	1.5	(0.52)
Hungary	**467**	(3.6)	491	(3.8)	497	(4.1)	**516**	(4.1)	**20.4**	(1.96)	**1.5**	(0.10)	4.1	(0.76)
Iceland	512	(3.2)	523	(3.2)	524	(3.4)	507	(3.9)	-1.9	(1.85)	**1.0**	(0.07)	0.0	(0.09)
Ireland	**495**	(3.8)	509	(3.7)	507	(3.7)	**509**	(3.9)	**4.1**	(1.73)	**1.2**	(0.08)	0.2	(0.19)
Italy	**459**	(4.3)	470	(4.3)	471	(4.2)	**480**	(3.6)	**8.9**	(1.82)	**1.2**	(0.08)	0.8	(0.32)
Japan	**504**	(5.5)	545	(4.9)	552	(4.4)	**554**	(6.7)	**21.4**	(2.46)	**1.8**	(0.12)	4.5	(0.95)
Korea	**531**	(3.9)	542	(3.6)	543	(3.9)	**559**	(4.6)	**13.0**	(1.93)	**1.2**	(0.06)	1.2	(0.36)
Mexico	**381**	(3.8)	399	(3.7)	408	(4.7)	**426**	(5.1)	**17.7**	(1.94)	**1.4**	(0.08)	4.6	(0.92)
New Zealand	521	(3.9)	527	(3.3)	536	(3.4)	526	(3.3)	3.0	(1.58)	**1.0**	(0.06)	0.1	(0.09)
Poland	**479**	(3.3)	489	(3.5)	503	(3.4)	**502**	(3.8)	**8.8**	(1.61)	**1.2**	(0.07)	1.0	(0.35)
Portugal	**452**	(4.2)	469	(4.4)	476	(4.8)	**477**	(4.0)	**11.0**	(1.61)	**1.3**	(0.08)	1.4	(0.40)
Slovak Republic	**488**	(3.7)	508	(2.6)	518	(4.4)	**530**	(4.1)	**17.3**	(1.66)	**1.5**	(0.10)	4.0	(0.76)
Sweden	507	(3.6)	516	(3.5)	514	(3.4)	509	(4.0)	-0.7	(1.79)	**1.0**	(0.07)	0.0	(0.04)
Switzerland	**501**	(4.1)	531	(4.0)	540	(4.7)	**542**	(4.6)	**15.7**	(1.59)	**1.5**	(0.09)	2.5	(0.47)
Turkey	439	(7.8)	434	(9.1)	434	(9.7)	443	(11.2)	1.1	(2.92)	**1.0**	(0.10)	0.0	(0.08)
United States	**473**	(4.0)	488	(3.4)	504	(4.1)	**484**	(3.9)	**5.5**	(1.46)	**1.3**	(0.08)	0.3	(0.18)
OECD average	***491***	*(0.8)*	*505*	*(0.8)*	*510*	*(0.9)*	***514***	*(0.9)*	***9.2***	*(0.38)*	***1.2***	*(0.02)*	*1.4*	*(0.09)*
Latvia	**475**	(4.4)	487	(4.5)	483	(5.6)	**501**	(5.4)	**10.1**	(2.10)	**1.3**	(0.14)	1.2	(0.48)
Liechtenstein	525	(11.5)	531	(10.3)	537	(9.7)	549	(10.8)	9.6	(6.84)	**1.1**	(0.26)	1.0	(1.39)
Russian Federation	**450**	(5.3)	473	(5.2)	479	(5.7)	**504**	(4.5)	**17.4**	(1.65)	**1.7**	(0.10)	4.9	(0.93)
Serbia	**437**	(4.7)	450	(4.6)	445	(4.4)	**448**	(5.1)	**4.3**	(1.78)	**1.1**	(0.07)	0.3	(0.24)
Thailand	**406**	(3.5)	416	(3.8)	426	(4.5)	**434**	(4.9)	**11.2**	(2.17)	**1.2**	(0.09)	1.8	(0.69)
Tunisia	**368**	(4.3)	368	(4.7)	368	(5.9)	**399**	(8.4)	**11.0**	(2.93)	**1.0**	(0.10)	2.2	(1.09)
Uruguay	**405**	(4.9)	431	(4.2)	442	(4.9)	**451**	(5.3)	**17.2**	(2.11)	**1.5**	(0.08)	3.2	(0.74)
United Kingdom[1]	520	(4.0)	522	(4.1)	529	(3.7)	527	(4.5)	**4.7**	(2.32)	**1.0**	(0.09)	0.3	(0.30)

Note: Statistically significant differences are marked in bold.
1. Response rate too low to ensure comparability.

Table 4.11

Index of attitudes towards computers and performance on the PISA mathematics scale, by national quarters of the index

Results based on students' self-reports

		Performance on the PISA mathematics scale, by national quarters of the index of attitudes towards computers								Change in the mathematics score per unit of the index of attitudes towards computers		Increased likelihood of students in the bottom quarter of this index distribution scoring in the bottom quarter of the national mathematics performance distribution		Explained variance in student performance (r-squared x 100)	
		Bottom quarter		Second quarter		Third quarter		Top quarter							
		Mean score	S.E.	Mean score	S.E.	Mean score	S.E.	Mean score	S.E.	Change	S.E.	Ratio	S.E.	%	S.E.
OECD countries	Australia	527	(3.2)	522	(3.0)	533	(2.9)	528	(2.5)	1.8	(1.23)	**1.0**	(0.05)	0.0	(0.05)
	Austria	**512**	(4.3)	513	(4.4)	509	(3.9)	**498**	(4.7)	-3.2	(1.84)	**0.9**	(0.07)	0.1	(0.14)
	Belgium	538	(3.5)	539	(3.7)	542	(3.5)	538	(3.2)	2.0	(1.37)	**1.0**	(0.05)	0.0	(0.05)
	Canada	**531**	(2.4)	537	(2.2)	542	(2.8)	**538**	(2.0)	**4.2**	(1.02)	**1.2**	(0.05)	0.2	(0.10)
	Czech Republic	524	(4.3)	526	(4.6)	532	(4.1)	527	(4.2)	1.2	(1.65)	**1.1**	(0.07)	0.0	(0.05)
	Denmark	512	(4.5)	519	(3.9)	518	(3.9)	516	(4.3)	1.3	(1.44)	**1.0**	(0.06)	0.0	(0.06)
	Finland	546	(3.0)	545	(2.5)	544	(3.1)	546	(3.0)	-0.7	(1.17)	**1.0**	(0.06)	0.0	(0.03)
	Germany	513	(4.1)	518	(4.2)	519	(5.1)	508	(4.8)	-0.4	(1.55)	**0.9**	(0.05)	0.0	(0.03)
	Greece	**444**	(4.6)	442	(4.9)	449	(4.9)	**458**	(5.2)	**5.6**	(1.90)	**1.1**	(0.07)	0.3	(0.22)
	Hungary	489	(4.0)	490	(4.2)	498	(4.2)	496	(3.4)	**3.3**	(1.55)	**1.2**	(0.07)	0.1	(0.13)
	Iceland	**518**	(3.3)	520	(3.4)	527	(3.8)	**503**	(3.1)	-3.3	(1.88)	**1.0**	(0.08)	0.1	(0.16)
	Ireland	**499**	(3.3)	504	(4.0)	510	(4.2)	**508**	(3.5)	**4.7**	(1.62)	**1.1**	(0.08)	0.3	(0.21)
	Italy	475	(3.8)	468	(3.9)	470	(3.9)	469	(4.9)	-2.3	(2.09)	**0.9**	(0.05)	0.1	(0.10)
	Japan	**521**	(6.1)	541	(5.2)	543	(4.9)	**550**	(5.3)	**10.6**	(2.08)	**1.4**	(0.11)	1.7	(0.65)
	Korea	542	(4.6)	544	(3.8)	547	(3.9)	543	(4.5)	2.0	(1.90)	**1.0**	(0.07)	0.0	(0.07)
	Mexico	**390**	(4.5)	397	(4.0)	404	(3.9)	**410**	(5.3)	**9.7**	(1.65)	**1.1**	(0.08)	1.1	(0.36)
	New Zealand	533	(3.4)	524	(4.3)	529	(4.1)	525	(3.6)	-2.3	(1.63)	**0.8**	(0.06)	0.1	(0.07)
	Poland	**480**	(4.9)	492	(3.9)	502	(4.2)	**499**	(4.1)	**8.0**	(2.00)	**1.3**	(0.10)	0.7	(0.36)
	Portugal	**458**	(4.7)	468	(4.7)	474	(4.8)	**473**	(4.8)	**7.1**	(1.91)	**1.3**	(0.11)	0.5	(0.30)
	Slovak Republic	508	(3.3)	506	(4.7)	514	(3.6)	513	(3.6)	**4.4**	(1.52)	**1.2**	(0.07)	0.2	(0.14)
	Sweden	**518**	(4.0)	514	(3.4)	514	(3.9)	**502**	(3.9)	**-5.1**	(1.56)	**0.9**	(0.06)	0.3	(0.20)
	Switzerland	522	(5.0)	527	(4.4)	537	(4.7)	529	(3.8)	**4.6**	(1.27)	**1.1**	(0.08)	0.3	(0.16)
	Turkey	431	(9.6)	434	(8.6)	435	(8.5)	437	(9.0)	2.3	(2.37)	**1.0**	(0.08)	0.0	(0.09)
	United States	**477**	(4.0)	484	(4.2)	497	(3.7)	**491**	(3.9)	**7.0**	(1.85)	**1.2**	(0.08)	0.5	(0.25)
	OECD average	***501***	***(0.9)***	***504***	***(0.9)***	***509***	***(0.9)***	***505***	***(0.9)***	***2.6***	***(0.34)***	***1.1***	***(0.01)***	***0.3***	***(0.04)***
Partner countries	Latvia	484	(5.2)	485	(5.1)	491	(4.3)	486	(5.2)	0.9	(2.35)	**1.1**	(0.09)	0.0	(0.08)
	Liechtenstein	543	(12.7)	543	(10.2)	545	(12.2)	514	(11.1)	-7.4	(7.04)	**0.9**	(0.19)	0.6	(1.09)
	Russian Federation	**464**	(5.8)	469	(5.2)	483	(5.6)	**486**	(5.0)	**9.7**	(1.84)	**1.2**	(0.08)	1.1	(0.41)
	Serbia	**437**	(4.4)	436	(4.7)	446	(5.0)	**451**	(4.5)	**6.5**	(1.81)	**1.2**	(0.08)	0.6	(0.31)
	Thailand	**411**	(3.6)	412	(4.1)	425	(4.4)	**433**	(4.1)	**11.5**	(2.04)	**1.1**	(0.08)	1.2	(0.40)
	Tunisia	**345**	(4.4)	372	(4.7)	388	(6.4)	**401**	(6.6)	**22.5**	(2.20)	**1.7**	(0.13)	6.1	(0.98)
	Uruguay	430	(3.8)	431	(4.4)	431	(4.3)	430	(5.9)	0.5	(2.11)	**1.0**	(0.06)	0.0	(0.03)
	United Kingdom[1]	521	(3.7)	523	(3.4)	530	(4.3)	526	(3.0)	**3.4**	(1.64)	**1.2**	(0.07)	0.1	(0.14)

Note: Statistically significant differences are marked in bold.

1. Response rate too low to ensure comparability.

Table B2.1

Index of ICT use for the Internet and entertainment and performance on the mathematics scale, by national quarters of the index

Results based on students' self-reports

		Index of ICT use for the Internet and entertainment															
		All students		Females		Males		Gender difference (M - F)		Bottom quarter		Second quarter		Third quarter		Top quarter	
		Mean index	S.E.	Mean index	S.E.	Mean index	S.E.	Dif.	S.E.	Mean index	S.E.	Mean index	S.E.	Mean index	S.E.	Mean index	S.E.
Adjudicated regions	Italy (Provincia Autonoma di Bolzano)	-0.29	(0.04)	-0.53	(0.03)	-0.01	(0.06)	**0.52**	(0.08)	-1.26	(0.03)	-0.53	(0.01)	-0.13	(0.01)	0.78	(0.04)
	Italy (Regione Lombardia)	-0.17	(0.03)	-0.41	(0.04)	0.07	(0.03)	**0.48**	(0.04)	-1.26	(0.03)	-0.47	(0.01)	0.04	(0.01)	1.01	(0.05)
	Italy (Regione Piemonte)	-0.12	(0.03)	-0.31	(0.04)	0.08	(0.04)	**0.39**	(0.05)	-1.20	(0.03)	-0.43	(0.01)	0.06	(0.01)	1.08	(0.05)
	Italy (Provincia Autonoma di Trento)	-0.26	(0.03)	-0.42	(0.04)	-0.06	(0.05)	**0.36**	(0.06)	-1.25	(0.03)	-0.52	(0.01)	-0.09	(0.01)	0.85	(0.06)
	Italy (Regione Toscana)	-0.15	(0.03)	-0.33	(0.03)	0.01	(0.06)	**0.34**	(0.07)	-1.27	(0.05)	-0.39	(0.01)	0.10	(0.01)	0.97	(0.04)
	Italy (Regione Veneto)	-0.24	(0.04)	-0.47	(0.05)	-0.01	(0.04)	**0.46**	(0.05)	-1.36	(0.03)	-0.49	(0.01)	0.00	(0.01)	0.91	(0.04)
	Italy (Other regions)	-0.16	(0.03)	-0.42	(0.04)	0.13	(0.03)	**0.54**	(0.04)	-1.39	(0.03)	-0.45	(0.01)	0.10	(0.01)	1.12	(0.03)
	United Kingdom (Scotland)	0.30	(0.03)	0.06	(0.03)	0.55	(0.04)	**0.48**	(0.04)	-0.79	(0.02)	-0.06	(0.01)	0.43	(0.01)	1.63	(0.03)
Non-adjudicated regions	Belgium (Flemish Community)	0.28	(0.02)	0.04	(0.02)	0.51	(0.03)	**0.48**	(0.03)	-0.78	(0.02)	-0.04	(0.00)	0.42	(0.00)	1.52	(0.02)
	Belgium (French Community)	-0.05	(0.03)	-0.38	(0.03)	0.25	(0.04)	**0.63**	(0.05)	-1.44	(0.03)	-0.40	(0.01)	0.18	(0.01)	1.47	(0.04)
	Belgium (German-speaking Community)	-0.05	(0.04)	-0.26	(0.04)	0.18	(0.05)	**0.44**	(0.07)	-1.21	(0.04)	-0.35	(0.01)	0.14	(0.01)	1.24	(0.05)
	Finland (Finnish speaking)	-0.14	(0.01)	-0.46	(0.01)	0.18	(0.02)	**0.64**	(0.03)	-0.96	(0.01)	-0.47	(0.00)	-0.07	(0.00)	0.94	(0.02)
	Finland (Swedish speaking)	0.00	(0.03)	-0.38	(0.02)	0.43	(0.05)	**0.81**	(0.05)	-0.93	(0.02)	-0.36	(0.01)	0.10	(0.01)	1.21	(0.06)

		Performance on the PISA mathematics scale, by national quarters of the index of ICT use for the Internet and entertainment								Change in the mathematics score per unit of the index of ICT use for the Internet and entertainment		Increased likelihood of students in the bottom quarter of the index of ICT use for the Internet and entertainment distribution scoring in the bottom quarter of the national mathematics performance distribution		Explained variance in student performance (r-squared x 100)	
		Bottom quarter		Second quarter		Third quarter		Top quarter							
		Mean score	S.E.	Mean score	S.E.	Mean score	S.E.	Mean score	S.E.	Effect	S.E.	Ratio	S.E.	%	S.E.
Adjudicated regions	Italy (Provincia Autonoma di Bolzano)	529	(7.4)	534	(6.5)	547	(9.0)	538	(4.4)	6.1	(3.41)	**1.4**	(0.13)	0.4	(0.45)
	Italy (Regione Lombardia)	515	(6.6)	526	(7.5)	517	(10.6)	531	(10.0)	5.7	(3.80)	**1.1**	(0.11)	0.4	(0.48)
	Italy (Regione Piemonte)	490	(5.8)	495	(7.3)	502	(7.3)	494	(6.7)	2.1	(2.63)	**1.1**	(0.12)	0.1	(0.15)
	Italy (Provincia Autonoma di Trento)	553	(5.6)	546	(6.6)	550	(5.5)	549	(5.3)	0.2	(2.93)	**0.9**	(0.14)	0.0	(0.11)
	Italy (Regione Toscana)	495	(6.2)	500	(5.2)	490	(7.6)	494	(5.2)	1.6	(2.71)	**0.9**	(0.11)	0.0	(0.13)
	Italy (Regione Veneto)	505	(8.4)	512	(7.0)	517	(5.7)	518	(8.8)	5.1	(3.66)	**1.2**	(0.17)	0.3	(0.49)
	Italy (Other regions)	436	(5.2)	458	(6.1)	454	(6.0)	446	(5.6)	3.3	(2.13)	**1.3**	(0.11)	0.1	(0.19)
	United Kingdom (Scotland)	528	(4.5)	528	(3.6)	522	(3.9)	520	(3.9)	-2.6	(1.94)	**1.0**	(0.07)	0.1	(0.16)
Non-adjudicated regions	Belgium (Flemish Community)	**539**	(4.1)	567	(3.9)	571	(3.6)	**566**	(3.5)	**9.5**	(1.66)	**1.4**	(0.09)	0.9	(0.30)
	Belgium (French Community)	**495**	(4.7)	508	(6.0)	516	(6.0)	**511**	(6.3)	**5.9**	(2.53)	**1.2**	(0.11)	0.5	(0.41)
	Belgium (German-speaking Community)	514	(7.6)	528	(7.8)	512	(8.2)	515	(7.0)	0.2	(3.52)	**1.0**	(0.15)	0.0	(0.11)
	Finland (Finnish speaking)	**543**	(3.2)	542	(3.1)	546	(2.9)	**552**	(3.4)	**5.0**	(1.52)	**1.1**	(0.07)	0.2	(0.14)
	Finland (Swedish speaking)	528	(5.2)	540	(6.2)	540	(4.6)	534	(4.5)	2.0	(2.65)	**1.1**	(0.13)	0.1	(0.15)

Note: Statistically significant differences are marked in bold.

Table B2.2

Index of ICT use for programs and software and performance on the PISA mathematics scale, by national quarters of the index

Results based on students' self-reports

		Index of ICT use for programs and software															
		All students		Females		Males		Gender difference (M - F)		Bottom quarter		Second quarter		Third quarter		Top quarter	
		Mean index	S.E.	Mean index	S.E.	Mean index	S.E.	Dif.	S.E.	Mean index	S.E.	Mean index	S.E.	Mean index	S.E.	Mean index	S.E.
Adjudicated regions	Italy (Provincia Autonoma di Bolzano)	0.02	(0.03)	-0.15	(0.03)	0.22	(0.05)	**0.37**	(0.05)	-0.94	(0.03)	-0.20	(0.01)	0.26	(0.01)	0.97	(0.04)
	Italy (Regione Lombardia)	0.14	(0.03)	-0.03	(0.04)	0.32	(0.03)	**0.35**	(0.04)	-1.02	(0.03)	-0.11	(0.01)	0.40	(0.01)	1.31	(0.06)
	Italy (Regione Piemonte)	0.17	(0.03)	0.08	(0.04)	0.27	(0.03)	**0.19**	(0.04)	-0.95	(0.03)	-0.07	(0.01)	0.42	(0.01)	1.29	(0.04)
	Italy (Provincia Autonoma di Trento)	0.07	(0.03)	-0.02	(0.03)	0.18	(0.05)	**0.20**	(0.05)	-1.00	(0.04)	-0.13	(0.01)	0.32	(0.01)	1.10	(0.04)
	Italy (Regione Toscana)	0.11	(0.04)	0.00	(0.04)	0.20	(0.06)	**0.20**	(0.07)	-1.08	(0.05)	-0.12	(0.01)	0.37	(0.01)	1.26	(0.05)
	Italy (Regione Veneto)	0.13	(0.03)	-0.01	(0.04)	0.26	(0.04)	**0.27**	(0.05)	-0.97	(0.03)	-0.09	(0.01)	0.38	(0.01)	1.21	(0.04)
	Italy (Other regions)	0.28	(0.03)	0.12	(0.03)	0.46	(0.04)	**0.34**	(0.05)	-0.94	(0.03)	-0.02	(0.01)	0.51	(0.01)	1.59	(0.04)
	United Kingdom (Scotland)	0.32	(0.03)	0.31	(0.03)	0.33	(0.03)	0.02	(0.04)	-0.75	(0.02)	0.11	(0.01)	0.55	(0.00)	1.37	(0.03)
Non-adjudicated regions	Belgium (Flemish Community)	-0.06	(0.02)	-0.17	(0.02)	0.05	(0.03)	**0.23**	(0.04)	-1.09	(0.02)	-0.26	(0.00)	0.18	(0.00)	0.94	(0.02)
	Belgium (French Community)	-0.38	(0.02)	-0.52	(0.03)	-0.25	(0.03)	**0.28**	(0.04)	-1.71	(0.02)	-0.65	(0.01)	-0.06	(0.01)	0.91	(0.04)
	Belgium (German-speaking Community)	-0.16	(0.04)	-0.29	(0.05)	-0.01	(0.05)	**0.27**	(0.07)	-1.35	(0.04)	-0.41	(0.01)	0.11	(0.01)	1.03	(0.05)
	Finland (Finnish speaking)	-0.27	(0.01)	-0.41	(0.02)	-0.13	(0.02)	**0.28**	(0.02)	-1.18	(0.01)	-0.48	(0.00)	-0.07	(0.00)	0.64	(0.02)
	Finland (Swedish speaking)	-0.39	(0.02)	-0.61	(0.03)	-0.15	(0.04)	**0.47**	(0.05)	-1.40	(0.03)	-0.62	(0.01)	-0.15	(0.01)	0.61	(0.03)

		Performance on the PISA mathematics scale, by national quarters of the index of ICT use for programs and software								Change in the mathematics score per unit of the index of ICT use for programs and software		Increased likelihood of students in the bottom quarter of the index of ICT use for programs and software distribution scoring in the bottom quarter of the national mathematics performance distribution		Explained variance in student performance (r-squared x 100)	
		Bottom quarter		Second quarter		Third quarter		Top quarter							
		Mean score	S.E.	Mean score	S.E.	Mean score	S.E.	Mean score	S.E.	Effect	S.E.	Ratio	S.E.	%	S.E.
Adjudicated regions	Italy (Provincia Autonoma di Bolzano)	533	(12.4)	537	(8.1)	545	(5.8)	534	(5.1)	3.1	(5.35)	**1.2**	(0.22)	0.1	(0.34)
	Italy (Regione Lombardia)	513	(8.5)	524	(8.6)	527	(5.8)	524	(10.6)	4.4	(3.65)	**1.1**	(0.12)	0.2	(0.38)
	Italy (Regione Piemonte)	496	(6.5)	500	(6.5)	504	(6.6)	482	(6.8)	-4.5	(2.84)	**1.0**	(0.15)	0.2	(0.31)
	Italy (Provincia Autonoma di Trento)	553	(6.2)	557	(5.3)	543	(5.4)	545	(5.7)	-3.2	(2.99)	**1.0**	(0.16)	0.1	(0.26)
	Italy (Regione Toscana)	499	(5.6)	507	(5.1)	489	(7.3)	484	(6.8)	-5.0	(2.68)	**0.8**	(0.13)	0.3	(0.35)
	Italy (Regione Veneto)	505	(8.0)	517	(6.2)	520	(7.5)	510	(7.3)	1.5	(3.45)	**1.2**	(0.14)	0.0	(0.18)
	Italy (Other regions)	**454**	(5.3)	464	(5.4)	447	(5.8)	**430**	(5.2)	**-7.7**	(2.02)	**0.9**	(0.08)	0.8	(0.41)
	United Kingdom (Scotland)	**530**	(4.0)	538	(3.9)	527	(3.6)	**503**	(4.0)	**-9.5**	(2.16)	**0.9**	(0.07)	1.0	(0.47)
Non-adjudicated regions	Belgium (Flemish Community)	551	(4.4)	568	(3.9)	575	(3.3)	550	(4.3)	3.9	(2.53)	**1.2**	(0.07)	0.1	(0.15)
	Belgium (French Community)	**505**	(5.4)	521	(6.1)	521	(5.8)	**488**	(6.3)	-3.3	(2.36)	**1.0**	(0.09)	0.1	(0.16)
	Belgium (German-speaking Community)	**515**	(7.4)	540	(5.9)	532	(7.5)	**487**	(8.6)	-6.4	(3.84)	**1.1**	(0.16)	0.4	(0.51)
	Finland (Finnish speaking)	539	(3.0)	548	(2.9)	551	(3.1)	545	(3.4)	3.4	(1.91)	**1.1**	(0.07)	0.1	(0.11)
	Finland (Swedish speaking)	525	(5.1)	546	(5.5)	544	(4.2)	528	(4.8)	1.3	(3.08)	**1.2**	(0.12)	0.0	(0.11)

Note: Statistically significant differences are marked in bold.

Table B2.3

Index of attitudes towards computers and performance on the PISA mathematics scale, by national quarters of the index

Results based on students' self-reports

		Index of attitudes towards computers															
		All students		Females		Males		Gender difference (M - F)		Bottom quarter		Second quarter		Third quarter		Top quarter	
		Mean index	S.E.	Mean index	S.E.	Mean index	S.E.	Dif.	S.E.	Mean index	S.E.	Mean index	S.E.	Mean index	S.E.	Mean index	S.E.
Adjudicated regions	Italy (Provincia Autonoma di Bolzano)	0.11	(0.03)	-0.14	(0.04)	0.40	(0.04)	**0.54**	(0.05)	-1.26	(0.04)	-0.16	(0.02)	0.52	(0.01)	1.34	(0.00)
	Italy (Regione Lombardia)	-0.19	(0.03)	-0.44	(0.04)	0.05	(0.04)	**0.49**	(0.05)	-1.33	(0.04)	-0.55	(0.01)	0.05	(0.01)	1.06	(0.03)
	Italy (Regione Piemonte)	-0.16	(0.03)	-0.33	(0.04)	0.03	(0.04)	**0.36**	(0.06)	-1.25	(0.03)	-0.52	(0.01)	0.07	(0.01)	1.05	(0.02)
	Italy (Provincia Autonoma di Trento)	-0.21	(0.03)	-0.41	(0.04)	0.03	(0.06)	**0.44**	(0.07)	-1.41	(0.05)	-0.54	(0.01)	0.05	(0.02)	1.09	(0.02)
	Italy (Regione Toscana)	-0.18	(0.02)	-0.37	(0.04)	0.00	(0.04)	**0.37**	(0.06)	-1.29	(0.02)	-0.53	(0.01)	0.06	(0.01)	1.07	(0.02)
	Italy (Regione Veneto)	-0.15	(0.04)	-0.42	(0.06)	0.10	(0.03)	**0.52**	(0.07)	-1.27	(0.04)	-0.50	(0.01)	0.09	(0.01)	1.06	(0.01)
	Italy (Other regions)	-0.02	(0.02)	-0.16	(0.03)	0.14	(0.03)	**0.30**	(0.04)	-1.12	(0.02)	-0.36	(0.01)	0.25	(0.01)	1.16	(0.01)
	United Kingdom (Scotland)	0.07	(0.02)	-0.09	(0.03)	0.23	(0.03)	**0.31**	(0.04)	-1.12	(0.02)	-0.29	(0.01)	0.41	(0.01)	1.27	(0.01)
Non-adjudicated regions	Belgium (Flemish Community)	0.16	(0.02)	-0.05	(0.03)	0.36	(0.03)	**0.40**	(0.03)	-1.11	(0.02)	-0.20	(0.01)	0.60	(0.01)	1.34	(0.00)
	Belgium (French Community)	0.08	(0.02)	-0.11	(0.03)	0.24	(0.03)	**0.36**	(0.05)	-1.27	(0.03)	-0.30	(0.01)	0.54	(0.01)	1.34	(0.00)
	Belgium (German-speaking Community)	0.28	(0.05)	0.19	(0.06)	0.38	(0.06)	**0.20**	(0.08)	-1.23	(0.05)	0.02	(0.02)	0.98	(0.03)	1.35	(0.00)
	Finland (Finnish speaking)	-0.37	(0.02)	-0.62	(0.02)	-0.12	(0.02)	**0.50**	(0.03)	-1.53	(0.02)	-0.73	(0.01)	-0.14	(0.01)	0.93	(0.01)
	Finland (Swedish speaking)	-0.48	(0.03)	-0.82	(0.04)	-0.10	(0.04)	**0.72**	(0.06)	-1.79	(0.04)	-0.87	(0.01)	-0.20	(0.02)	0.95	(0.02)

		Performance on the PISA mathematics scale, by national quarters of the index of attitudes towards computers								Change in the mathematics score per unit of the index of attitudes towards computers		Increased likelihood of students in the bottom quarter of the index of attitudes towards computers distribution scoring in the bottom quarter of the national mathematics performance distribution		Explained variance in student performance (r-squared x 100)	
		Bottom quarter		Second quarter		Third quarter		Top quarter							
		Mean score	S.E.	Mean score	S.E.	Mean score	S.E.	Mean score	S.E.	Effect	S.E.	Ratio	S.E.	%	S.E.
Adjudicated regions	Italy (Provincia Autonoma di Bolzano)	539	(8.8)	535	(7.1)	543	(8.6)	535	(5.0)	0.7	(3.47)	**1.0**	(0.14)	0.0	(0.18)
	Italy (Regione Lombardia)	519	(8.9)	520	(8.5)	522	(10.0)	528	(8.1)	2.5	(3.24)	**1.0**	(0.17)	0.1	(0.20)
	Italy (Regione Piemonte)	498	(7.7)	490	(7.6)	495	(6.0)	500	(4.9)	1.7	(2.75)	**0.9**	(0.11)	0.0	(0.14)
	Italy (Provincia Autonoma di Trento)	546	(6.4)	542	(7.1)	555	(6.3)	556	(5.6)	2.9	(3.28)	**1.1**	(0.16)	0.2	(0.40)
	Italy (Regione Toscana)	503	(5.8)	495	(5.7)	493	(6.6)	492	(5.7)	-2.9	(2.85)	**0.8**	(0.12)	0.1	(0.21)
	Italy (Regione Veneto)	**506**	(7.2)	511	(6.6)	514	(7.5)	**525**	(8.3)	**9.1**	(3.14)	**1.2**	(0.16)	1.0	(0.68)
	Italy (Other regions)	452	(5.5)	447	(5.8)	451	(5.2)	447	(6.8)	-1.1	(2.92)	**0.9**	(0.08)	0.0	(0.11)
	United Kingdom (Scotland)	521	(3.7)	523	(3.4)	530	(4.3)	526	(3.0)	**3.4**	(1.64)	**1.2**	(0.07)	0.1	(0.14)
Non-adjudicated regions	Belgium (Flemish Community)	**565**	(4.0)	563	(3.9)	564	(4.1)	**554**	(4.1)	-2.3	(1.66)	**0.9**	(0.06)	0.1	(0.08)
	Belgium (French Community)	**504**	(5.7)	507	(5.4)	506	(5.9)	**515**	(5.4)	**5.0**	(2.00)	**1.0**	(0.10)	0.3	(0.22)
	Belgium (German-speaking Community)	516	(8.3)	534	(7.6)	519	(7.7)	507	(7.7)	0.8	(4.22)	**1.1**	(0.18)	0.0	(0.21)
	Finland (Finnish speaking)	548	(3.4)	545	(3.0)	545	(2.9)	546	(3.0)	-1.2	(1.26)	**0.9**	(0.06)	0.0	(0.04)
	Finland (Swedish speaking)	525	(5.6)	536	(5.4)	546	(5.1)	535	(5.1)	4.4	(2.33)	**1.2**	(0.16)	0.4	(0.36)

Note: Statistically significant differences are marked in bold.

Table B2.4
Index of confidence in routine ICT tasks and performance on the PISA mathematics scale, by national quarters of the index
Results based on students' self-reports

		Index of confidence in routine ICT tasks															
		All students		Females		Males		Gender difference (M - F)		Bottom quarter		Second quarter		Third quarter		Top quarter	
		Mean index	S.E.	Mean index	S.E.	Mean index	S.E.	Dif.	S.E.	Mean index	S.E.	Mean index	S.E.	Mean index	S.E.	Mean index	S.E.
Adjudicated regions	Italy (Provincia Autonoma di Bolzano)	0.04	(0.02)	-0.21	(0.03)	0.31	(0.04)	**0.52**	(0.05)	-1.17	(0.03)	-0.24	(0.01)	0.75	(0.01)	0.82	(0.00)
	Italy (Regione Lombardia)	-0.05	(0.04)	-0.14	(0.05)	0.05	(0.07)	**0.19**	(0.08)	-1.36	(0.07)	-0.30	(0.01)	0.66	(0.02)	0.82	(0.00)
	Italy (Regione Piemonte)	-0.08	(0.04)	-0.22	(0.06)	0.08	(0.06)	**0.29**	(0.09)	-1.41	(0.04)	-0.35	(0.01)	0.63	(0.02)	0.82	(0.00)
	Italy (Provincia Autonoma di Trento)	0.08	(0.03)	-0.08	(0.05)	0.27	(0.03)	**0.35**	(0.05)	-1.18	(0.04)	-0.10	(0.03)	0.80	(0.00)	0.82	(0.00)
	Italy (Regione Toscana)	-0.19	(0.04)	-0.28	(0.05)	-0.10	(0.07)	**0.18**	(0.09)	-1.56	(0.03)	-0.49	(0.01)	0.49	(0.02)	0.81	(0.00)
	Italy (Regione Veneto)	-0.06	(0.03)	-0.18	(0.04)	0.06	(0.06)	**0.24**	(0.07)	-1.40	(0.04)	-0.32	(0.01)	0.68	(0.02)	0.82	(0.00)
	Italy (Other regions)	-0.27	(0.03)	-0.40	(0.03)	-0.12	(0.04)	**0.28**	(0.05)	-1.68	(0.02)	-0.58	(0.01)	0.37	(0.02)	0.81	(0.00)
	United Kingdom (Scotland)	0.25	(0.02)	0.16	(0.03)	0.34	(0.02)	**0.19**	(0.03)	-0.92	(0.03)	0.30	(0.02)	0.81	(0.00)	0.82	(0.00)
Non-adjudicated regions	Belgium (Flemish Community)	0.26	(0.01)	0.15	(0.02)	0.38	(0.02)	**0.23**	(0.03)	-0.90	(0.02)	0.34	(0.01)	0.81	(0.00)	0.82	(0.00)
	Belgium (French Community)	-0.10	(0.03)	-0.26	(0.04)	0.04	(0.05)	**0.30**	(0.05)	-1.59	(0.04)	-0.31	(0.01)	0.69	(0.01)	0.82	(0.00)
	Belgium (German-speaking Community)	0.02	(0.04)	-0.10	(0.05)	0.14	(0.06)	**0.25**	(0.08)	-1.40	(0.05)	-0.15	(0.02)	0.80	(0.00)	0.82	(0.00)
	Finland (Finnish speaking)	0.09	(0.02)	-0.29	(0.02)	0.47	(0.02)	**0.75**	(0.03)	-1.25	(0.02)	-0.02	(0.01)	0.80	(0.00)	0.82	(0.00)
	Finland (Swedish speaking)	-0.09	(0.03)	-0.45	(0.04)	0.32	(0.03)	**0.77**	(0.06)	-1.51	(0.03)	-0.34	(0.02)	0.70	(0.02)	0.82	(0.00)

		Performance on the PISA mathematics scale, by national quarters of the index of confidence in routine ICT tasks								Change in the mathematics score per unit of the index of confidence in routine ICT tasks		Increased likelihood of students in the bottom quarter of the index of confidence in routine ICT tasks distribution scoring in the bottom quarter of the national mathematics performance distribution		Explained variance in student performance (r-squared x 100)	
		Bottom quarter		Second quarter		Third quarter		Top quarter							
		Mean score	S.E.	Mean score	S.E.	Mean score	S.E.	Mean score	S.E.	Effect	S.E.	Ratio	S.E.	%	S.E.
Adjudicated regions	Italy (Provincia Autonoma di Bolzano)	**504**	(5.6)	524	(6.2)	557	(7.8)	**564**	(7.9)	**31.0**	(3.39)	**2.1**	(0.22)	10.0	(1.82)
	Italy (Regione Lombardia)	**484**	(9.9)	519	(7.8)	544	(8.2)	**542**	(8.9)	**29.6**	(4.25)	**1.9**	(0.24)	9.3	(2.68)
	Italy (Regione Piemonte)	**452**	(6.9)	497	(6.1)	514	(7.3)	**520**	(6.1)	**29.2**	(2.66)	**2.4**	(0.23)	10.4	(1.72)
	Italy (Provincia Autonoma di Trento)	**533**	(6.2)	548	(7.1)	558	(7.5)	**559**	(8.8)	**14.3**	(3.72)	**1.3**	(0.18)	2.8	(1.41)
	Italy (Regione Toscana)	**452**	(6.2)	493	(5.4)	516	(5.9)	**520**	(6.1)	**27.3**	(2.52)	**2.2**	(0.24)	10.0	(1.80)
	Italy (Regione Veneto)	**483**	(9.0)	505	(5.6)	530	(6.7)	**536**	(7.0)	**25.4**	(3.17)	**2.0**	(0.19)	8.3	(1.94)
	Italy (Other regions)	**400**	(6.1)	444	(4.6)	472	(6.0)	**479**	(6.0)	**30.1**	(2.44)	**2.4**	(0.16)	11.6	(1.48)
	United Kingdom (Scotland)	**491**	(4.5)	527	(3.7)	540	(4.2)	**540**	(4.7)	**28.1**	(2.46)	**2.0**	(0.14)	7.3	(1.12)
Non-adjudicated regions	Belgium (Flemish Community)	**521**	(4.6)	565	(5.1)	579	(4.7)	**581**	(5.8)	**36.7**	(2.65)	**2.0**	(0.11)	8.8	(1.16)
	Belgium (French Community)	**456**	(7.1)	513	(4.7)	530	(6.3)	**535**	(5.9)	**32.9**	(2.99)	**2.4**	(0.17)	11.5	(1.73)
	Belgium (German-speaking Community)	**473**	(7.0)	521	(6.1)	538	(10.4)	**542**	(7.7)	**29.9**	(3.13)	**2.0**	(0.27)	9.0	(2.11)
	Finland (Finnish speaking)	**515**	(3.1)	547	(3.1)	561	(3.4)	**559**	(3.2)	**21.5**	(1.54)	**1.7**	(0.09)	5.5	(0.81)
	Finland (Swedish speaking)	**498**	(5.4)	537	(5.0)	555	(5.7)	**551**	(5.3)	**24.0**	(2.92)	**2.0**	(0.22)	8.7	(2.00)

Note: Statistically significant differences are marked in bold.

Table B2.5

Index of confidence in Internet ICT tasks and performance on the PISA mathematics scale, by national quarters of the index

Results based on students' self-reports

		Index of confidence in Internet ICT tasks															
		All students		Females		Males		Gender difference (M - F)		Bottom quarter		Second quarter		Third quarter		Top quarter	
		Mean index	S.E.	Mean index	S.E.	Mean index	S.E.	Dif.	S.E.	Mean index	S.E.	Mean index	S.E.	Mean index	S.E.	Mean index	S.E.
Adjudicated regions	Italy (Provincia Autonoma di Bolzano)	-0.09	(0.02)	-0.32	(0.04)	0.17	(0.04)	**0.49**	(0.07)	-1.33	(0.03)	-0.40	(0.01)	0.50	(0.02)	0.88	(0.00)
	Italy (Regione Lombardia)	-0.28	(0.04)	-0.48	(0.05)	-0.08	(0.06)	**0.41**	(0.08)	-1.69	(0.04)	-0.67	(0.01)	0.38	(0.02)	0.88	(0.00)
	Italy (Regione Piemonte)	-0.29	(0.04)	-0.48	(0.05)	-0.08	(0.04)	**0.40**	(0.06)	-1.65	(0.03)	-0.64	(0.02)	0.25	(0.03)	0.88	(0.00)
	Italy (Provincia Autonoma di Trento)	-0.20	(0.03)	-0.42	(0.04)	0.05	(0.05)	**0.48**	(0.07)	-1.51	(0.03)	-0.55	(0.02)	0.38	(0.03)	0.88	(0.00)
	Italy (Regione Toscana)	-0.31	(0.04)	-0.42	(0.05)	-0.20	(0.07)	**0.22**	(0.08)	-1.67	(0.04)	-0.66	(0.01)	0.23	(0.02)	0.88	(0.00)
	Italy (Regione Veneto)	-0.32	(0.05)	-0.54	(0.06)	-0.10	(0.05)	**0.44**	(0.06)	-1.69	(0.04)	-0.70	(0.01)	0.24	(0.02)	0.88	(0.00)
	Italy (Other regions)	-0.44	(0.04)	-0.62	(0.05)	-0.22	(0.04)	**0.40**	(0.06)	-1.90	(0.03)	-0.82	(0.01)	0.10	(0.02)	0.88	(0.00)
	United Kingdom (Scotland)	0.28	(0.02)	0.15	(0.03)	0.40	(0.02)	**0.25**	(0.03)	-0.88	(0.02)	0.23	(0.02)	0.87	(0.00)	0.88	(0.00)
Non-adjudicated regions	Belgium (Flemish Community)	0.41	(0.01)	0.31	(0.02)	0.50	(0.02)	**0.19**	(0.03)	-0.73	(0.02)	0.61	(0.01)	0.87	(0.00)	0.88	(0.00)
	Belgium (French Community)	-0.02	(0.03)	-0.15	(0.04)	0.09	(0.04)	**0.24**	(0.05)	-1.47	(0.04)	-0.23	(0.01)	0.73	(0.01)	0.88	(0.00)
	Belgium (German-speaking Community)	0.14	(0.04)	0.06	(0.05)	0.22	(0.06)	**0.16**	(0.07)	-1.21	(0.05)	0.01	(0.02)	0.87	(0.00)	0.88	(0.00)
	Finland (Finnish speaking)	0.06	(0.01)	-0.34	(0.02)	0.46	(0.01)	**0.79**	(0.02)	-1.08	(0.01)	-0.26	(0.01)	0.68	(0.01)	0.88	(0.00)
	Finland (Swedish speaking)	0.11	(0.02)	-0.19	(0.03)	0.45	(0.03)	**0.64**	(0.04)	-1.08	(0.03)	-0.13	(0.01)	0.76	(0.02)	0.88	(0.00)

		Performance on the PISA mathematics scale, by national quarters of the index of confidence in Internet ICT tasks								Change in the mathematics score per unit of the index of confidence in Internet ICT tasks		Increased likelihood of students in the bottom quarter of the index of confidence in Internet ICT tasks distribution scoring in the bottom quarter of the national mathematics performance distribution		Explained variance in student performance (r-squared x 100)	
		Bottom quarter		Second quarter		Third quarter		Top quarter							
		Mean score	S.E.	Mean score	S.E.	Mean score	S.E.	Mean score	S.E.	Effect	S.E.	Ratio	S.E.	%	S.E.
Adjudicated regions	Italy (Provincia Autonoma di Bolzano)	**513**	(6.9)	530	(5.5)	552	(8.7)	**554**	(7.6)	**18.8**	(2.69)	**1.7**	(0.21)	4.2	(1.08)
	Italy (Regione Lombardia)	**497**	(9.4)	513	(7.8)	530	(7.5)	**549**	(9.8)	**19.4**	(2.93)	**1.5**	(0.16)	5.1	(1.45)
	Italy (Regione Piemonte)	**469**	(5.8)	489	(6.9)	506	(6.6)	**519**	(6.1)	**20.7**	(2.55)	**1.7**	(0.20)	5.9	(1.38)
	Italy (Provincia Autonoma di Trento)	**538**	(5.7)	541	(6.4)	554	(6.7)	**565**	(5.6)	**9.7**	(3.41)	**1.3**	(0.18)	1.6	(1.00)
	Italy (Regione Toscana)	**470**	(6.9)	487	(7.0)	503	(5.1)	**521**	(4.7)	**20.3**	(2.73)	**1.6**	(0.17)	5.9	(1.51)
	Italy (Regione Veneto)	**489**	(8.4)	505	(6.1)	522	(7.3)	**539**	(7.6)	**19.8**	(2.84)	**1.7**	(0.18)	6.0	(1.62)
	Italy (Other regions)	**418**	(6.1)	440	(5.1)	461	(4.7)	**477**	(5.5)	**20.6**	(2.34)	**1.6**	(0.13)	6.3	(1.29)
	United Kingdom (Scotland)	**511**	(4.0)	527	(4.0)	531	(3.8)	**530**	(4.0)	**11.9**	(2.18)	**1.5**	(0.10)	1.3	(0.48)
Non-adjudicated regions	Belgium (Flemish Community)	**529**	(3.9)	570	(4.1)	573	(3.8)	**574**	(3.8)	**29.9**	(2.19)	**1.7**	(0.10)	5.3	(0.75)
	Belgium (French Community)	**473**	(7.8)	505	(5.8)	525	(6.9)	**533**	(7.0)	**25.8**	(3.69)	**1.8**	(0.16)	6.8	(1.77)
	Belgium (German-speaking Community)	**494**	(7.1)	517	(7.6)	533	(8.3)	**536**	(9.6)	**21.4**	(4.41)	**1.4**	(0.20)	4.2	(1.79)
	Finland (Finnish speaking)	**534**	(3.1)	542	(3.2)	551	(3.6)	**556**	(4.0)	**11.5**	(1.76)	**1.2**	(0.08)	1.3	(0.41)
	Finland (Swedish speaking)	**516**	(5.3)	535	(5.3)	546	(5.8)	**544**	(6.1)	**16.4**	(3.33)	**1.4**	(0.17)	2.9	(1.15)

Note: Statistically significant differences are marked in bold.

Table B2.6

Index of confidence in high-level ICT tasks and performance on the PISA mathematics scale, by national quarters of the index

Results based on students' self-reports

		Index of confidence in high-level ICT tasks															
		All students		Females		Males		Gender difference (M - F)		Bottom quarter		Second quarter		Third quarter		Top quarter	
		Mean index	S.E.	Mean index	S.E.	Mean index	S.E.	Dif.	S.E.	Mean index	S.E.	Mean index	S.E.	Mean index	S.E.	Mean index	S.E.
Adjudicated regions	Italy (Provincia Autonoma di Bolzano)	0.02	(0.03)	-0.31	(0.03)	0.38	(0.04)	**0.69**	(0.05)	-1.02	(0.02)	-0.33	(0.01)	0.22	(0.01)	1.20	(0.04)
	Italy (Regione Lombardia)	-0.12	(0.03)	-0.34	(0.03)	0.10	(0.04)	**0.44**	(0.04)	-1.18	(0.03)	-0.44	(0.01)	0.10	(0.01)	1.05	(0.04)
	Italy (Regione Piemonte)	-0.12	(0.03)	-0.36	(0.05)	0.14	(0.04)	**0.49**	(0.07)	-1.19	(0.03)	-0.44	(0.01)	0.08	(0.01)	1.06	(0.04)
	Italy (Provincia Autonoma di Trento)	-0.14	(0.03)	-0.39	(0.04)	0.16	(0.05)	**0.56**	(0.06)	-1.25	(0.04)	-0.48	(0.01)	0.07	(0.01)	1.11	(0.04)
	Italy (Regione Toscana)	-0.19	(0.03)	-0.43	(0.05)	0.02	(0.04)	**0.46**	(0.05)	-1.26	(0.02)	-0.51	(0.01)	0.01	(0.01)	0.99	(0.03)
	Italy (Regione Veneto)	-0.18	(0.03)	-0.45	(0.03)	0.08	(0.04)	**0.52**	(0.04)	-1.23	(0.02)	-0.49	(0.01)	0.01	(0.01)	0.98	(0.03)
	Italy (Other regions)	-0.16	(0.03)	-0.38	(0.03)	0.10	(0.04)	**0.48**	(0.05)	-1.30	(0.02)	-0.48	(0.01)	0.05	(0.01)	1.11	(0.03)
	United Kingdom (Scotland)	0.31	(0.03)	0.09	(0.03)	0.53	(0.03)	**0.45**	(0.04)	-0.84	(0.02)	-0.03	(0.01)	0.51	(0.01)	1.58	(0.02)
Non-adjudicated regions	Belgium (Flemish Community)	0.04	(0.02)	-0.22	(0.02)	0.29	(0.02)	**0.51**	(0.03)	-1.00	(0.01)	-0.27	(0.00)	0.23	(0.00)	1.20	(0.02)
	Belgium (French Community)	0.04	(0.03)	-0.18	(0.03)	0.24	(0.04)	**0.43**	(0.03)	-1.15	(0.03)	-0.26	(0.01)	0.26	(0.01)	1.34	(0.03)
	Belgium (German-speaking Community)	0.05	(0.04)	-0.16	(0.04)	0.28	(0.06)	**0.44**	(0.08)	-1.14	(0.04)	-0.32	(0.01)	0.28	(0.02)	1.40	(0.04)
	Finland (Finnish speaking)	-0.04	(0.02)	-0.48	(0.02)	0.42	(0.02)	**0.90**	(0.03)	-1.15	(0.02)	-0.39	(0.01)	0.16	(0.01)	1.24	(0.02)
	Finland (Swedish speaking)	-0.14	(0.03)	-0.55	(0.03)	0.31	(0.04)	**0.86**	(0.05)	-1.31	(0.03)	-0.47	(0.01)	0.10	(0.01)	1.11	(0.04)

		Performance on the PISA mathematics scale, by national quarters of the index of confidence in high-level ICT tasks								Change in the mathematics score per unit of the index of confidence in high-level ICT tasks		Increased likelihood of students in the bottom quarter of the index of confidence in high-level ICT tasks distribution scoring in the bottom quarter of the national mathematics performance distribution		Explained variance in student performance (r-squared x 100)	
		Bottom quarter		Second quarter		Third quarter		Top quarter							
		Mean score	S.E.	Mean score	S.E.	Mean score	S.E.	Mean score	S.E.	Effect	S.E.	Ratio	S.E.	%	S.E.
Adjudicated regions	Italy (Provincia Autonoma di Bolzano)	**512**	(7.2)	535	(5.1)	535	(6.2)	**568**	(9.5)	**23.0**	(4.01)	**1.7**	(0.18)	6.0	(1.90)
	Italy (Regione Lombardia)	**508**	(7.8)	519	(8.9)	525	(7.5)	**537**	(10.1)	**11.3**	(4.36)	**1.2**	(0.15)	1.3	(0.99)
	Italy (Regione Piemonte)	**489**	(5.9)	491	(7.1)	492	(6.3)	**511**	(8.0)	**9.5**	(3.53)	**1.1**	(0.13)	1.0	(0.78)
	Italy (Provincia Autonoma di Trento)	**542**	(6.5)	542	(6.0)	550	(5.4)	**564**	(6.1)	**6.9**	(3.40)	**1.1**	(0.16)	0.8	(0.78)
	Italy (Regione Toscana)	**486**	(5.9)	491	(5.7)	499	(6.2)	**505**	(6.0)	**8.3**	(2.82)	**1.1**	(0.16)	0.8	(0.55)
	Italy (Regione Veneto)	**493**	(8.3)	518	(7.0)	518	(5.4)	**524**	(8.3)	**12.3**	(3.48)	**1.5**	(0.15)	1.7	(0.97)
	Italy (Other regions)	**440**	(5.9)	450	(5.6)	448	(5.7)	**458**	(5.2)	**7.6**	(2.06)	**1.2**	(0.10)	0.7	(0.35)
	United Kingdom (Scotland)	520	(4.0)	522	(4.1)	529	(3.7)	527	(4.5)	**4.7**	(2.32)	**1.0**	(0.09)	0.3	(0.30)
Non-adjudicated regions	Belgium (Flemish Community)	**554**	(3.2)	563	(3.8)	561	(3.4)	**568**	(4.1)	**5.8**	(2.13)	**1.1**	(0.07)	0.3	(0.20)
	Belgium (French Community)	498	(7.3)	516	(4.8)	514	(6.0)	509	(6.0)	**6.3**	(3.20)	**1.2**	(0.11)	0.4	(0.42)
	Belgium (German-speaking Community)	510	(7.1)	524	(7.3)	538	(7.6)	506	(7.8)	0.5	(3.99)	**1.0**	(0.15)	0.0	(0.15)
	Finland (Finnish speaking)	**540**	(3.1)	540	(3.1)	544	(3.3)	**559**	(3.4)	**7.7**	(1.54)	**1.0**	(0.07)	0.8	(0.31)
	Finland (Swedish speaking)	**524**	(5.9)	534	(4.9)	543	(5.9)	**539**	(4.7)	**8.2**	(2.84)	**1.1**	(0.14)	1.0	(0.67)

Note: Statistically significant differences are marked in bold.

Annex C

THE DEVELOPMENT OF PISA: A COLLABORATIVE EFFORT

Members of the PISA Governing Board

Chair: Ryo Watanabe

Australia: Wendy Whitham

Austria: Helmut Bachmann and Jürgen Horschinegg

Belgium: Dominique Barthélémy, Christiane Blondin and Liselotte van de Perre

Brazil: Eliezer Pacheco

Canada: Satya Brink and Dianne Pennock

Czech Republic: Jan Koucky

Denmark: Jørgen Balling Rasmussen

Finland: Jari Rajanen

France: Gérard Bonnet

Germany: Hans Konrad Koch, Elfriede Ohrnberger and Botho Priebe

Greece: Vassilis Koulaidis

Hong Kong-China: Esther Ho Sui Chu

Hungary: Péter Vári

Iceland: Júlíus K. Björnsson

Indonesia: Bahrul Hayat

Ireland: Gerry Shiel

Italy: Giacomo Elias and Angela Vegliante

Japan: Ryo Watanabe

Korea: Kye Young Lee

Latvia: Andris Kangro

Luxembourg: Michel Lanners

Macao-China: Lam Fat Lo

Mexico: Felipe Martínez Rizo

Netherlands: Jules L. Peschar

New Zealand: Lynne Whitney

Norway: Alette Schreiner

Poland: Stanislaw Drzazdzewski

Portugal: Glória Ramalho

Russian Federation: Galina Kovalyova

Serbia: Dragica Pavlovic Babic

Slovak Republic: Vladimir Repas

Spain: Carme Amorós Basté, Guillermo Gil and Josu Sierra Orrantia

Sweden: Anita Wester

Switzerland: Katrin Holenstein and Heinz Rhyn

Thailand: Sunee Klainin

Tunisia: Néjib Ayed

Turkey: Sevki Karaca and Ruhi Kilç

United Kingdom: Lorna Bertrand and Liz Levy

United States: Mariann Lemke and Elois Scott

Uruguay: Pedro Ravela

Special Advisor: Eugene Owen

PISA 2003 National Project Managers

Australia: John Cresswell and Sue Thomson

Austria: Günter Haider and Claudia Reiter

Belgium: Luc van de Poele

Brazil: Mariana Migliari

Canada: Tamara Knighton and Dianne Pennock

Czech Republic: Jana Paleckova

Denmark: Jan Mejding

Finland: Jouni Välijärvi

France: Anne-Laure Monnier

Germany: Manfred Prenzel

Greece: Vassilia Hatzinikita

Hong Kong-China: Esther Ho Sui Chu

Hungary: Péter Vári

Iceland: Almar Midvik Halldorsson

Indonesia: Bahrul Hayat

Ireland: Judith Cosgrove

Italy: Maria Teresa Siniscalco

Japan: Ryo Watanabe

Korea: Mee-Kyeong Lee

Latvia: Andris Kangro

Luxembourg: Iris Blanke

Macao-China: Esther Ho Sui Chu (2003), Lam Fat Lo (2006)

Mexico: Rafael Vidal

Netherlands: Erna Gille

New Zealand: Fiona Sturrock

Norway: Marit Kjaernsli

Poland: Michal Federowicz

Portugal: Lídia Padinha

Russian Federation: Galina Kovalyova

Serbia: Dragica Pavlovic Babic

Slovak Republic: Paulina Korsnakova

Spain: Guillermo Gil

Sweden: Karin Taube

Switzerland: Huguette McCluskey

Thailand: Sunee Klainin

Tunisia: Néjib Ayed

Turkey: Sevki Karaca

United Kingdom: Rachael Harker and Graham Thorpe

United States: Mariann Lemke

Uruguay: Pedro Ravela

OECD Secretariat

Andreas Schleicher (overall co-ordination of PISA and member country relations)

John Cresswell (project management)

Juliet Evans (administrative support)

Miyako Ikeda (project management)

Kate Lancaster (editorial support)

Claire Shewbridge (project management)

Sophie Vayssettes (statistical support)

PISA Expert Groups

PISA Editorial Group

Wendy Whitham (Chair) (Australia)

Stanislaw Drzazdzewski (Poland)

Jürgen Horschinegg (Austria)

Dianne Pennock (Canada)

Heinz Rhyn (Switzerland)

Gerry Shiel (Ireland)

Mathematics Expert Group

Jan de Lange (Chair) (Utrecht University, Netherlands)

Werner Blum (Chair) (University of Kassel, Germany)

Vladimir Burjan (National Institute for Education, Slovak Republic)

Sean Close (St Patrick's College, Ireland)

John Dossey (Consultant, United States)

Mary Lindquist (Columbus State University, United States)

Zbigniew Marciniak (Warsaw University, Poland)

Mogens Niss (Roskilde University, Denmark)

Kyung-Mee Park (Hongik University, Korea)

Luis Rico (University of Granada, Spain)

Yoshinori Shimizu (Tokyo Gakugei University, Japan)

Reading Expert Group

Irwin Kirsch (Chair) (Educational Testing Service, United States)

Marilyn Binkley (National Center for Educational Statistics, United States)

Alan Davies (University of Edinburgh, United Kingdom)

Stan Jones (Statistics Canada, Canada)

John de Jong (Language Testing Services, Netherlands)

Dominique Lafontaine (Université de Liège Sart Tilman, Belgium)

Pirjo Linnakylä (University of Jyväskylä, Finland)

Martine Rémond (Institut National de Recherche Pédagogique, France)

Science Expert Group

Wynne Harlen (Chair) (University of Bristol, United Kingdom)

Peter Fensham (Monash University, Australia)

Raul Gagliardi (University of Geneva, Switzerland)

Svein Lie (University of Oslo, Norway)

Manfred Prenzel (Universität Kiel, Germany)

Senta A. Raizen (National Center for Improving Science Education (NCISE), United States)

Donghee Shin (KICE, Korea)

Elizabeth Stage (University of California, United States)

Problem Solving Expert Group

John Dossey (Chair) (Consultant, United States)

Beno Csapo (University of Szeged, Hungary)

Jan De Lange (Utrecht University, Netherlands)

Eckhard Klieme (German Institute for International Educational Research, Germany)

Wynne Harlen (University of Bristol, United Kingdom)

Ton de Jong (University of Twente, Netherlands)

Irwin Kirsch (Educational Training Service, United States)

Stella Vosniadou (University of Athens, Greece)

PISA Technical Advisory Group

Keith Rust (Chair) (Westat)

Ray Adams (ACER, Australia)

Pierre Foy (Statistics Canada, Canada)

Aletta Grisay (Belgium)

Larry Hedges (University of Chicago, United States)

Eugene Johnson (American Institutes for Research, United States)

John de Jong (Language Testing Services, Netherlands)

Irwin Kirsch (Educational Testing Service, United States)

Steve May (Ministry of Education, New Zealand)

Christian Monseur (HallStat SPRL, Belgium)

Norman Verhelst (Citogroep, Netherlands)

J. Douglas Willms (University of New Brunswick, Canada)

PISA Consortium

Australian Council for Educational Research

Ray Adams (Project Director of the PISA Consortium)

Alla Berezner (data management, data analysis)

Eveline Gerbhardt (data processing, data analysis)

Marten Koomen (management)

Dulce Lay (data processing)

Le Tu Luc (data processing)

Greg Macaskill (data processing)

Barry McCrae (science instruments, test development mathematics and problem solving)

Martin Murphy (field operations and sampling)

Van Nguyen (data processing)

Alla Routitsky (data processing)

Wolfram Schulz (Coordinator questionnaire development, data processing, data analysis)

Ross Turner (Coordinator test development)

Maurice Walker (sampling, data processing, questionnaire development)

Margaret Wu (test development mathematics and problem solving, data analysis)

John Cresswell (test development science)

Juliette Mendelovits (test development reading)

Joy McQueen (test development reading)

Beatrice Halleux (translation quality control)

Westat

Nancy Caldwell (Director of the PISA Consortium for field operations and quality monitoring)

Ming Chen (weighting)

Fran Cohen (weighting)

Susan Fuss (weighting)

Brice Hart (weighting)

Sharon Hirabayashi (weighting)

Sheila Krawchuk (sampling and weighting)

Christian Monseur (consultant) (weighting)

Phu Nguyen (weighting)

Mats Nyfjall (weighting)

Merl Robinson (field operations and quality monitoring)

Keith Rust (Director of the PISA Consortium for sampling and weighting)

Leslie Wallace (weighting)

Erin Wilson (weighting)

Citogroep

Steven Bakker (science test development)

Bart Bossers (reading test development)

Truus Decker (mathematics test development)

Janny Harmsen (office/meeting support)

Erna van Hest (reading test development and quality monitoring)

Kees Lagerwaard (mathematics test development)

Gerben van Lent (mathematics test development)

Ger Limpens (mathematical test development)

Ico de Roo (science test development)

Maria van Toor (office support and quality monitoring)

Norman Verhelst (technical advice, data analysis)

Educational Testing Service

Irwin Kirsch (reading test development)

National Institute for Educational Policy Research of Japan

Hanako Senuma (mathematics test development)

Other experts

Cordula Artelt (questionnaire development)

Aletta Grisay (technical advice, data analysis, translation, questionnaire development)

Donald Hirsch (editorial review)

Peter Poole (University of Leeds, problem-solving item development)

Bronwen Swinnerton (University of Leeds, problem-solving item development)

John Threlfall (University of Leeds, problem-solving item development)

Kai von Ahlefeld (layout)

Katja Hettler (layout)

OECD PUBLICATIONS, 2, rue André-Pascal, 75775 PARIS CEDEX 16
PRINTED IN FRANCE
(98 2006 01 1 P) ISBN 92-64-03608-3 – No. 54931 2006